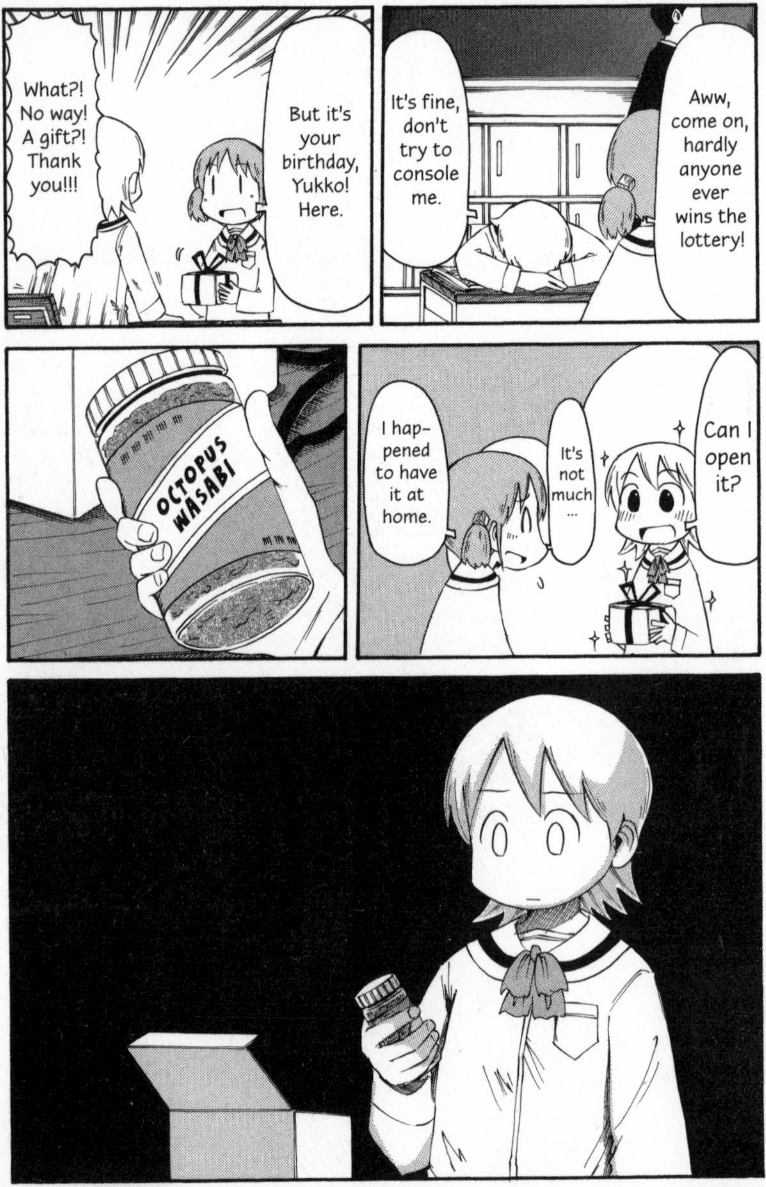
Aww, come on, hardly anyone ever wins the lottery!
It's fine, don't try to console me.
But it's your birthday, Yukko! Here.
What?! No way! A gift?! Thank you!!!
Can I open it?
It's not much...
I hap-pened to have it at home.
OCTOPUS WASABI

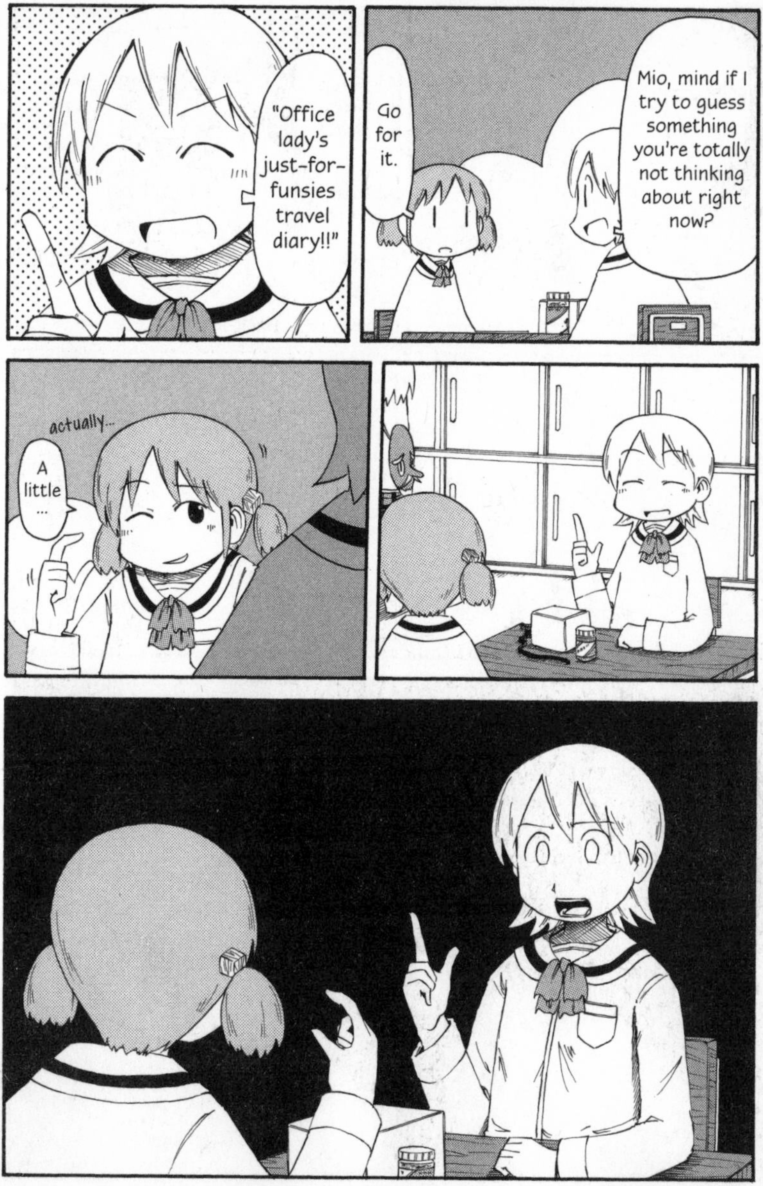
Mio, mind if I try to guess something you're totally not thinking about right now?
Go for it.
"Office lady's just-for-funsies travel diary!!"
actually...
A little ...

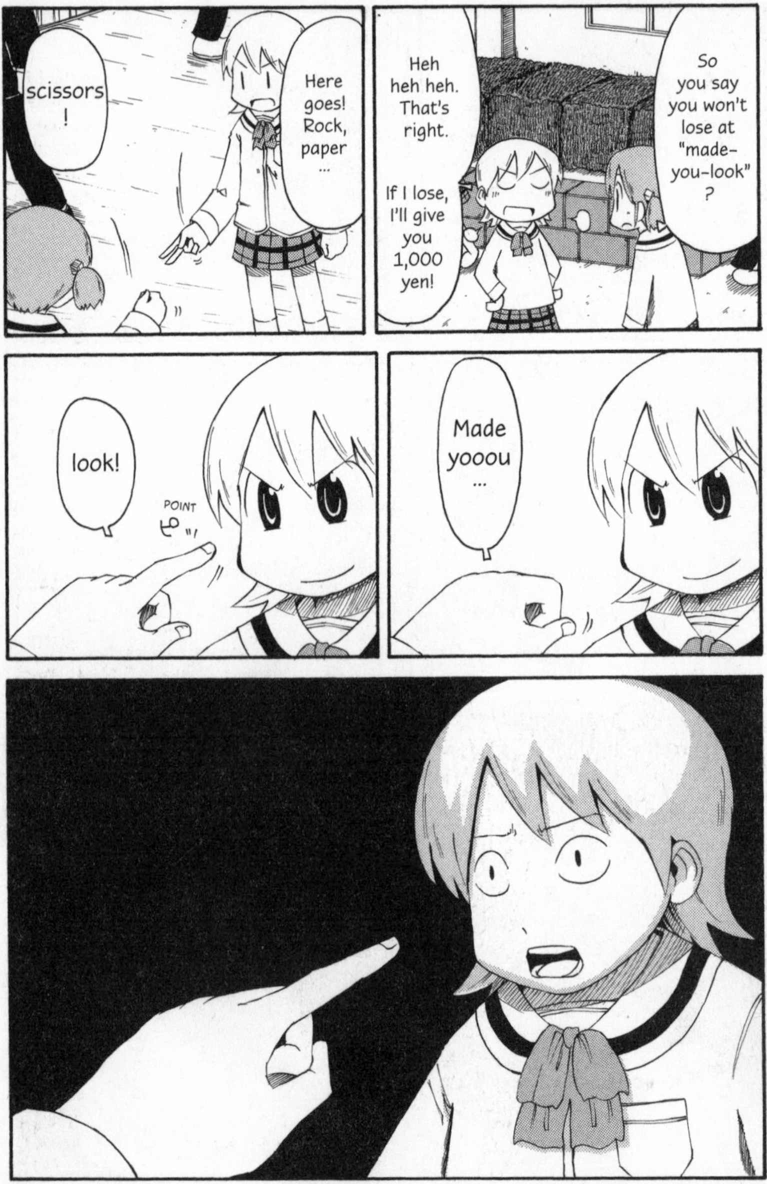
So you say you won't lose at "made-you-look"?
Heh heh heh. That's right.
If I lose, I'll give you 1,000 yen!
Here goes! Rock, paper...
scissors!
Made yooou...
look!
POINT

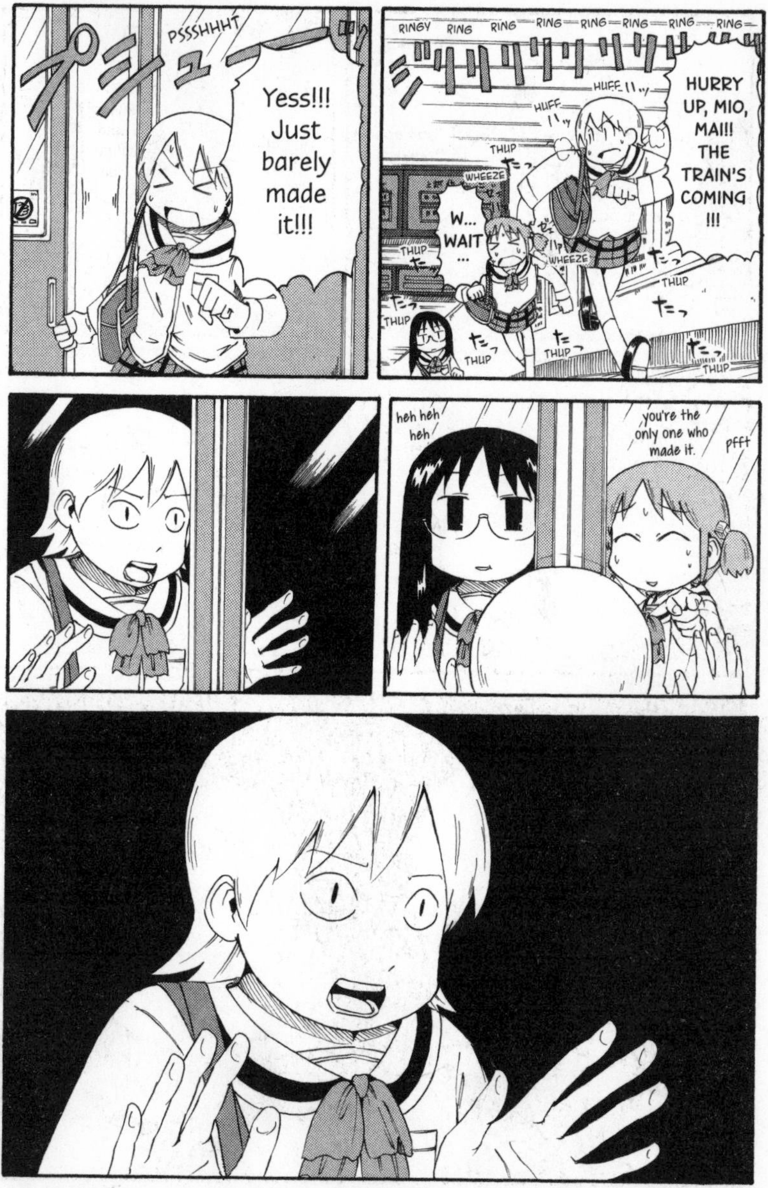
RINGY RING RING RING RING RING RING RING
HURRY UP, MIO, MAI!! THE TRAIN'S COMING !!!
HUFF
HUFF
THUP
WHEEZE
W... WAIT ...
WHEEZE
THUP
PSSSHHHT
Yess!!! Just barely made it!!!
you're the only one who made it.
pfft
heh heh heh

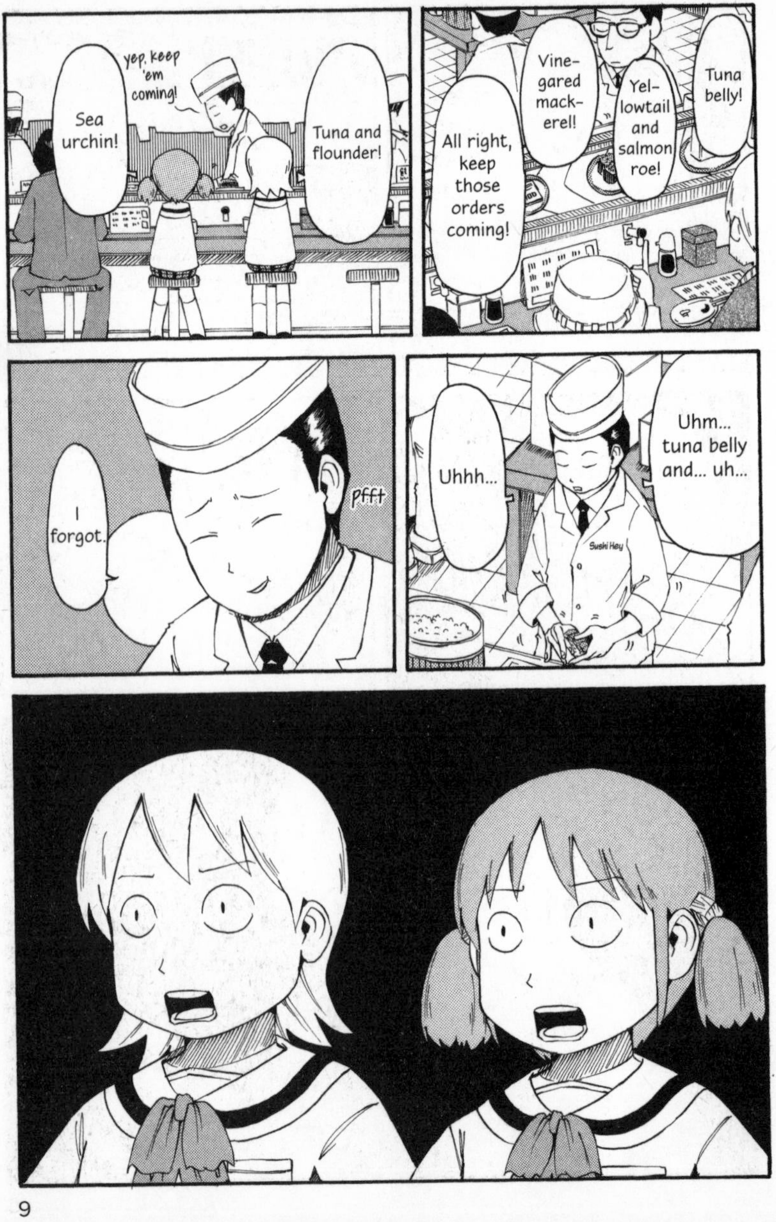
Tuna belly!
Yellowtail and salmon roe!
Vinegared mackerel!
All right, keep those orders coming!
Tuna and flounder!
yep, keep 'em coming!
Sea urchin!
Uhm... tuna belly and... uh...
Uhhh...
Sushi Hey
pfft
I forgot.

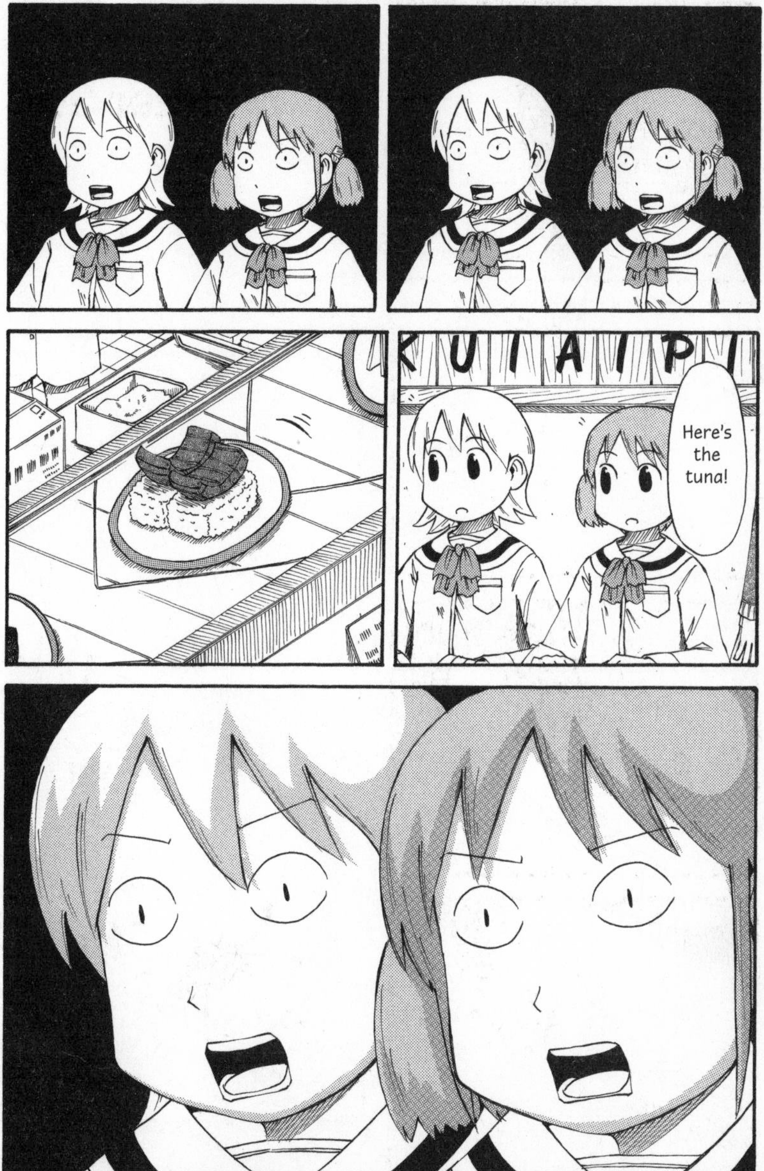
KUIAIPI
Here's the tuna!

chapter 35: end

chapter 36

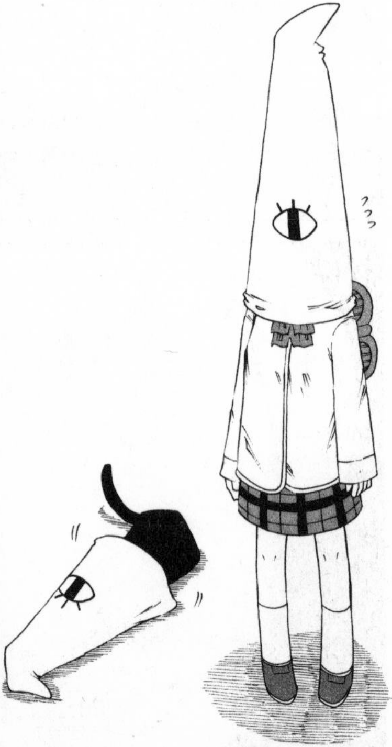

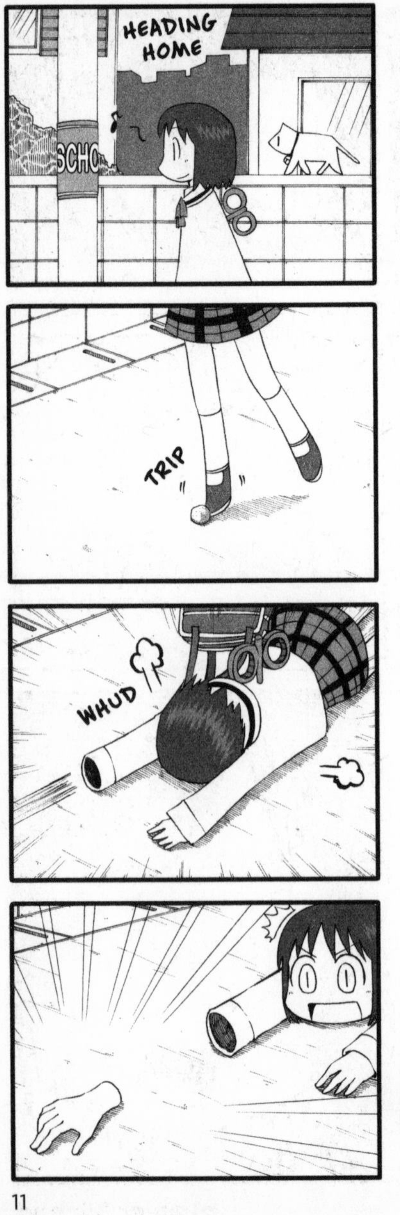

HEADING HOME
SCHO
TRIP
WHUD

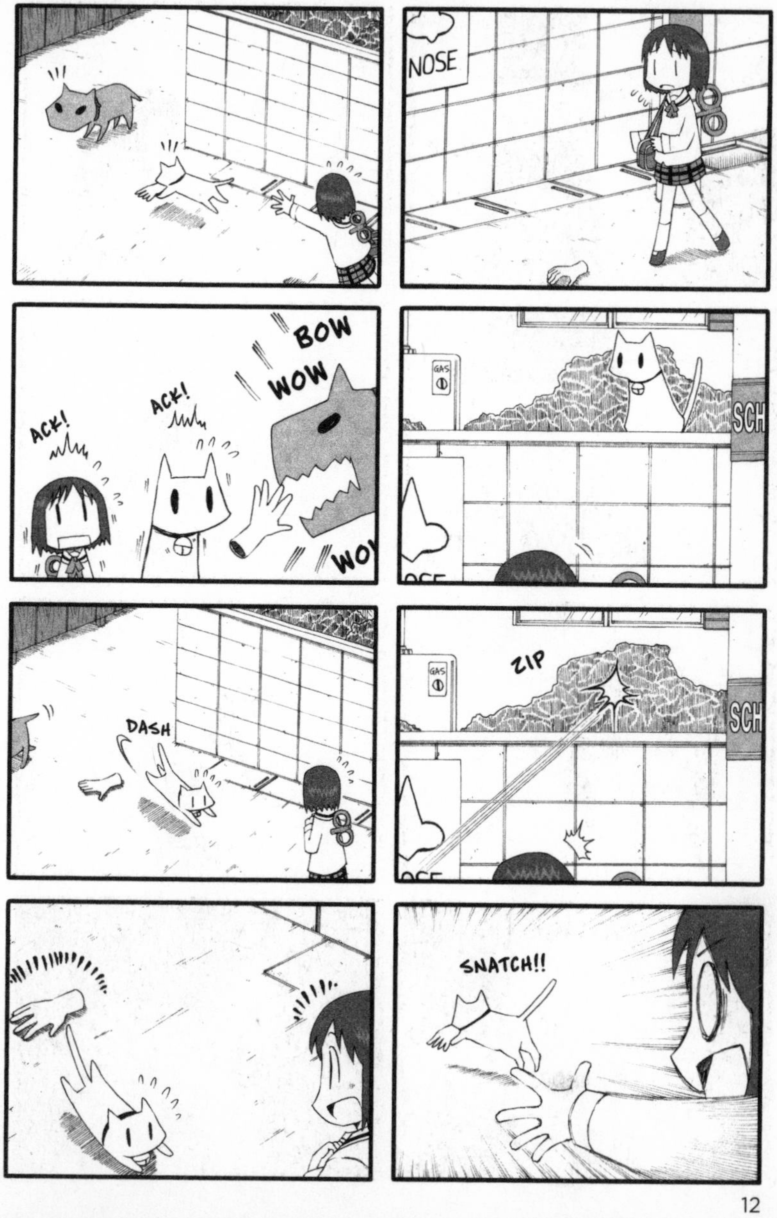
NOSE
GAS
SCH
BOW
WOW
ACK!
ACK!
WO
GAS
ZIP
SCH
DASH
SNATCH!!

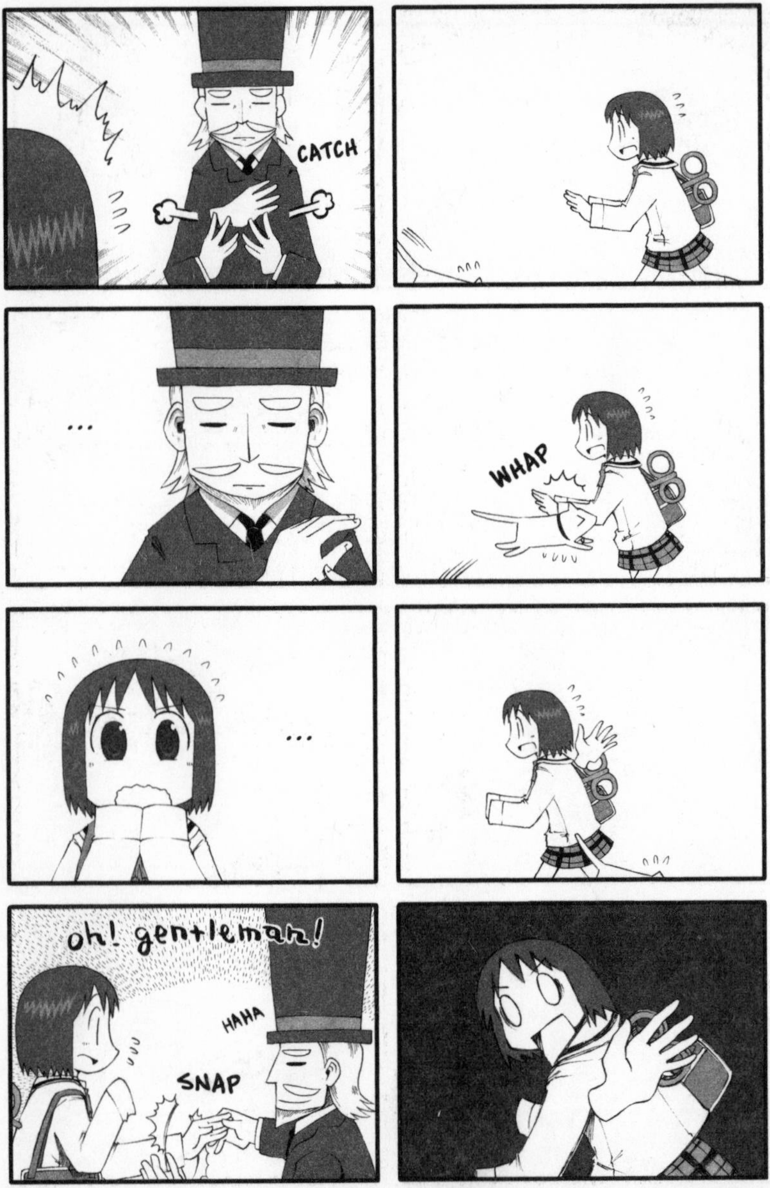
CATCH
WHAP
...
...
oh! gentleman!
HAHA
SNAP

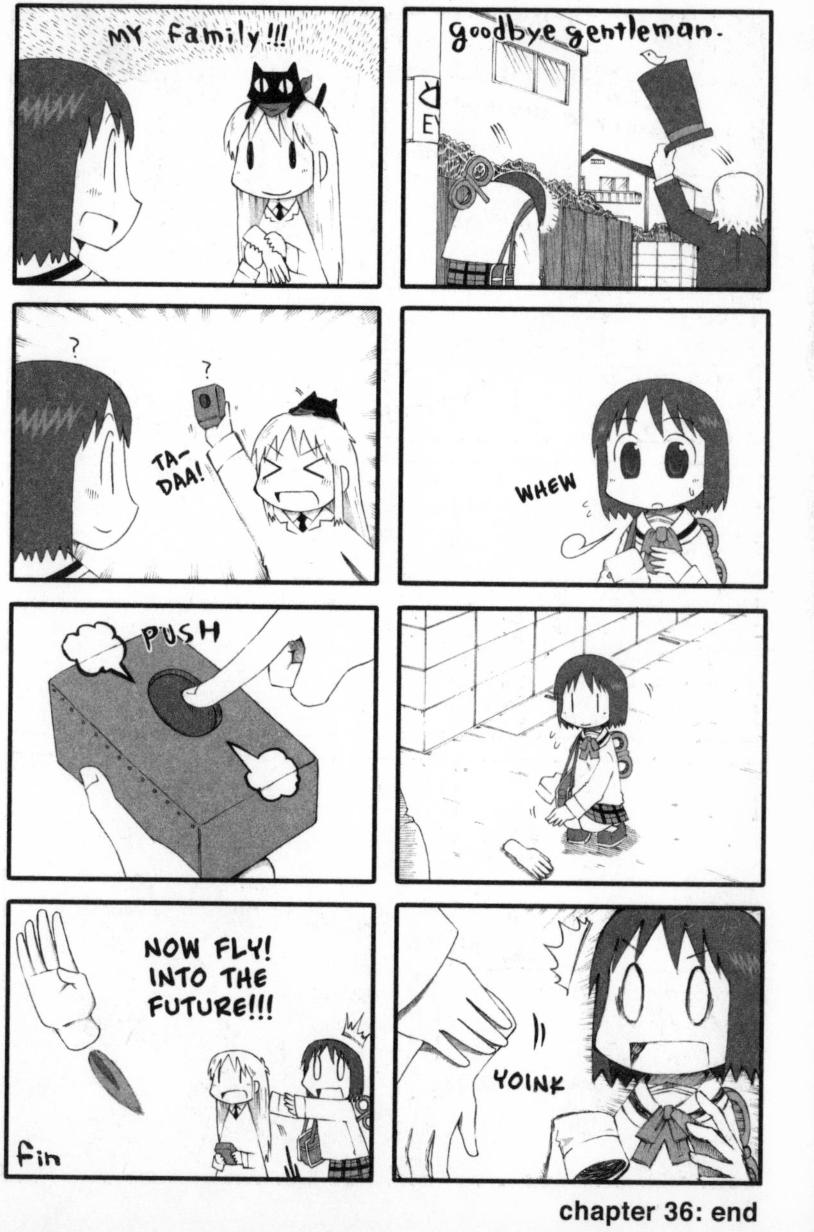
goodbye gentleman.
MY family!!!
WHEW
?
?
TA-DAA!
PUSH
YOINK
NOW FLY! INTO THE FUTURE!!!
fin

chapter 36: end

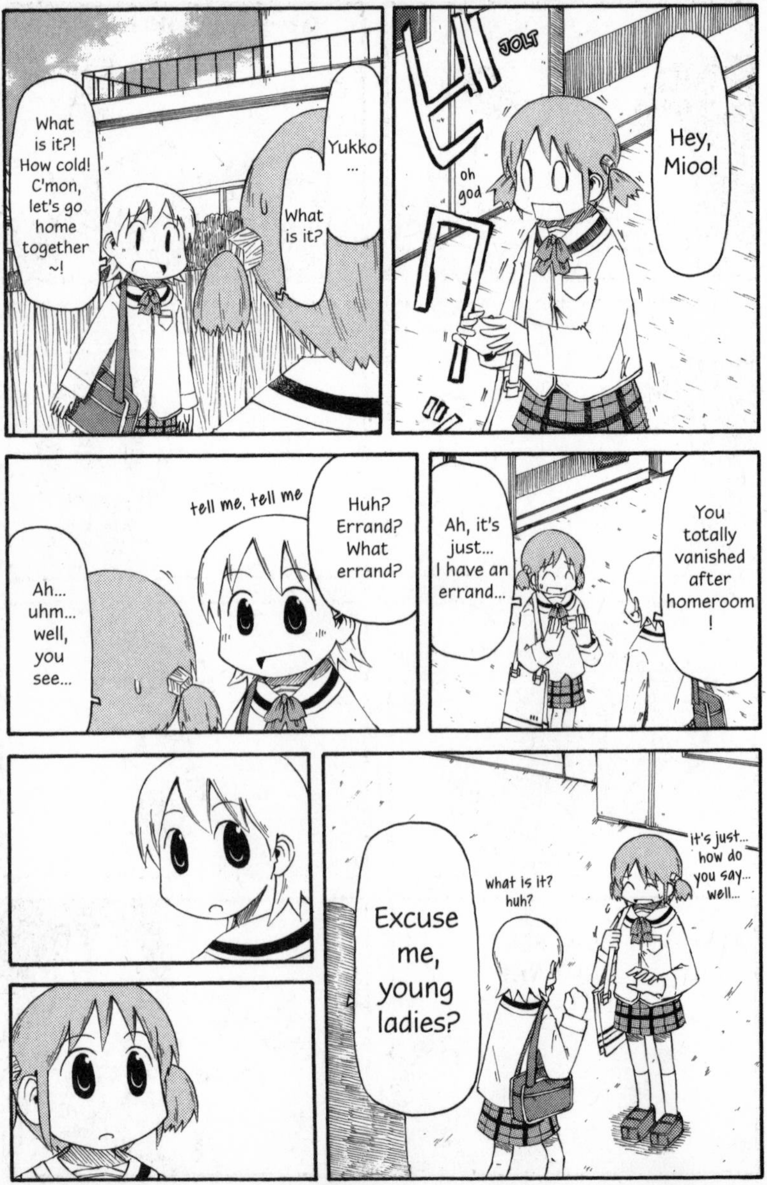
Hey, Mioo!
JOLT
oh god
Yukko ...
What is it?
What is it?! How cold! C'mon, let's go home together ~!
You totally vanished after homeroom!
Ah, it's just... I have an errand...
Huh? Errand? What errand?
tell me, tell me
Ah... uhm... well, you see...
it's just... how do you say... well...
what is it? huh?
Excuse me, young ladies?

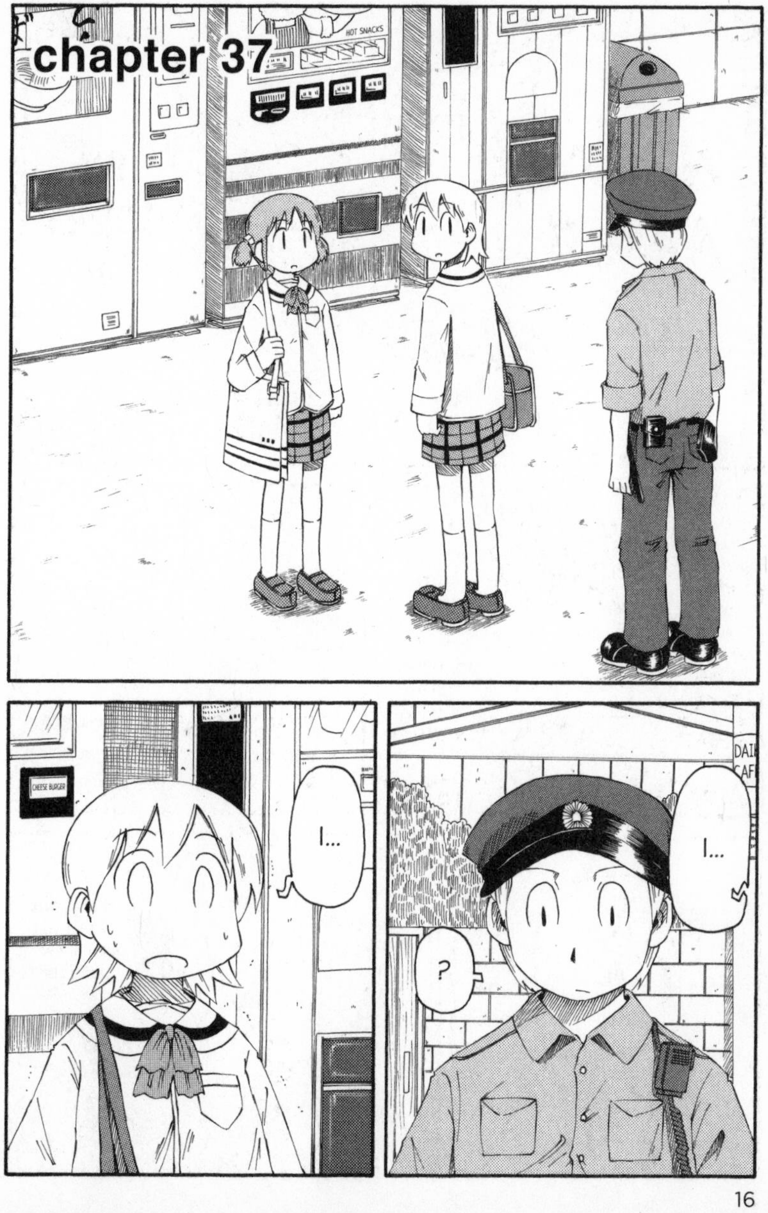
chapter 37
HOT SNACKS
I...
?
CHEESE BURGER
I...

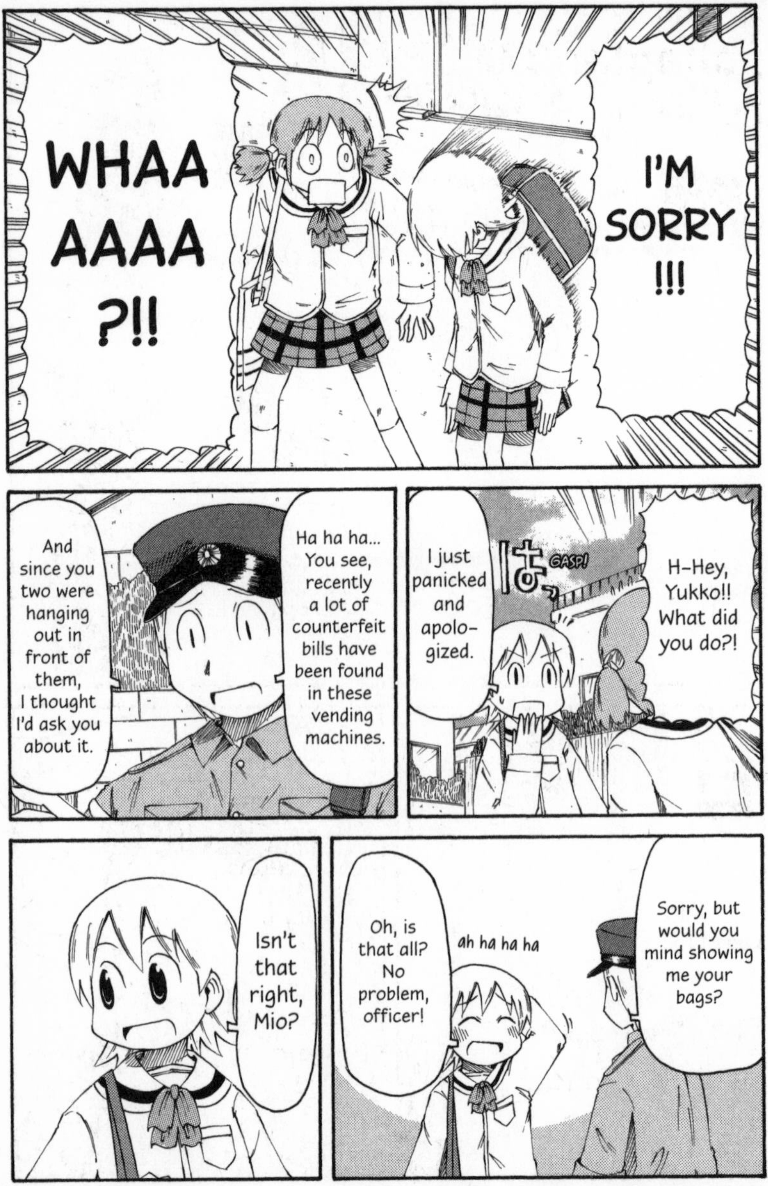
I'M SORRY!!!
WHAAAAAA?!!
H-Hey, Yukko!! What did you do?!
は
GASP!
I just panicked and apologized.
Ha ha ha... You see, recently a lot of counterfeit bills have been found in these vending machines.
And since you two were hanging out in front of them, I thought I'd ask you about it.
Sorry, but would you mind showing me your bags?
ah ha ha ha
Oh, is that all? No problem, officer!
Isn't that right, Mio?

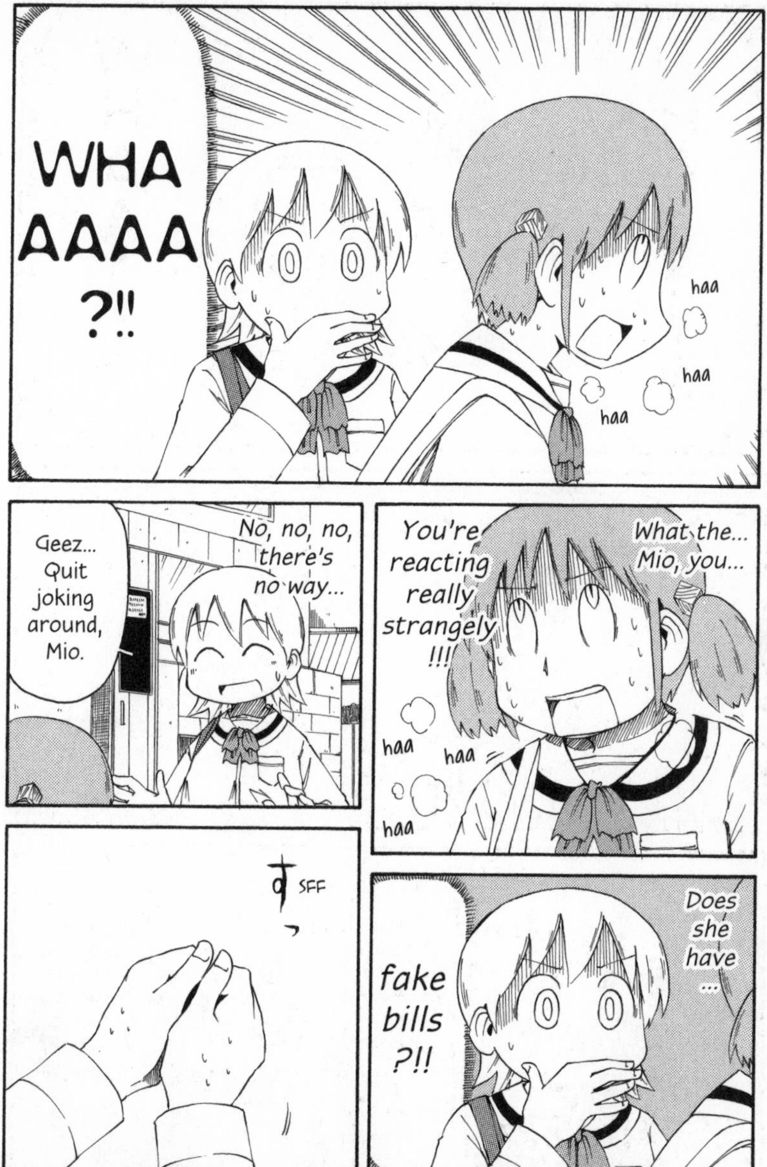
WHA AAAA ?!!
haa
haa
haa
What the... Mio, you...
You're reacting really strangely!!!
haa
haa
haa
No, no, no, there's no way...
Geez... Quit joking around, Mio.
Does she have...
fake bills ?!!
すっ
SFF

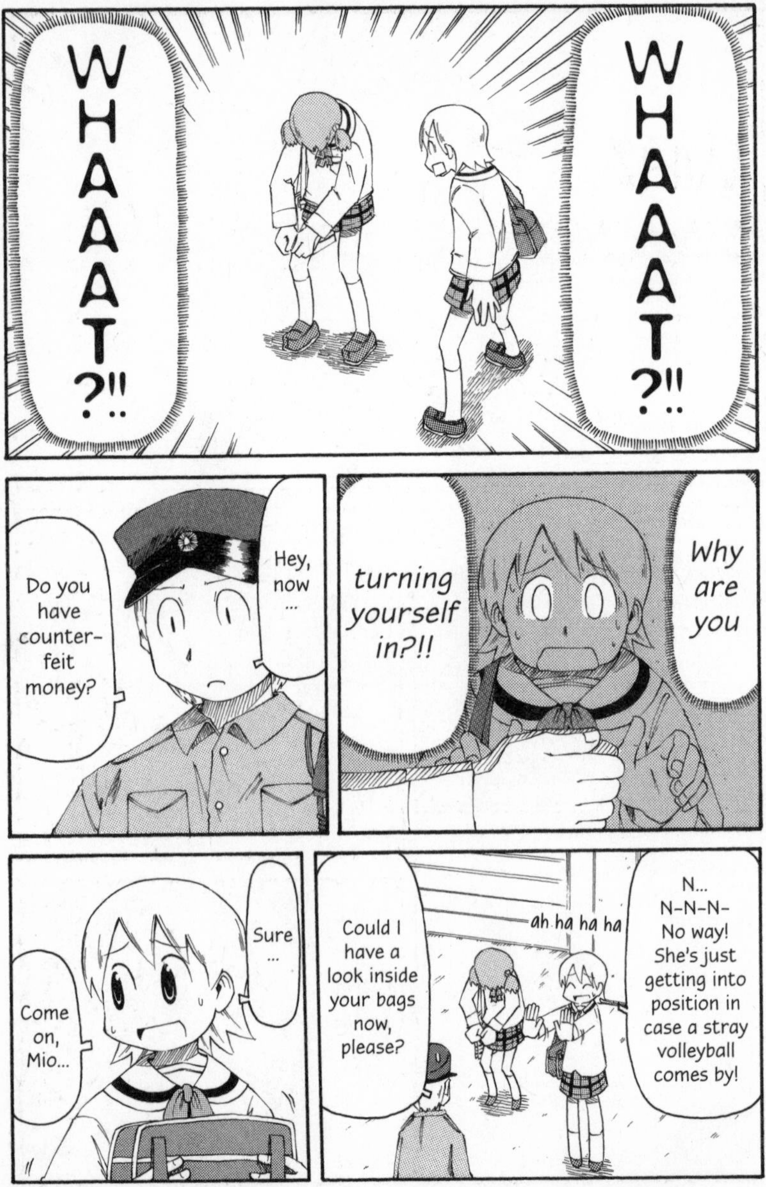
WHAAAT?!!
WHAAAT?!!
Why are you
turning yourself in?!!
Hey, now ...
Do you have counter-feit money?
N... N-N-N- No way! She's just getting into position in case a stray volleyball comes by!
ah ha ha ha
Could I have a look inside your bags now, please?
Sure ...
Come on, Mio...

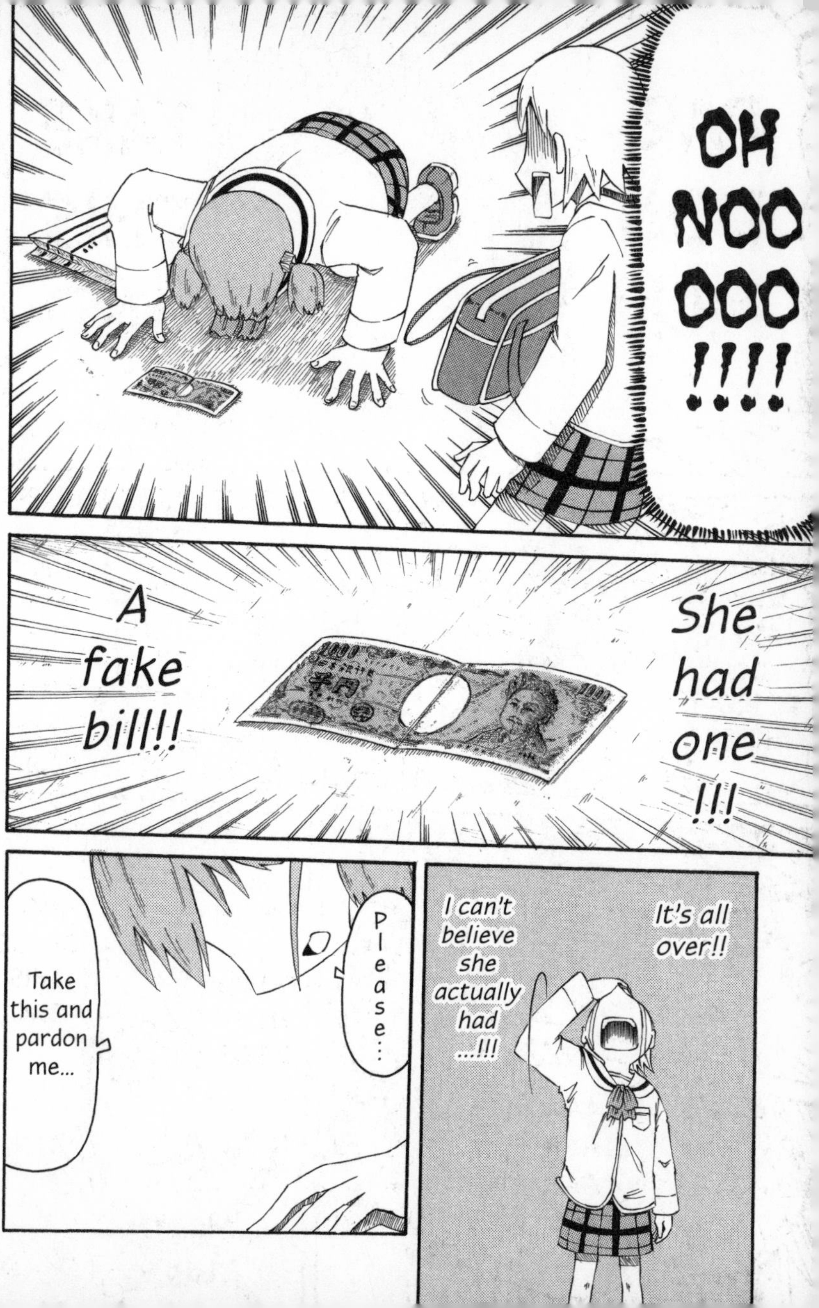
OH NOOOOO!!!!
She had one!!!
A fake bill!!
It's all over!!
I can't believe she actually had ...!!!
Please…
Take this and pardon me...

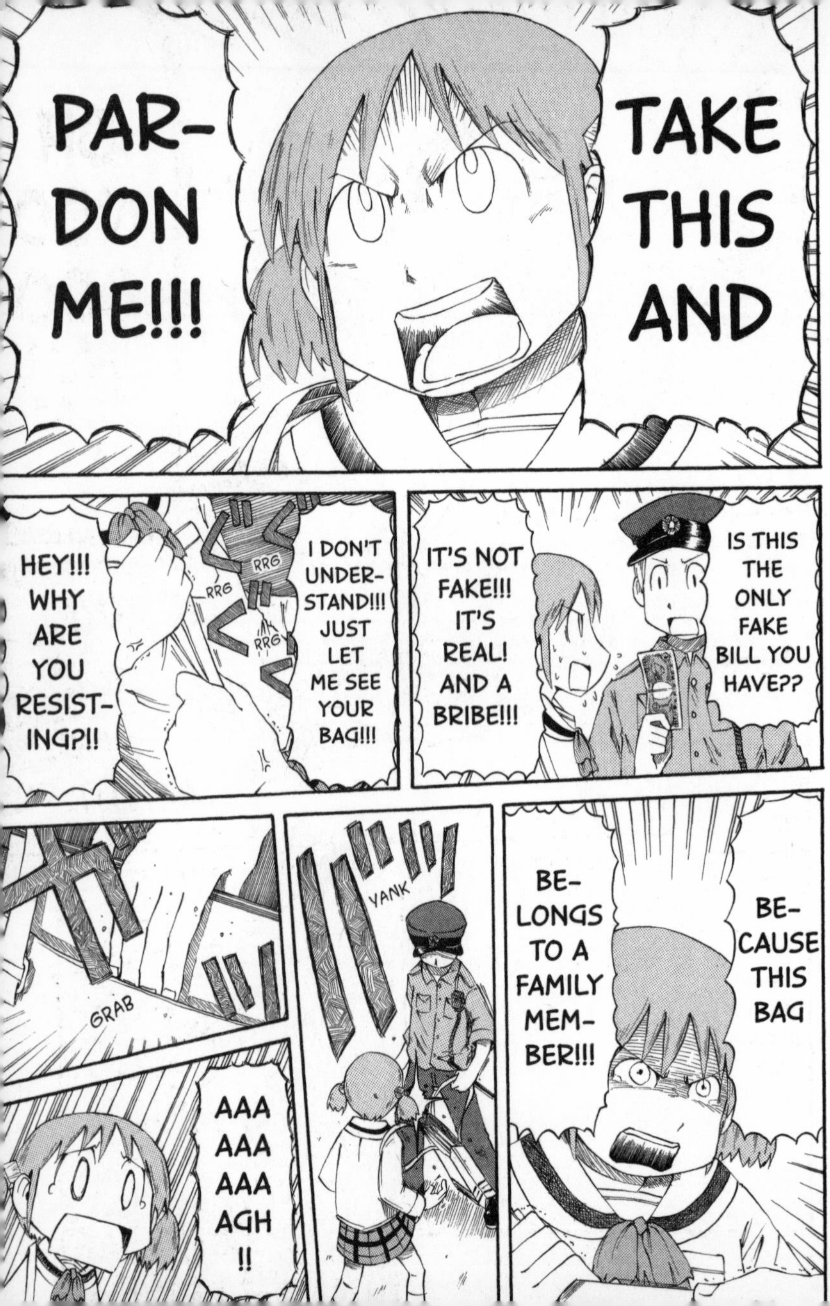
TAKE THIS AND
PARDON ME!!!
IS THIS THE ONLY FAKE BILL YOU HAVE??
IT'S NOT FAKE!!! IT'S REAL! AND A BRIBE!!!
I DON'T UNDERSTAND!!! JUST LET ME SEE YOUR BAG!!!
RRG
RRG
RRG
HEY!!! WHY ARE YOU RESISTING?!!
BECAUSE THIS BAG
BELONGS TO A FAMILY MEMBER!!!
YANK
GRAB
AAAAAAAAAAAGH !!

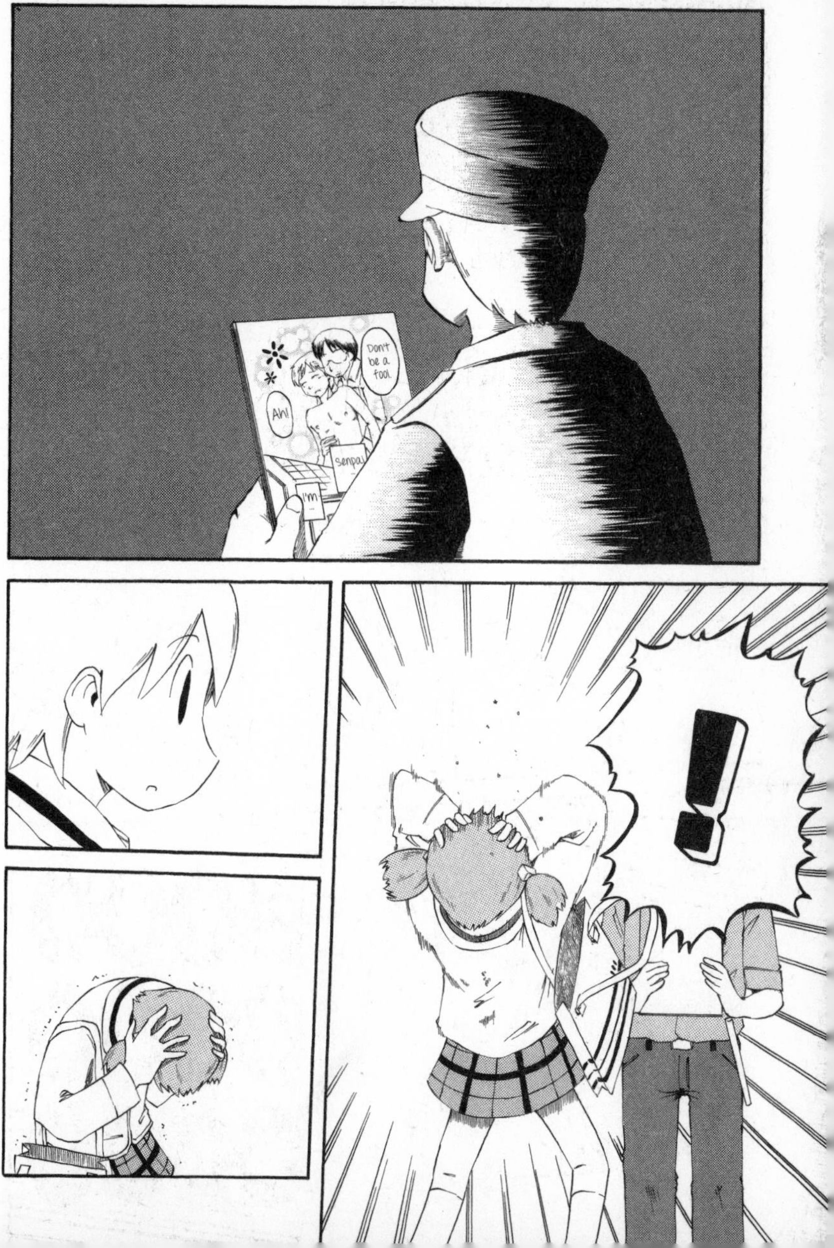
Don't be a fool.
Ah!
senpai...
I'm...
!

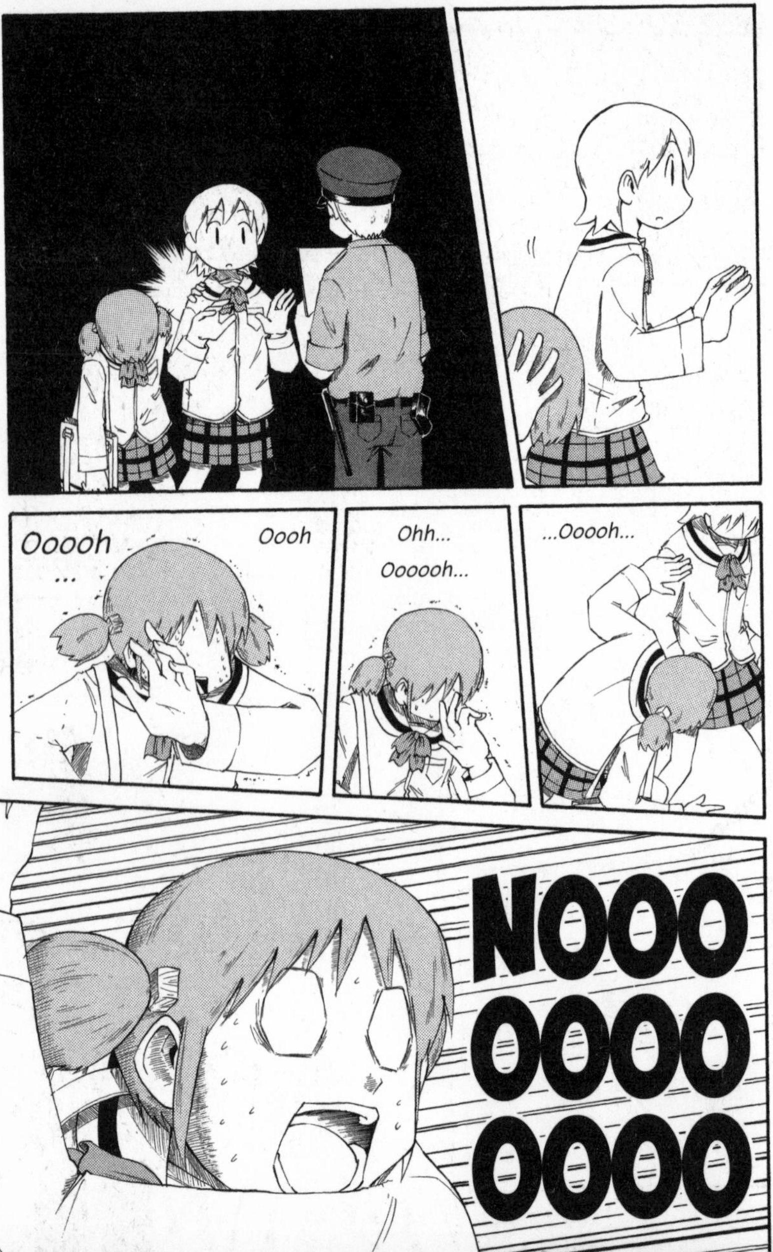
...Ooooh...
Ohh...
Oooooh...
Oooh
Ooooh
...
NOOOOOOOOOOO

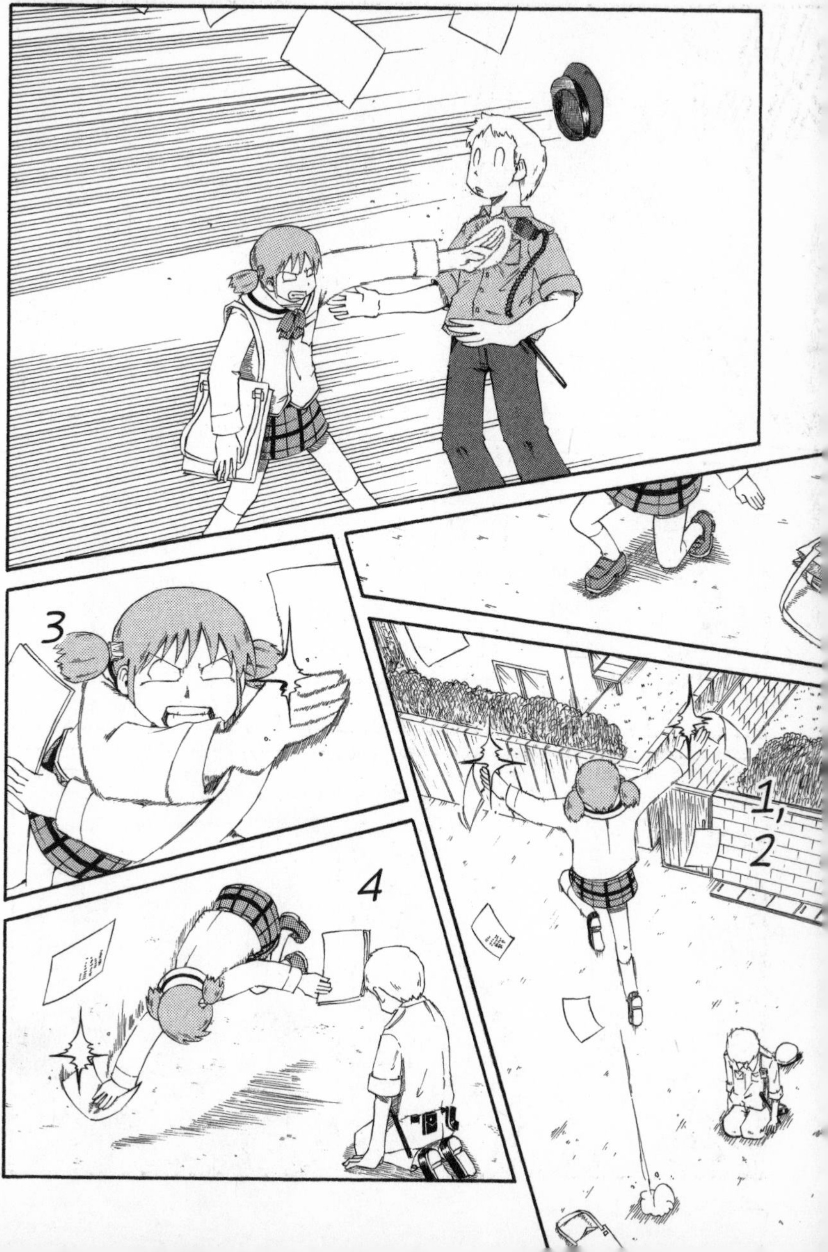
1,
2
3
4

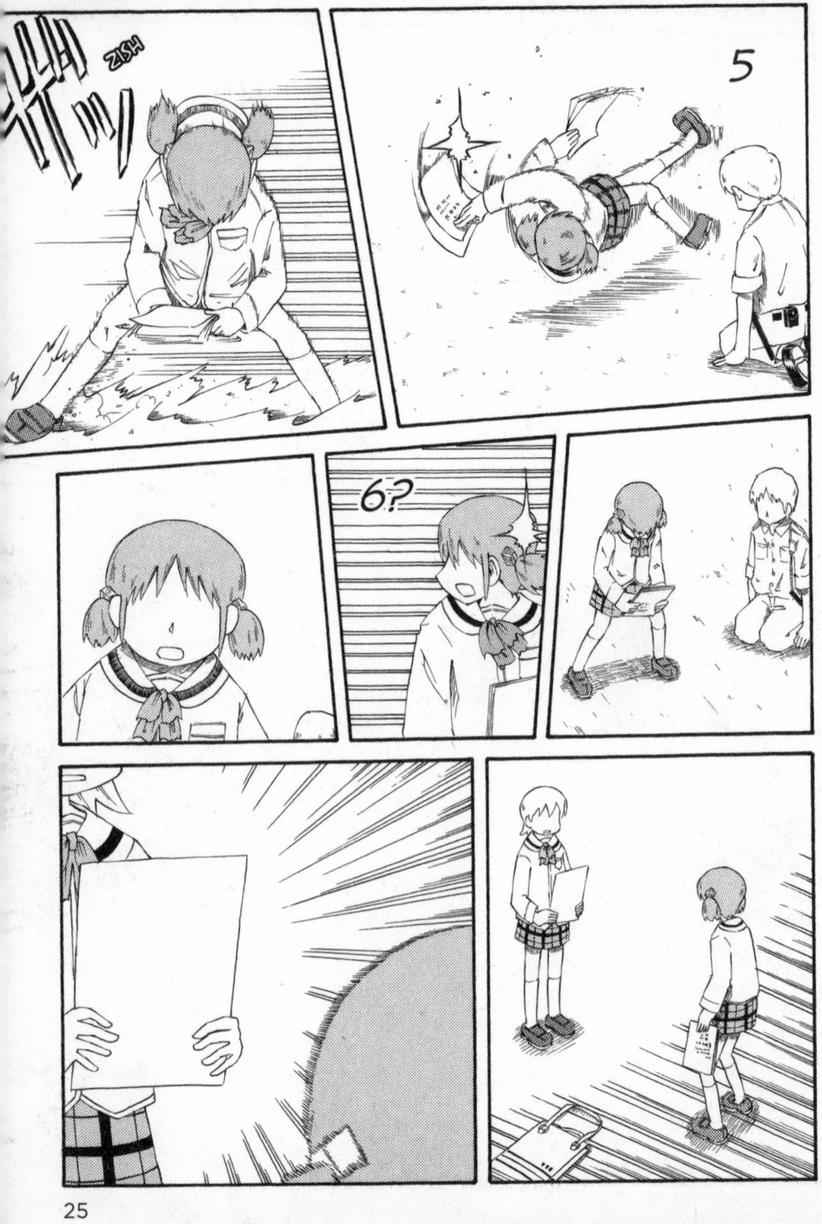
5
ZISH
6?

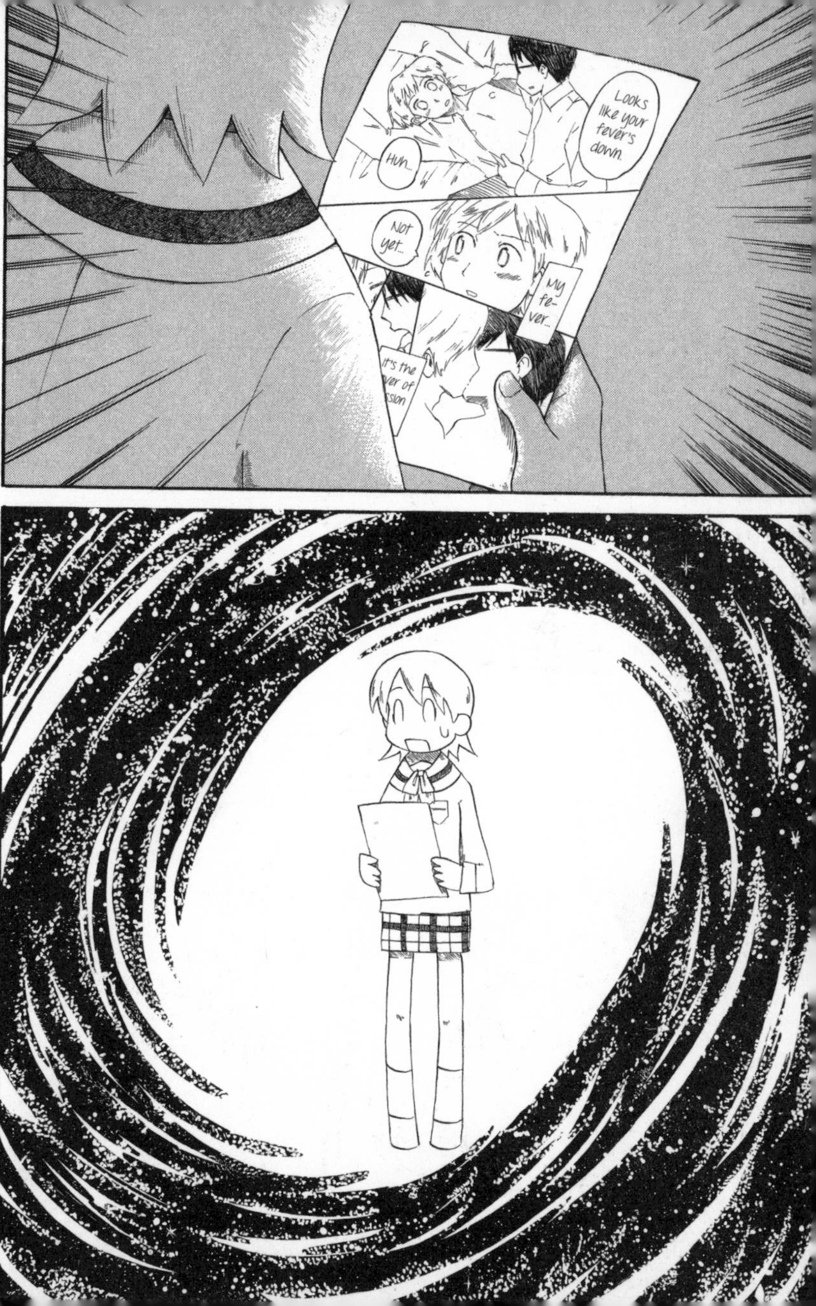
Looks like your fever's down.
Huh...
Not yet...
My fever...
It's the ver of ssion

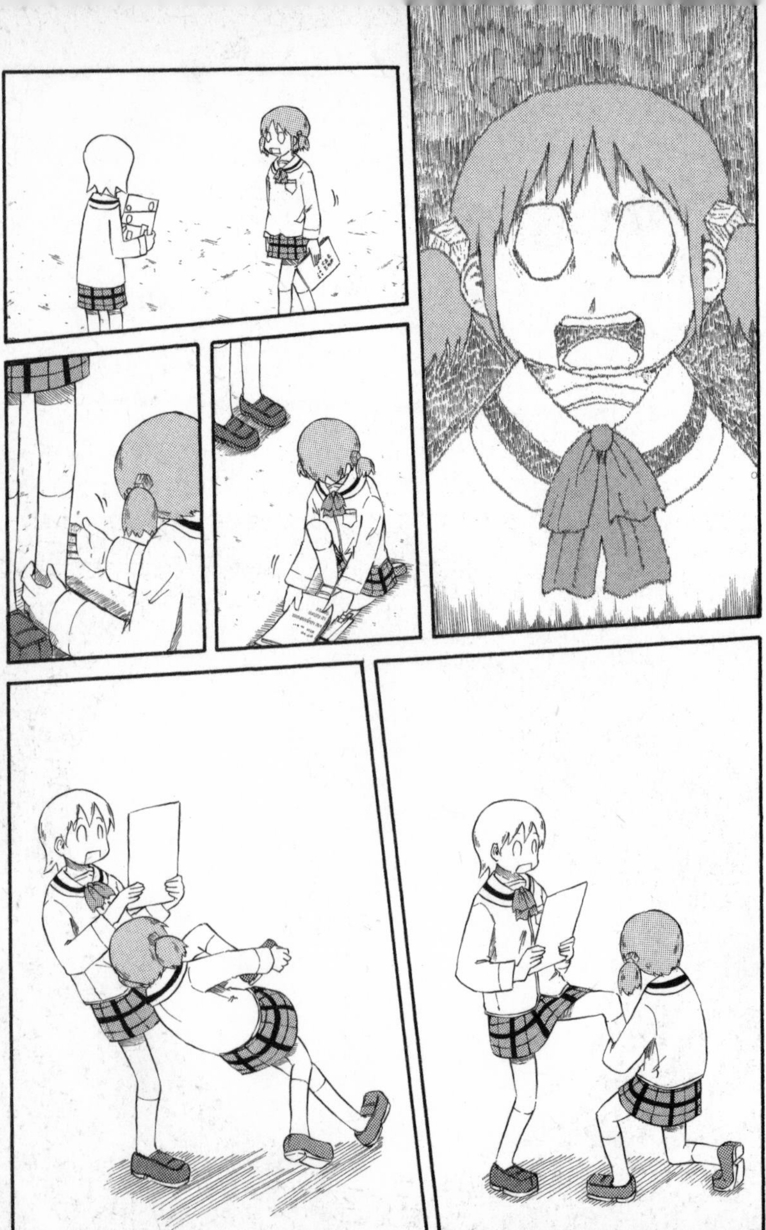

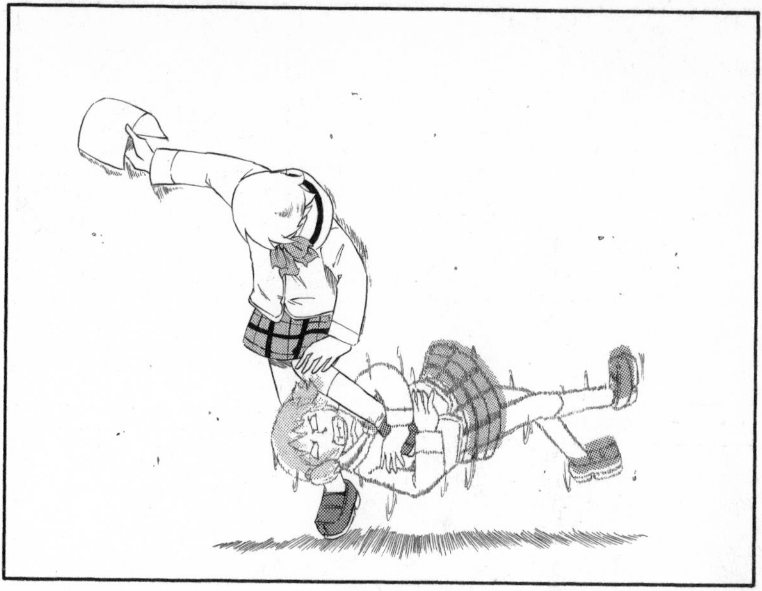

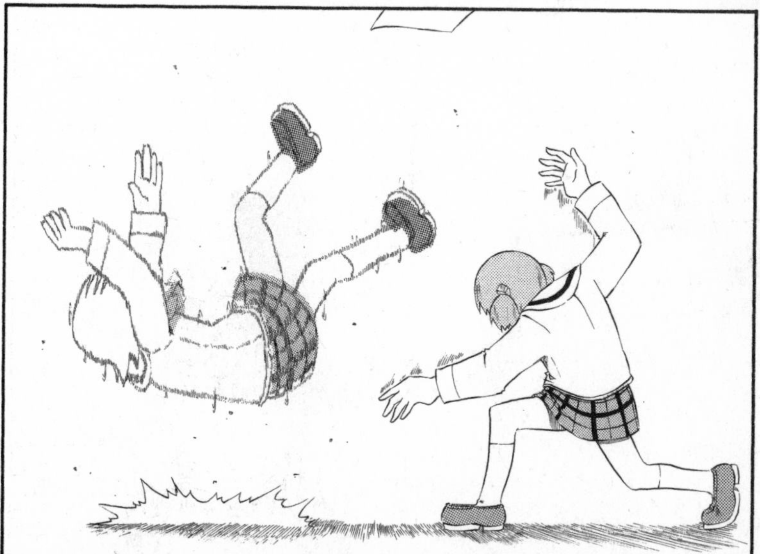

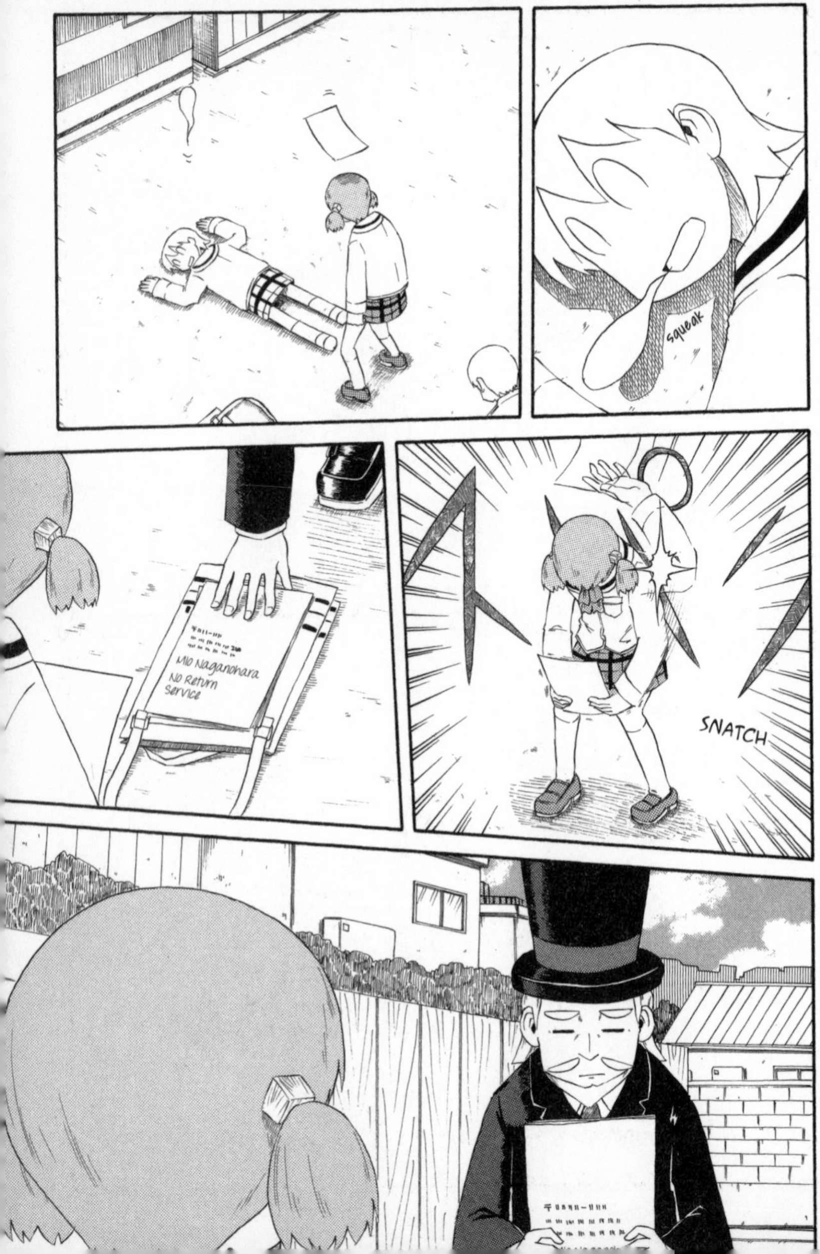
squeak
SNATCH
Mio Naganohara
No Return
Service

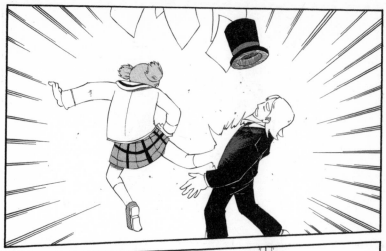

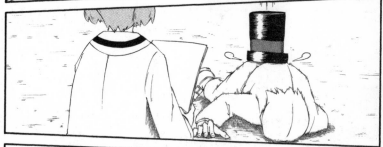

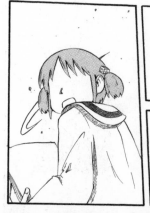

1, 2, 3,
4, 5......

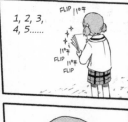

FLIP パ〇チ

パ〇チ
FLIP パ〇チ
FLIP

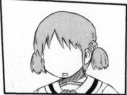

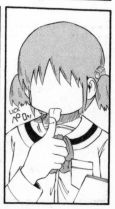

LICK
ペ〇ッ

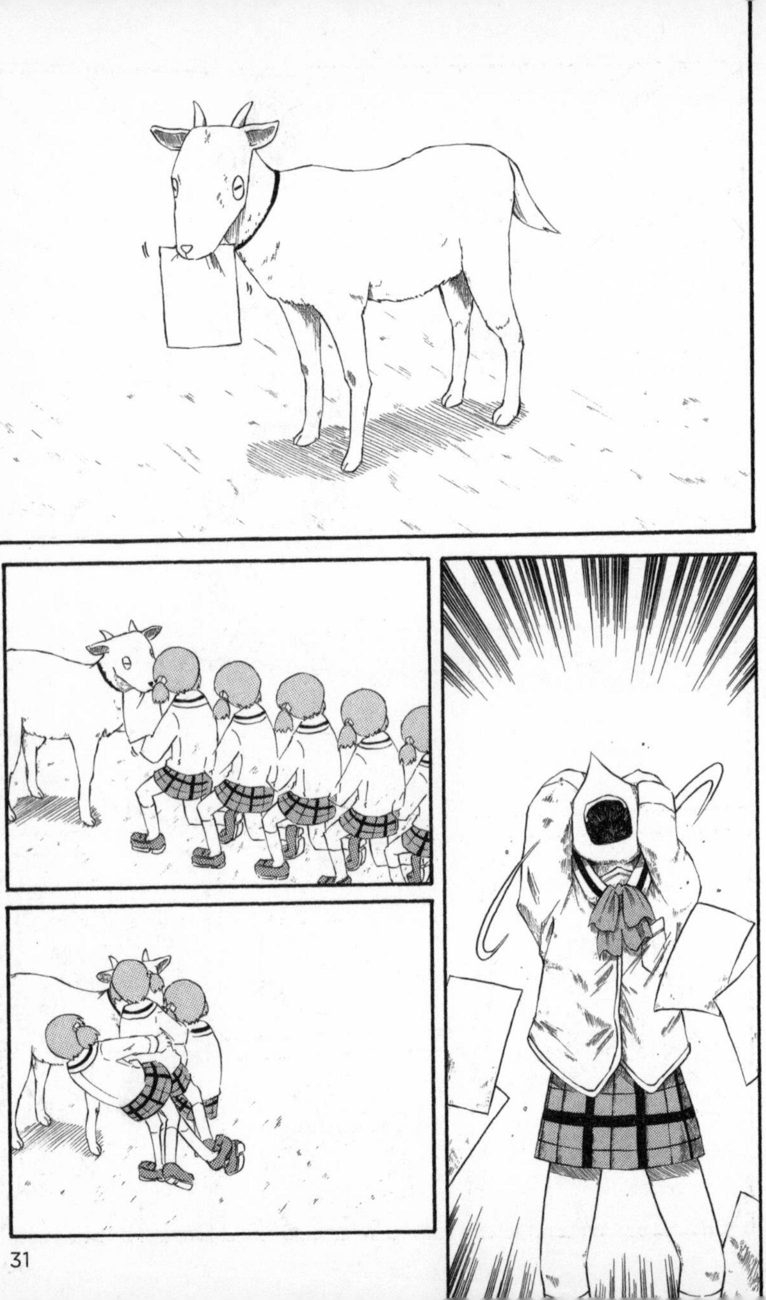

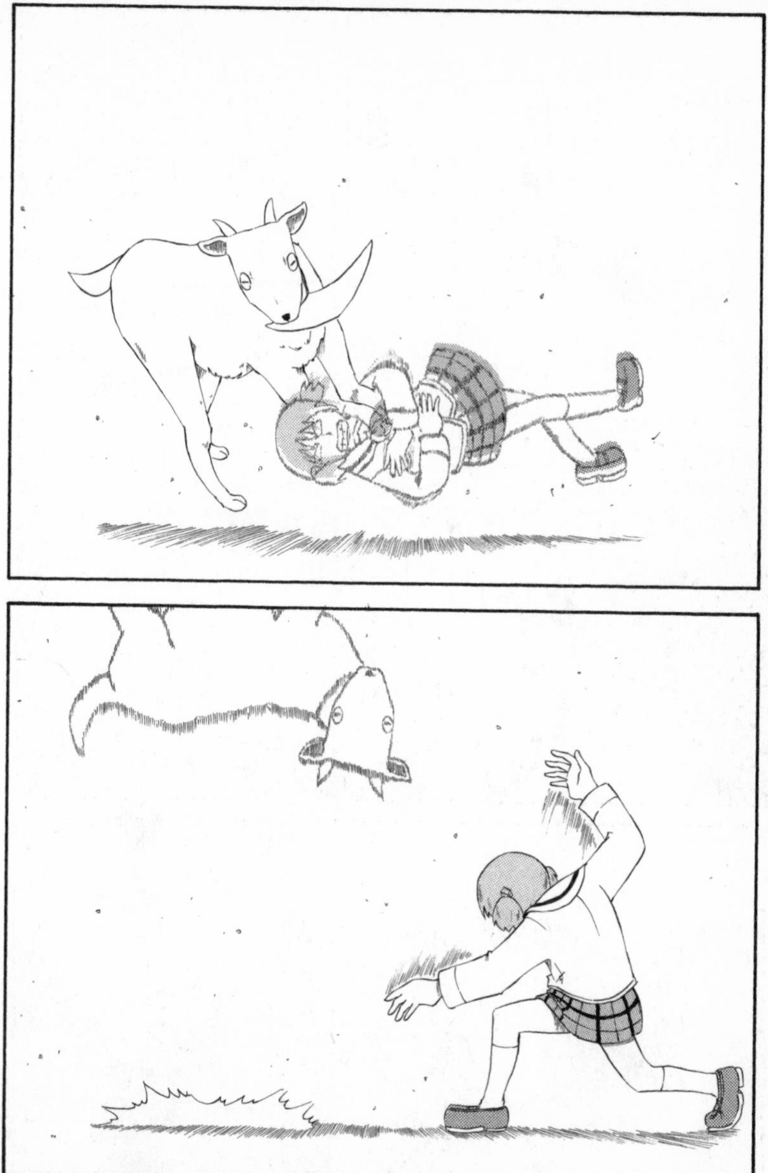

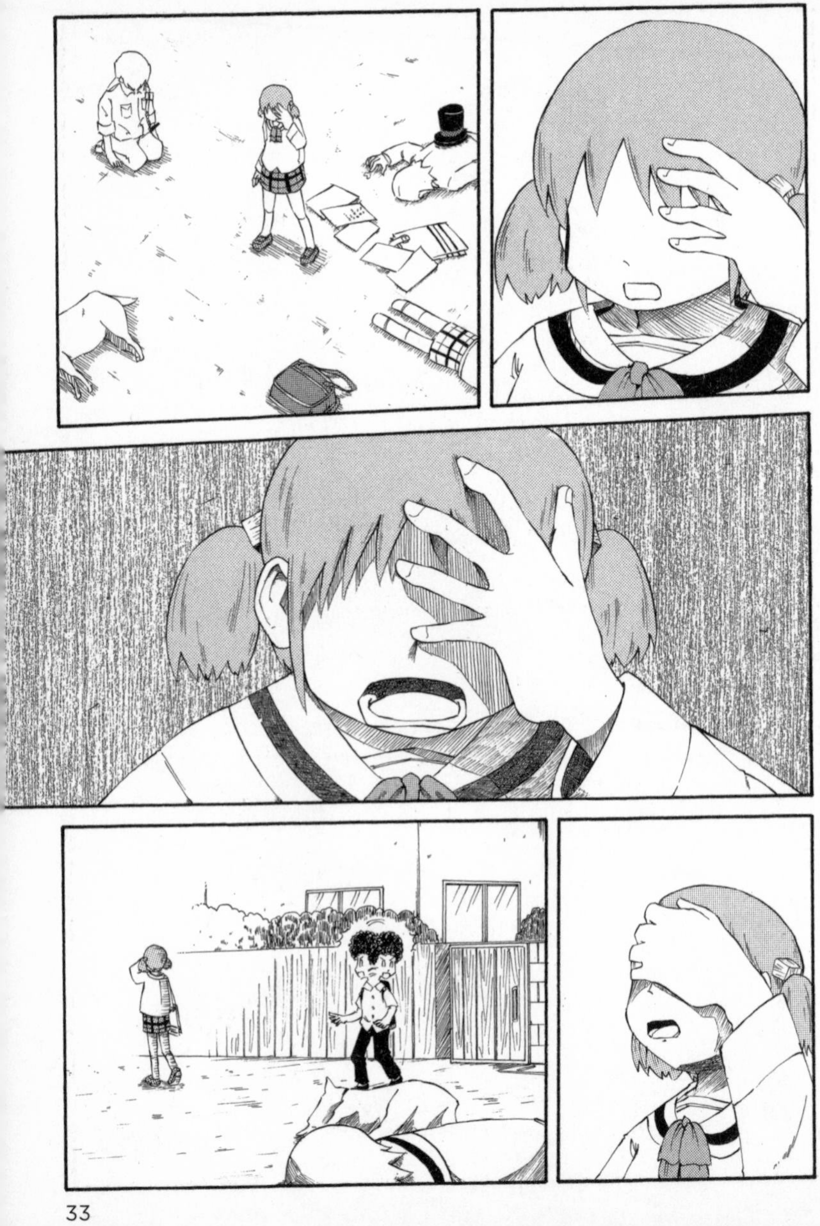

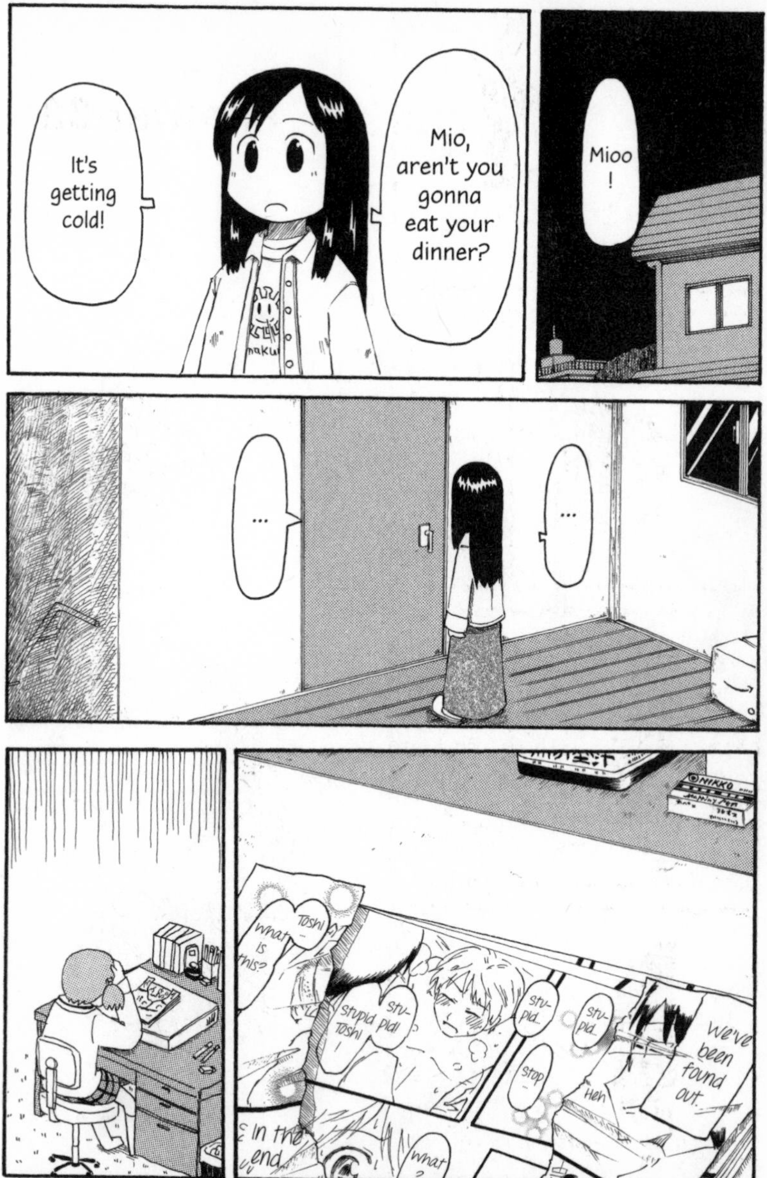
Mioo !
Mio, aren't you gonna eat your dinner?
It's getting cold!
...
...
We've been found out.
Stu-pid...
Stu-pid...
Heh
Stop...
Stu-pid!
Stupid Toshi!
Toshi...
what is this?
What?
In the end

chapter 37: end

chapter 38

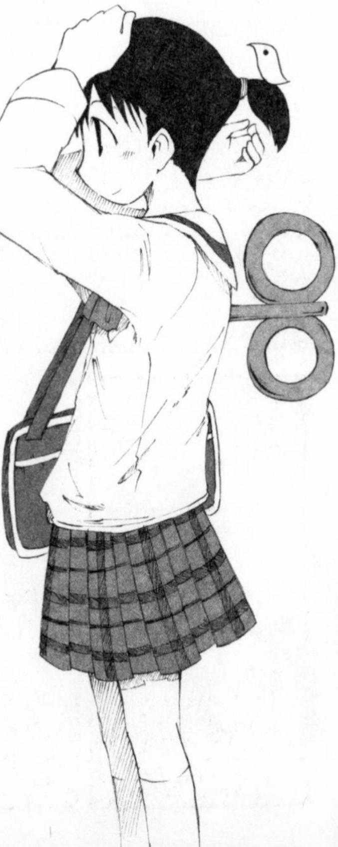

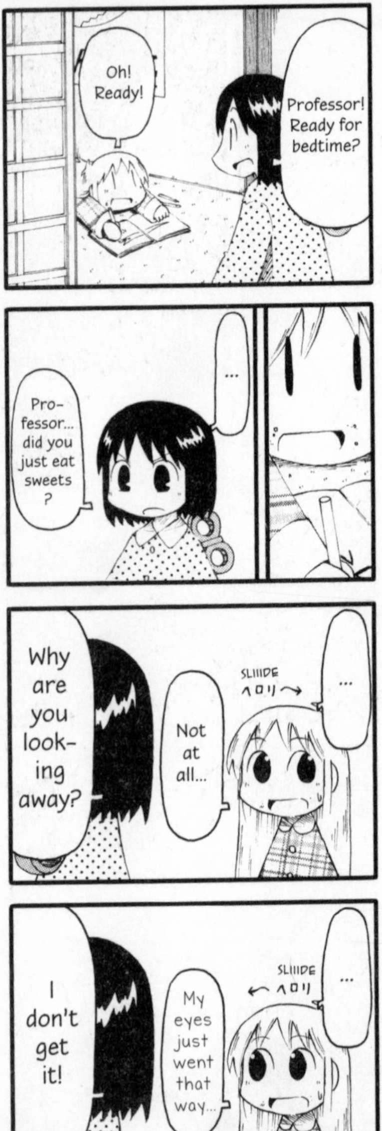

Professor! Ready for bedtime?
Oh! Ready!
...
Pro-fessor... did you just eat sweets?
SLIIIDE ヘロリ
...
Not at all...
Why are you look-ing away?
SLIIIDE ヘロリ
...
My eyes just went that way...
I don't get it!

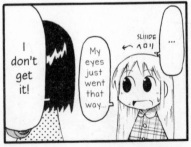

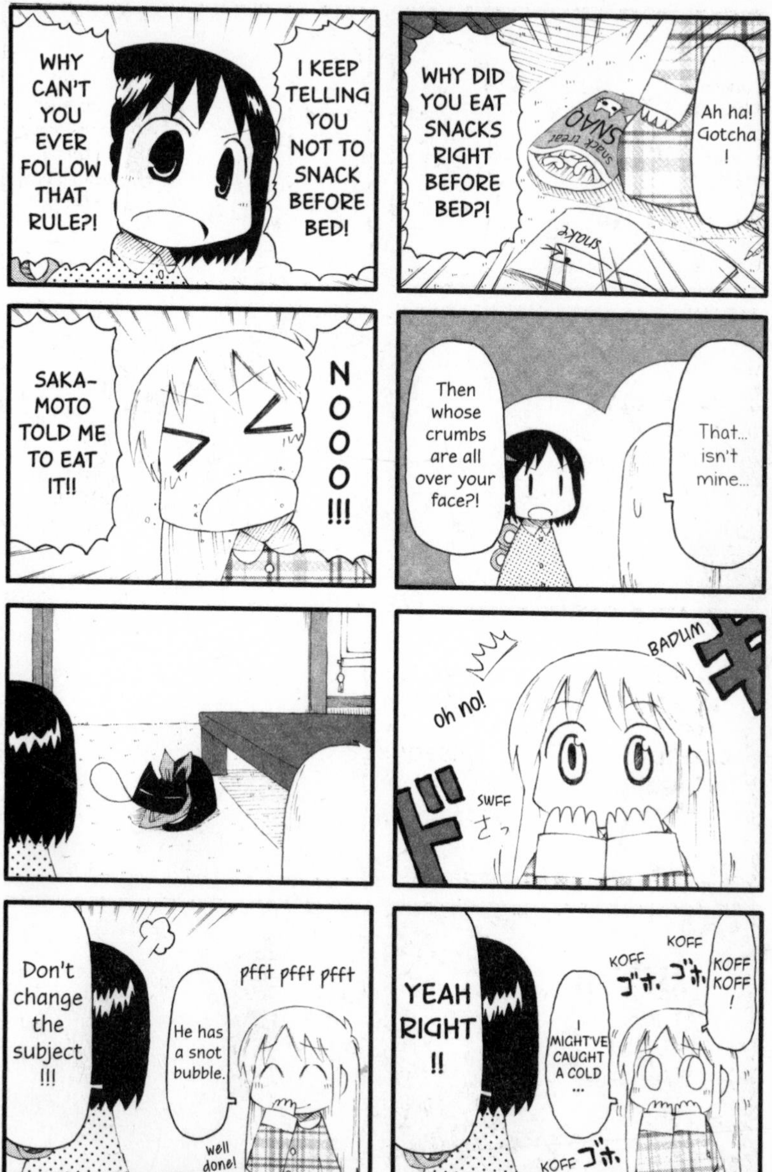

Ah ha! Gotcha!
WHY DID YOU EAT SNACKS RIGHT BEFORE BED?!
I KEEP TELLING YOU NOT TO SNACK BEFORE BED!
WHY CAN'T YOU EVER FOLLOW THAT RULE?!
That... isn't mine...
Then whose crumbs are all over your face?!
NOOOO!!!
SAKAMOTO TOLD ME TO EAT IT!!
BADUM
oh no!
SWFF
さっ
KOFF KOFF!
KOFF ゴホ
KOFF ゴホ
I MIGHT'VE CAUGHT A COLD ...
YEAH RIGHT!!
KOFF ゴホ
pfft pfft pfft
He has a snot bubble.
Don't change the subject!!!
well done!

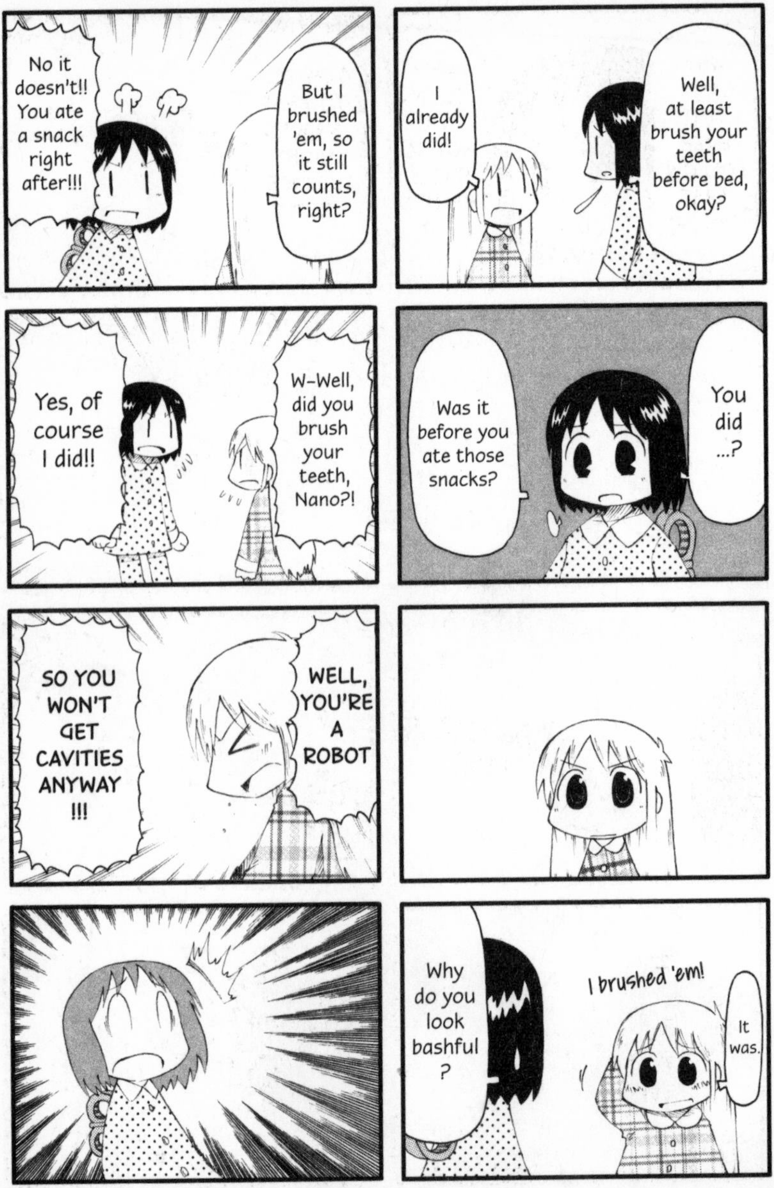
Well, at least brush your teeth before bed, okay?
I already did!
But I brushed 'em, so it still counts, right?
No it doesn't!! You ate a snack right after!!!
You did ...?
Was it before you ate those snacks?
W-Well, did you brush your teeth, Nano?!
Yes, of course I did!!
WELL, YOU'RE A ROBOT
SO YOU WON'T GET CAVITIES ANYWAY !!!
It was.
I brushed 'em!
Why do you look bashful ?

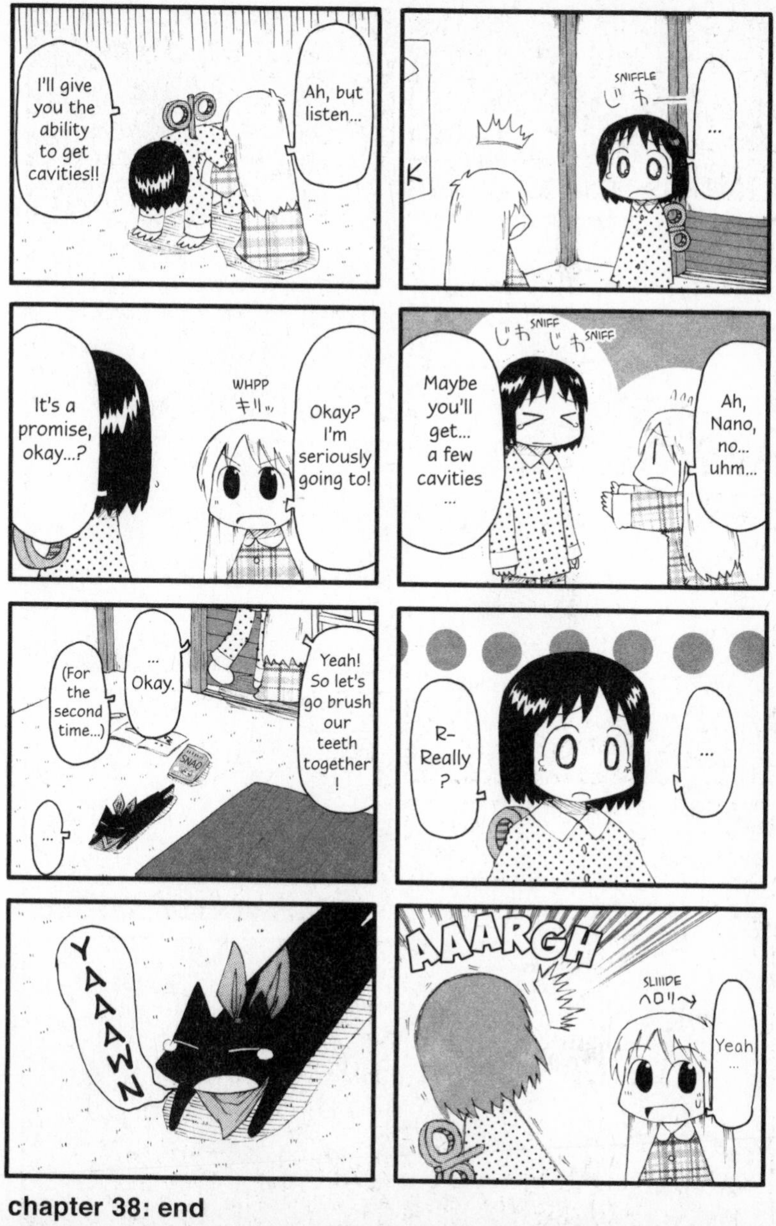
SNIFFLE
じわー
...
SNIFF
じわ
SNIFF
じわ
Ah, Nano, no... uhm...
Maybe you'll get... a few cavities ...
...
R-Really?
AAARGH
SLIIIDE
ヘロリ→
Yeah ...
Ah, but listen...
I'll give you the ability to get cavities!!
WHPP
キリッ
Okay? I'm seriously going to!
It's a promise, okay...?
Yeah! So let's go brush our teeth together!
... Okay.
(For the second time...)
SNAO
...
YAAAWN

chapter 38: end

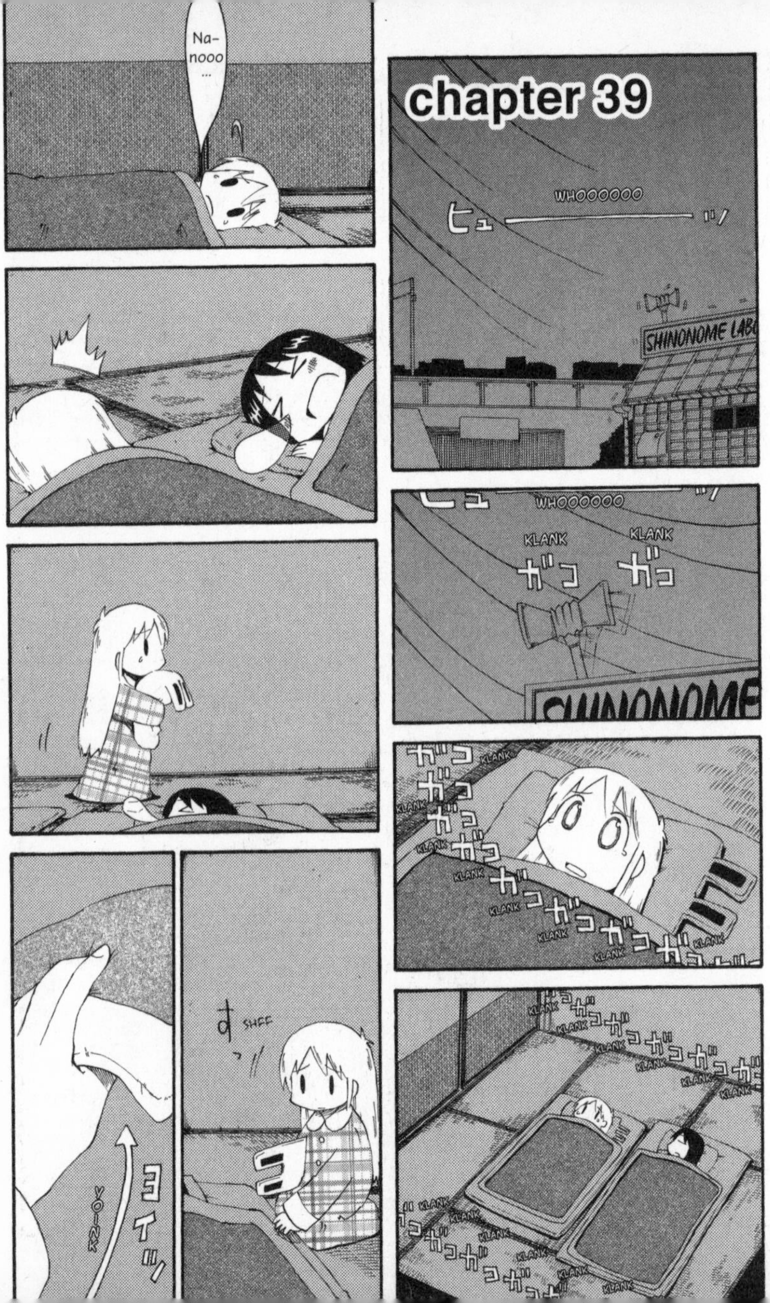
chapter 39
ヒュー ッ
WHOOOOOOO
WHOOOOOOO
ガコ ガコ
KLANK KLANK
SHINONOME LABO
KLANK
KLANK
Na-nooo ...
すっ
SHFF
ヨイッ
YOINK

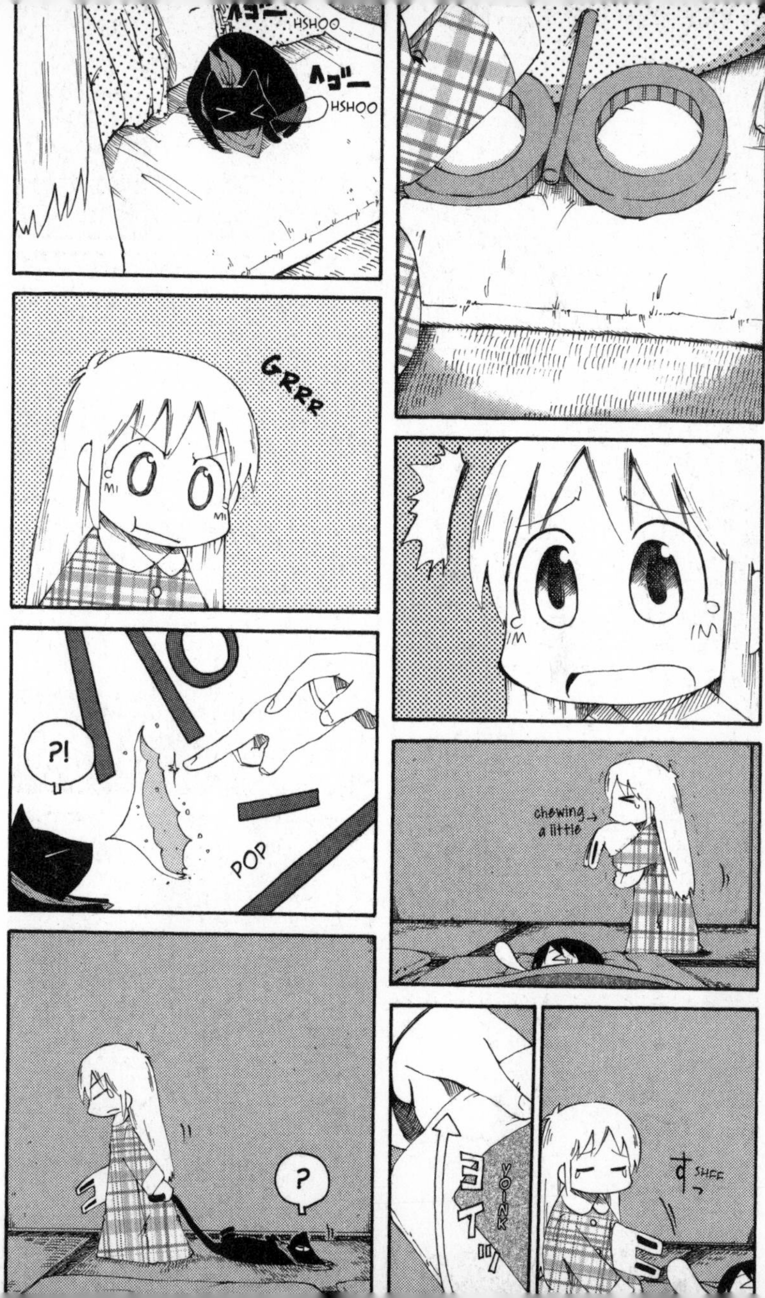

ヘゴー
HSHOO
ヘゴー
HSHOO
GRRR
chewing a little
?!
POP
ヨイ
VOINK
す
SHFF
?

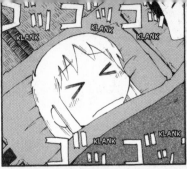

SQUEEEEZE
NNN NGH ...
KLANK
KLANK
KLANK
KLANK
KLANK
...
SQUEEEEEEZE
WHOOOOOOOO
KLANK
KLANK
KLANK
KLANK
SHINONOME
Hey ... Na-nooo ...
Na-noooo!
KLANK
KLANK
KLANK
KLANK
KLANK
KLANK
KLANK
KLANK
Mmm...? Whas happenin? Professor?

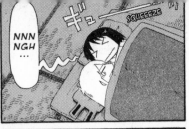

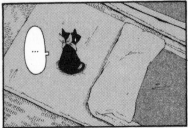

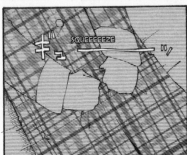

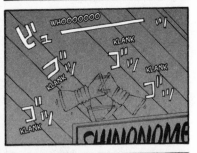

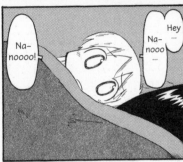

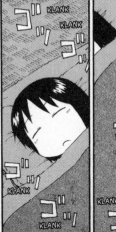

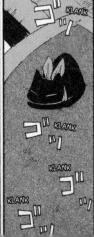

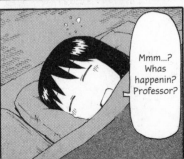

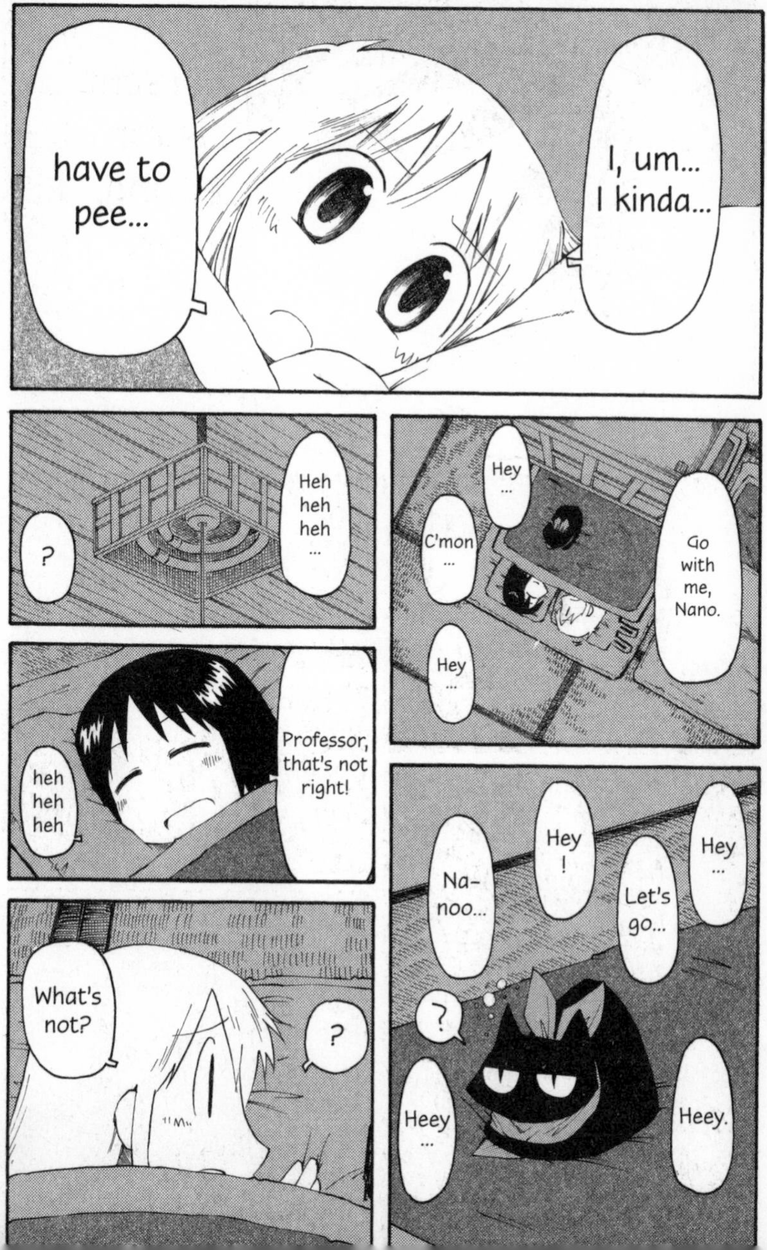
I, um... I kinda...
have to pee...
Hey ...
Go with me, Nano.
C'mon ...
Hey ...
Heh heh heh ...
?
Professor, that's not right!
heh heh heh
Hey ...
Let's go...
Hey !
Na-noo...
?
Heey.
Heey ...
?
What's not?

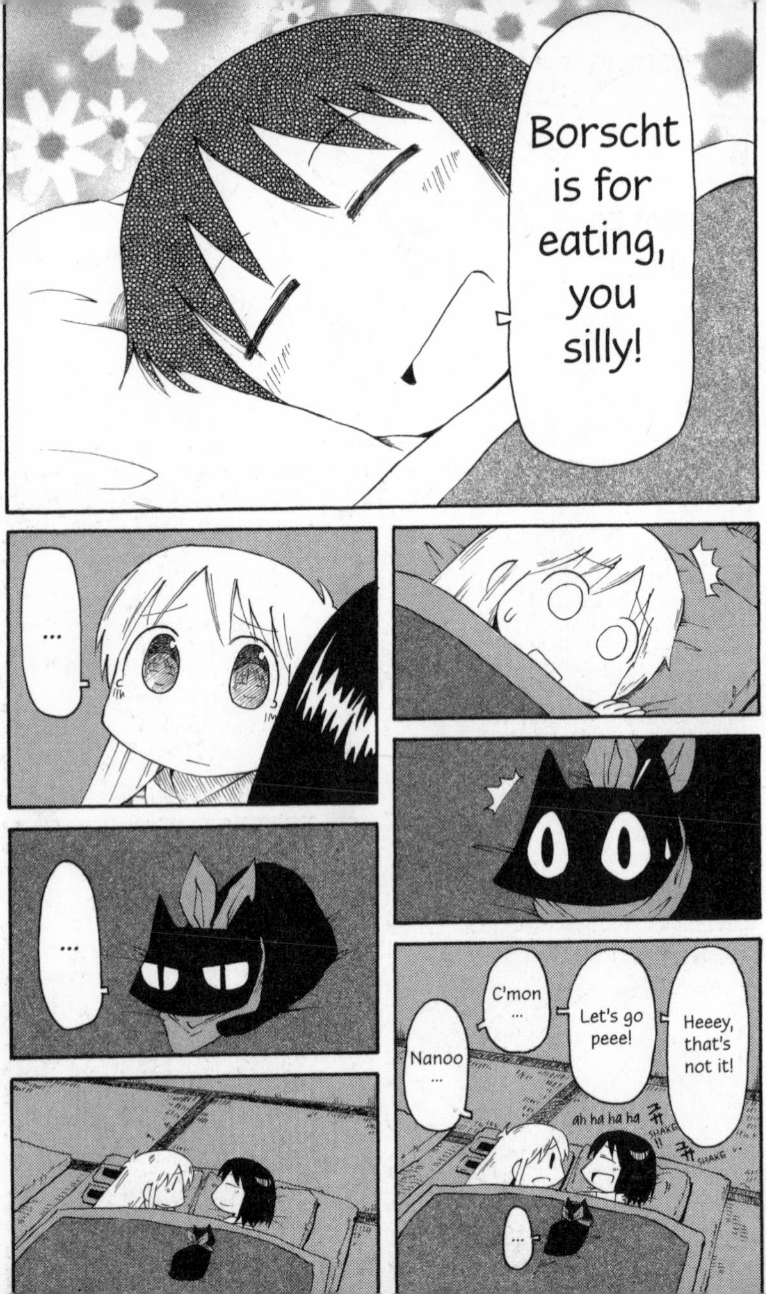
Borscht is for eating, you silly!
...
...
Heeey, that's not it!
Let's go peee!
C'mon ...
Nanoo ...
ah ha ha ha
SHAKE
SHAKE
...

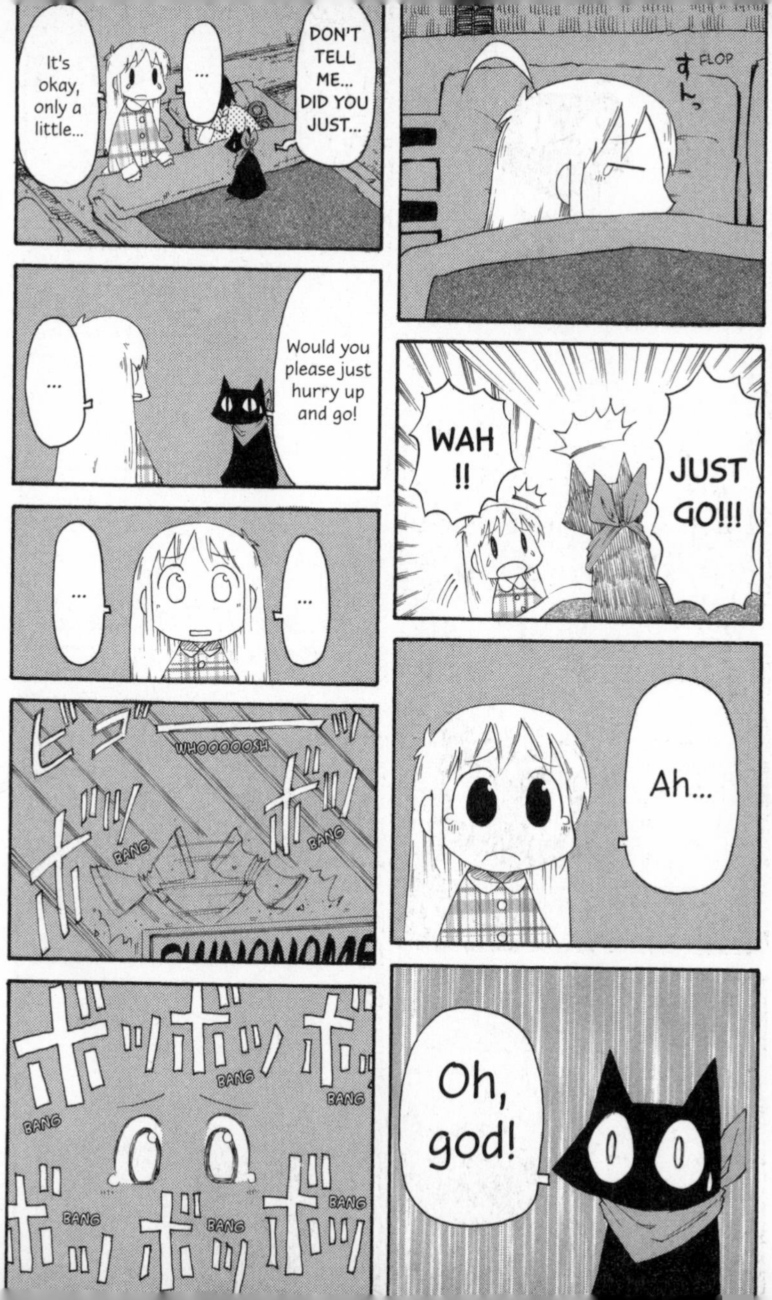
FLOP
WAH !!
JUST GO!!!
Ah...
Oh, god!
DON'T TELL ME... DID YOU JUST...
...
It's okay, only a little...
Would you please just hurry up and go!
...
...
...
WHOOOOOSH
BANG
BANG
BANG
BANG
BANG
BANG
BANG
BANG

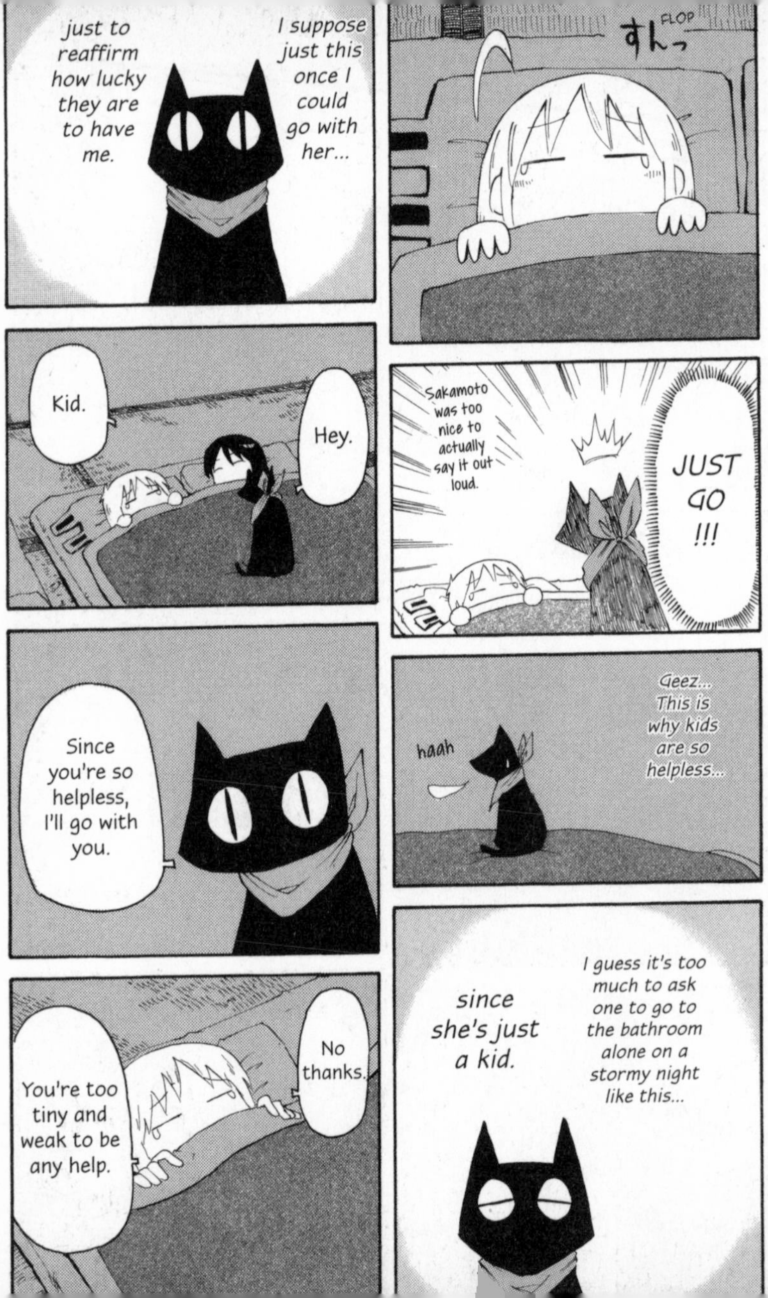
FLOP
すんっ
Sakamoto was too nice to actually say it out loud.
JUST GO !!!
haah
Geez... This is why kids are so helpless...
I guess it's too much to ask one to go to the bathroom alone on a stormy night like this...
since she's just a kid.
I suppose just this once I could go with her...
just to reaffirm how lucky they are to have me.
Hey.
Kid.
Since you're so helpless, I'll go with you.
No thanks.
You're too tiny and weak to be any help.

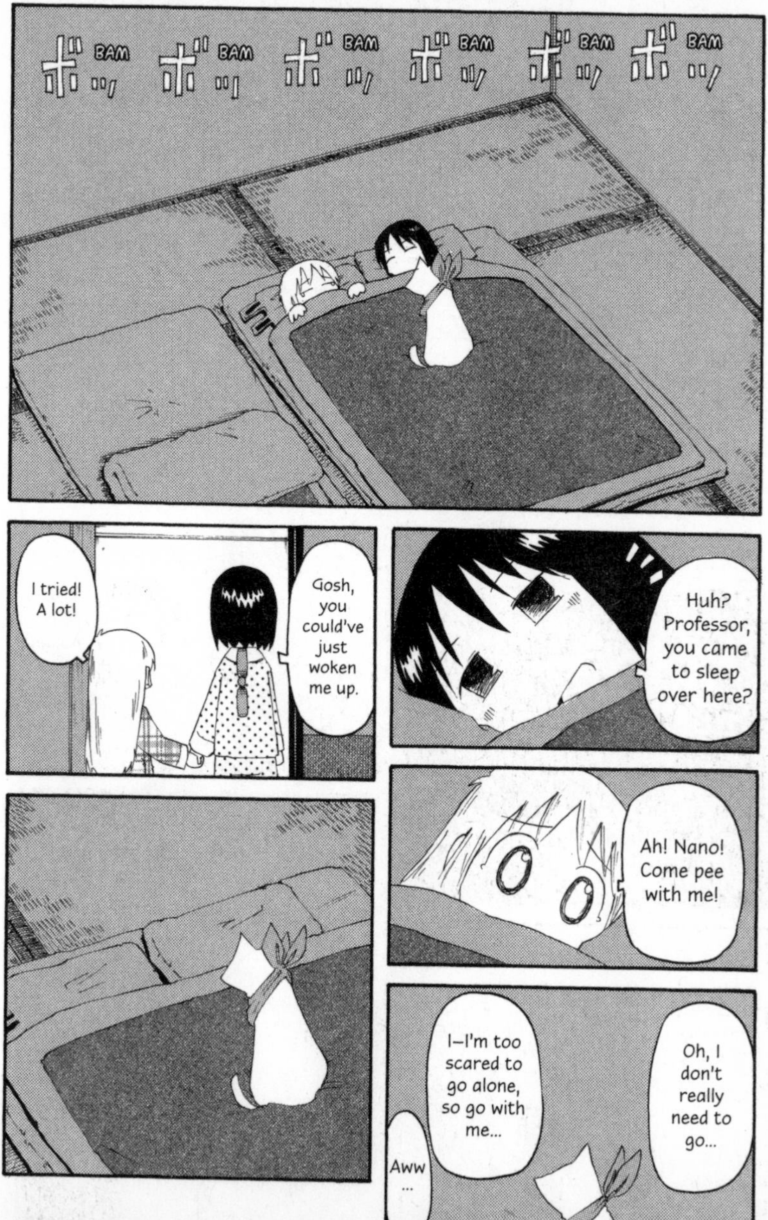
BAM
BAM
BAM
BAM
BAM
BAM
Huh? Professor, you came to sleep over here?
Gosh, you could've just woken me up.
I tried! A lot!
Ah! Nano! Come pee with me!
Oh, I don't really need to go...
I–I'm too scared to go alone, so go with me...
Aww ...

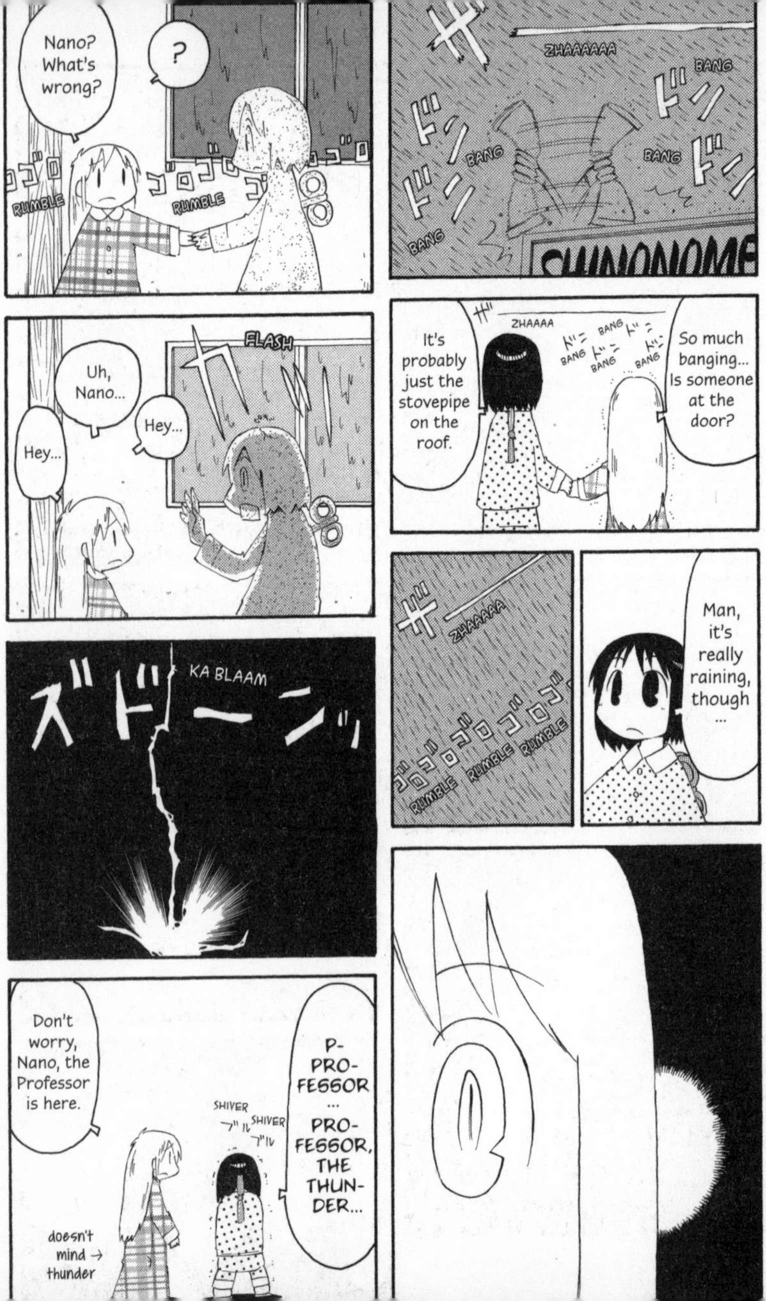
ZHAAAAAAA
BANG
BANG
BANG
BANG
SHINONOME
ZHAAAA
BANG BANG BANG BANG BANG
So much banging... Is someone at the door?
It's probably just the stovepipe on the roof.
Man, it's really raining, though ...
ZHAAAAAA
RUMBLE RUMBLE RUMBLE
?
Nano? What's wrong?
RUMBLE
RUMBLE
FLASH
Hey...
Uh, Nano...
Hey...
KA BLAAM
P-PRO-FESSOR... PRO-FESSOR, THE THUN-DER...
SHIVER SHIVER
Don't worry, Nano, the Professor is here.
doesn't mind → thunder

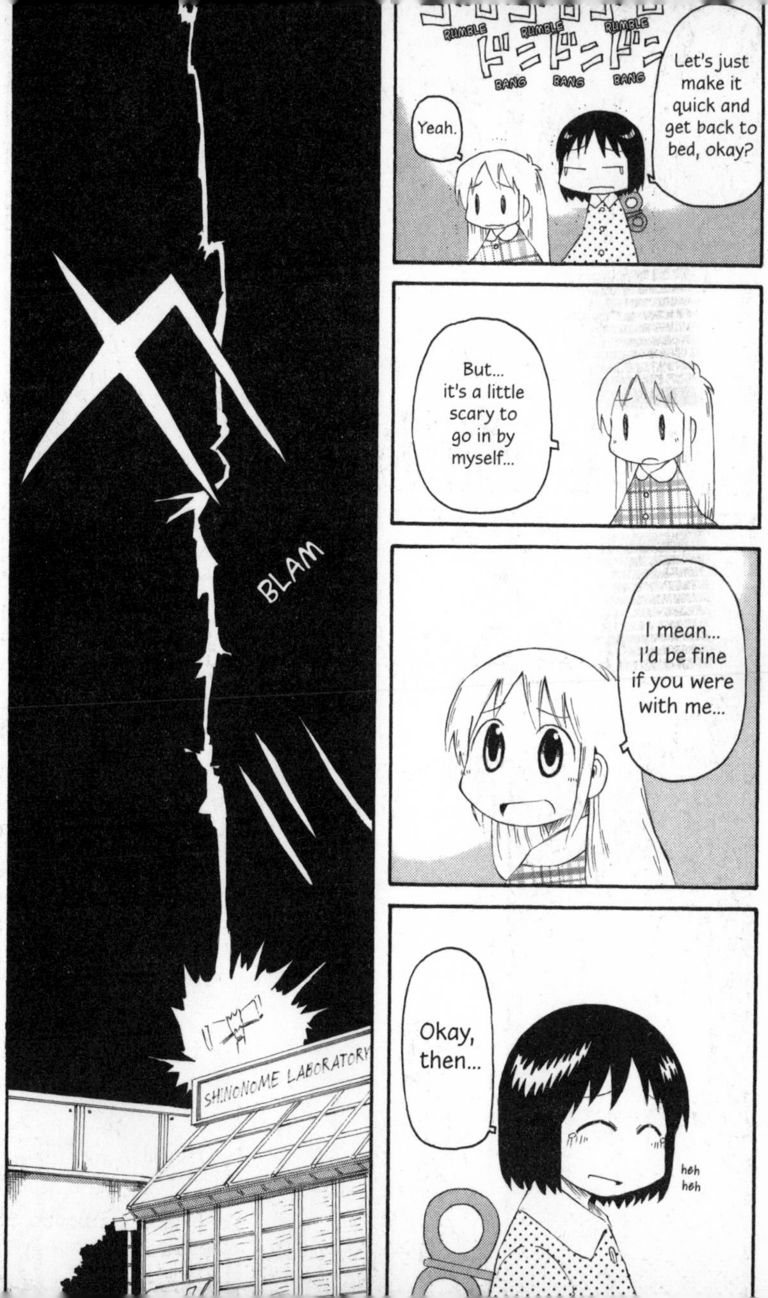
RUMBLE RUMBLE RUMBLE
ドンドンドン
BANG BANG BANG
Let's just make it quick and get back to bed, okay?
Yeah.
But... it's a little scary to go in by myself...
I mean... I'd be fine if you were with me...
Okay, then...
heh heh
BLAM
SHINONOME LABORATORY

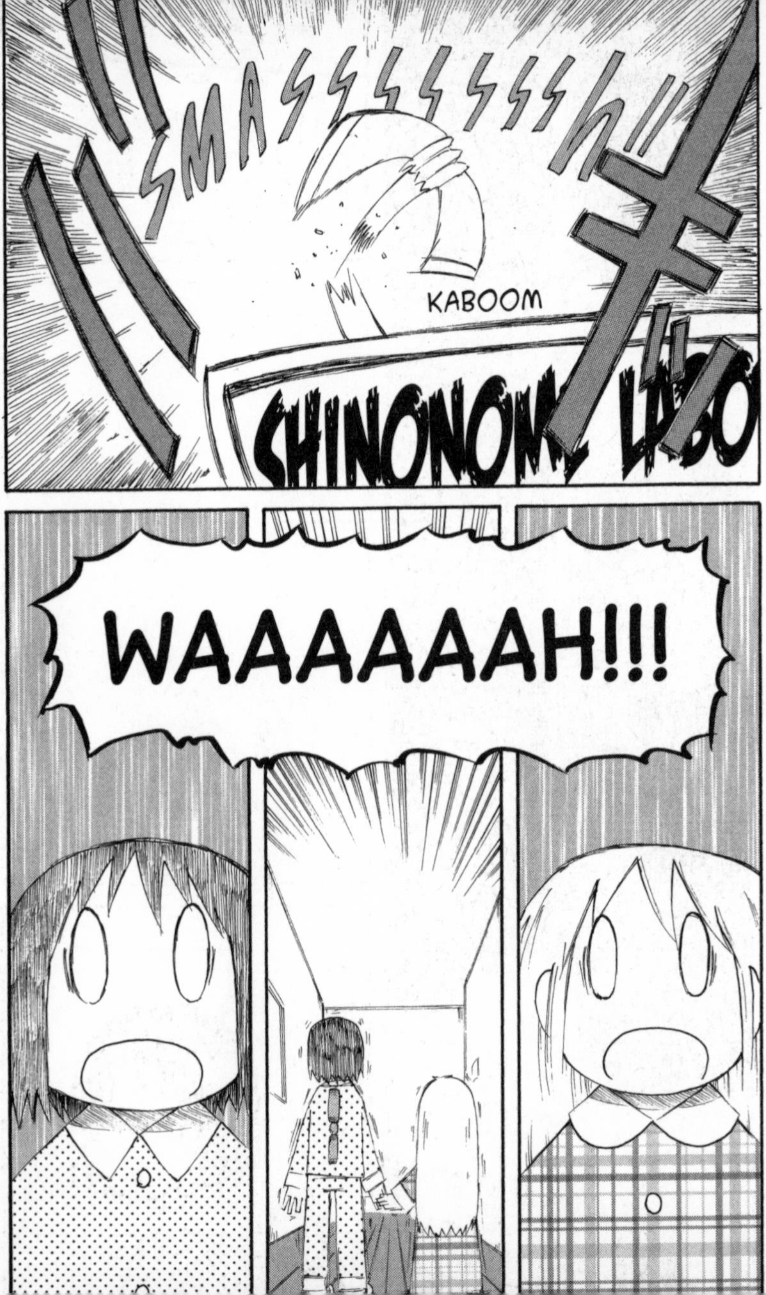
SMASSSSSSSh!!
KABOOM
WAAAAAAH!!!

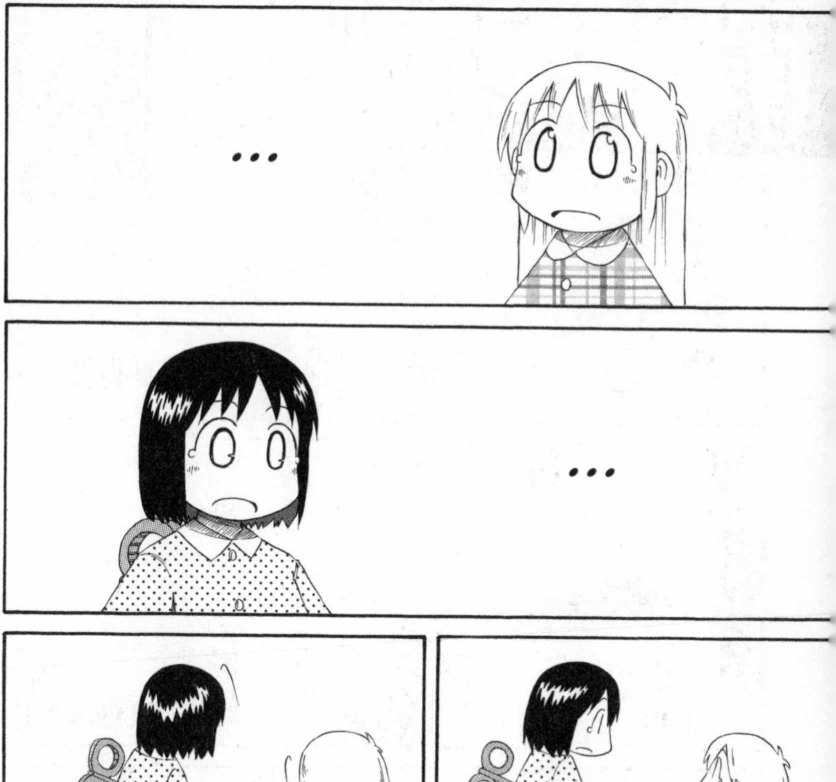
...
...

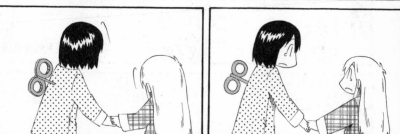

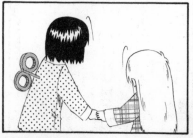

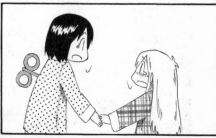

chapter 39: end

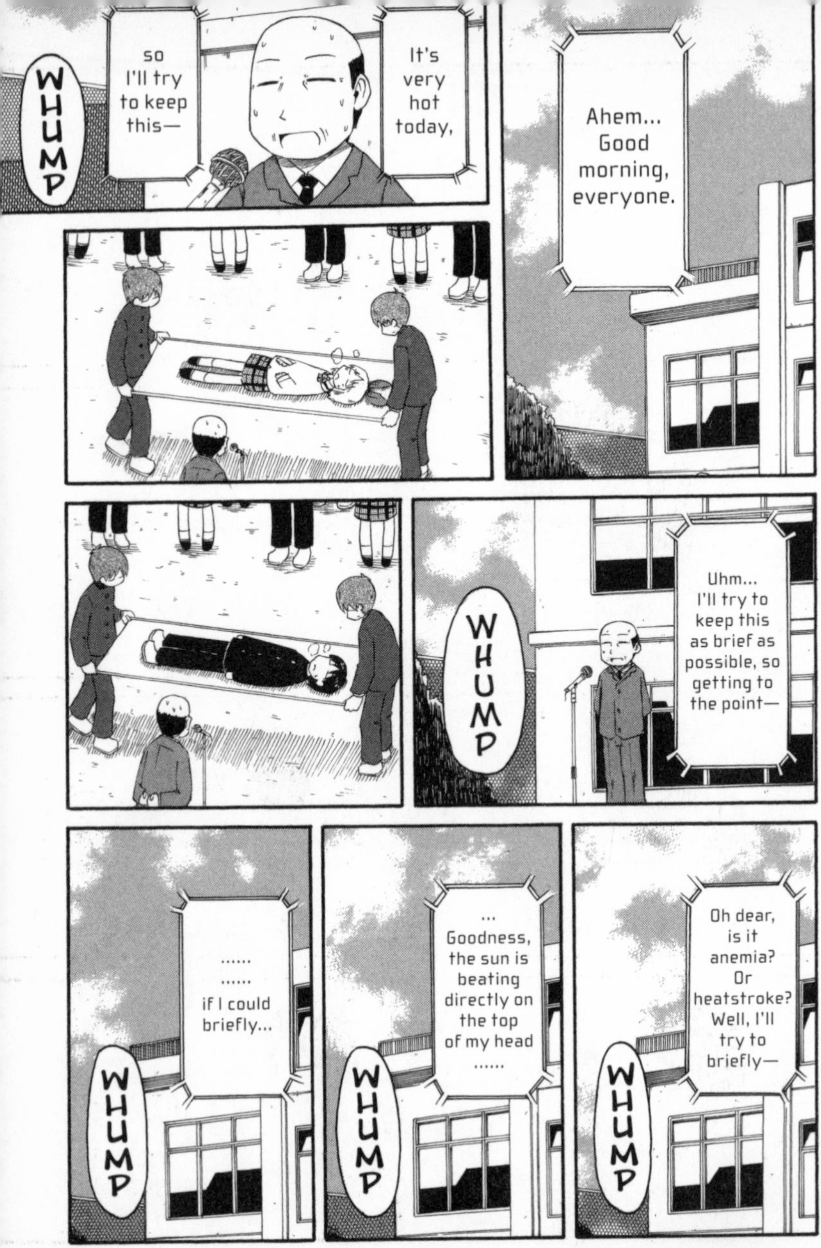
Ahem... Good morning, everyone.
It's very hot today,
so I'll try to keep this—
WHUMP
Uhm... I'll try to keep this as brief as possible, so getting to the point—
WHUMP
Oh dear, is it anemia? Or heatstroke? Well, I'll try to briefly—
WHUMP
... Goodness, the sun is beating directly on the top of my head ......
WHUMP
.... if I could briefly...
WHUMP

chapter 40

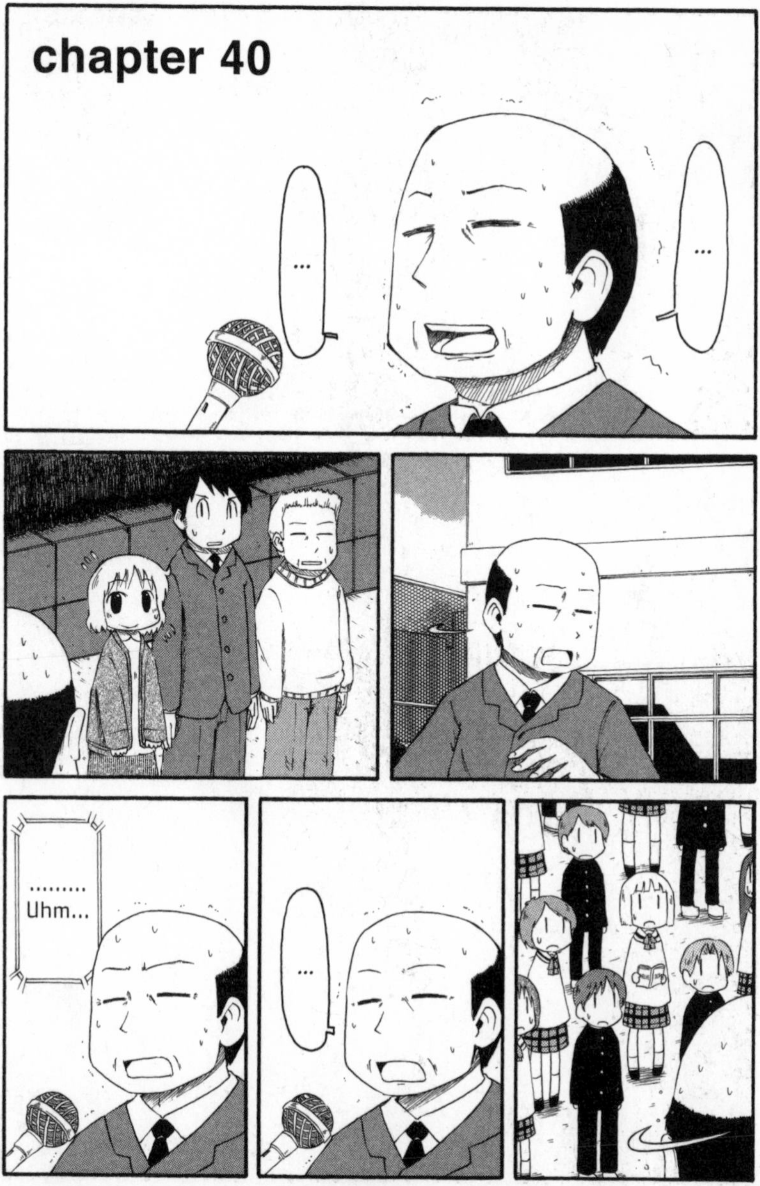

...
...
...
....
Uhm...

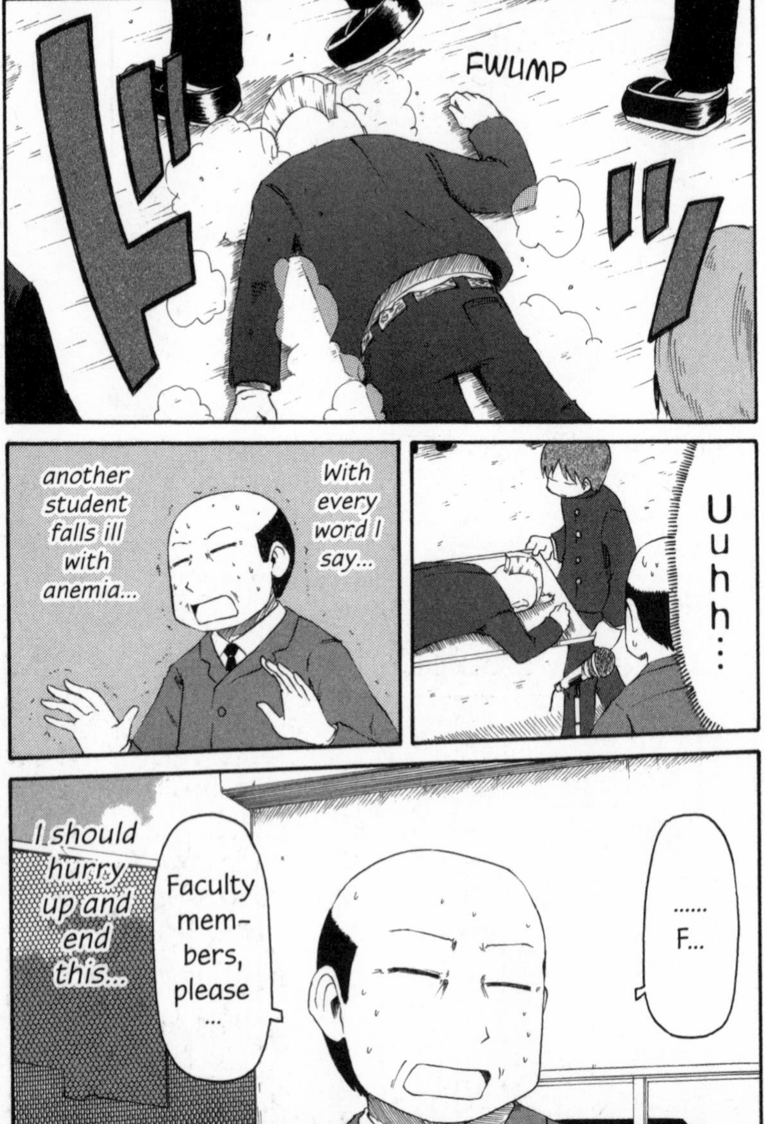
FWUMP
Uuhh...
With every word I say...
another student falls ill with anemia...
...... F...
Faculty mem-bers, please ...
I should hurry up and end this...

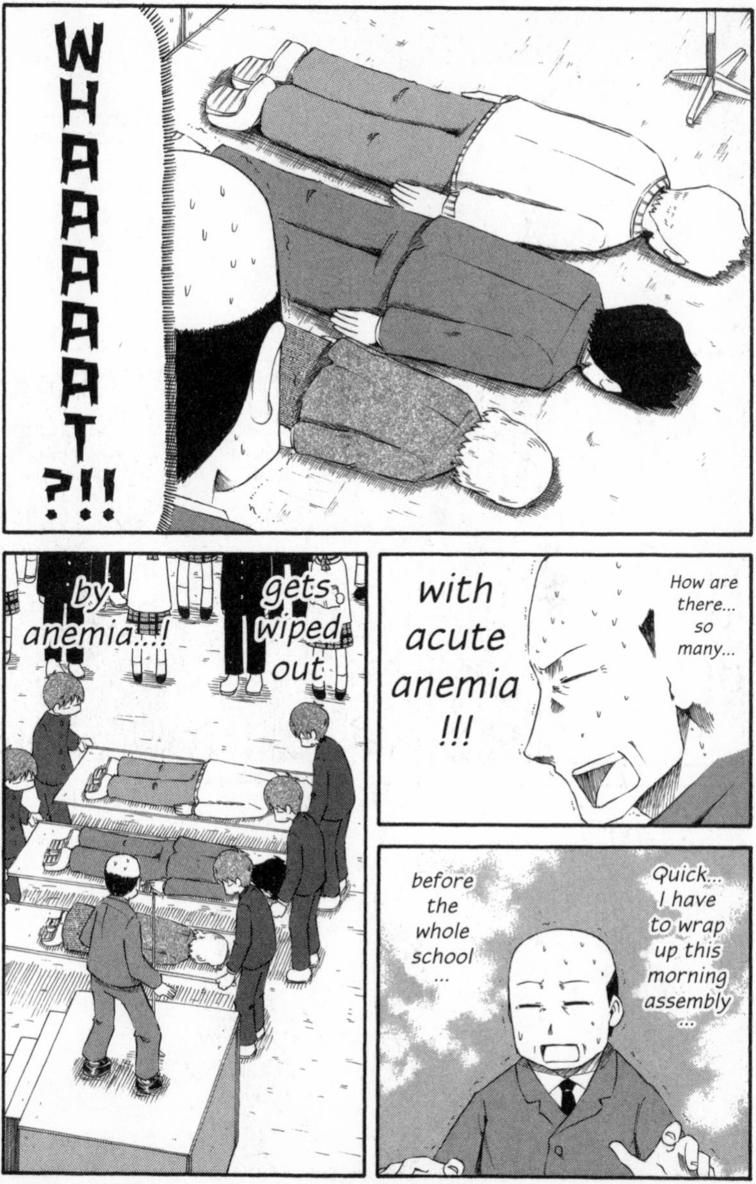
WHAAAAAT?!!
How are there... so many...
with acute anemia!!!
Quick... I have to wrap up this morning assembly...
before the whole school...
gets wiped out
by anemia...!

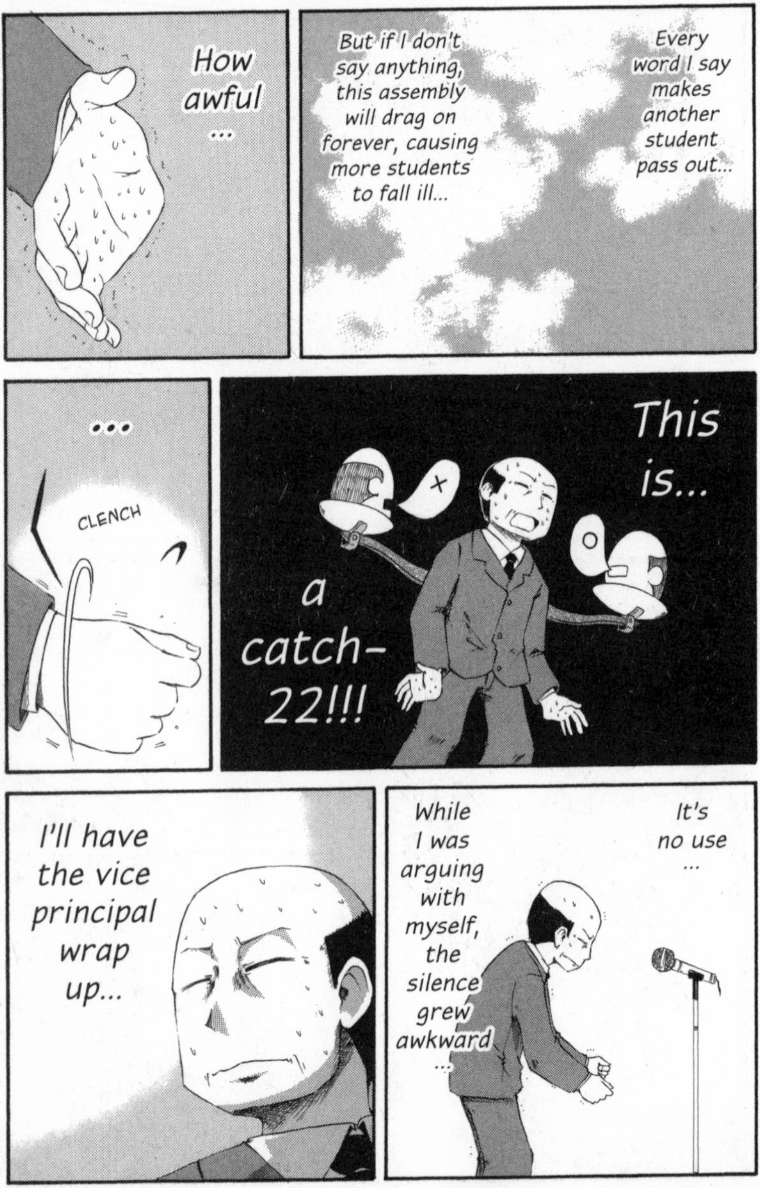
Every word I say makes another student pass out...
But if I don't say anything, this assembly will drag on forever, causing more students to fall ill...
How awful ...
This is...
a catch-22!!!
...
CLENCH
It's no use ...
While I was arguing with myself, the silence grew awkward ...
I'll have the vice principal wrap up...

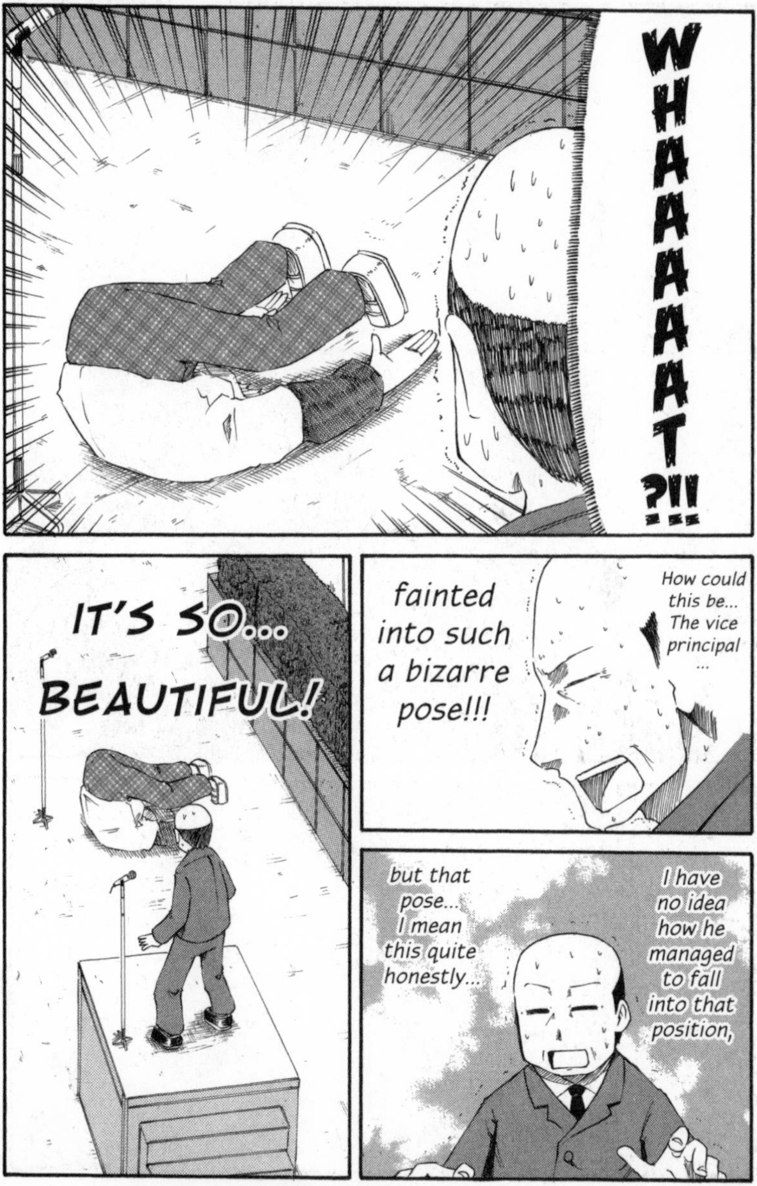
WHAAAAAT?!!
How could this be... The vice principal ...
fainted into such a bizarre pose!!!
I have no idea how he managed to fall into that position,
but that pose... I mean this quite honestly...
IT'S SO... BEAUTIFUL!

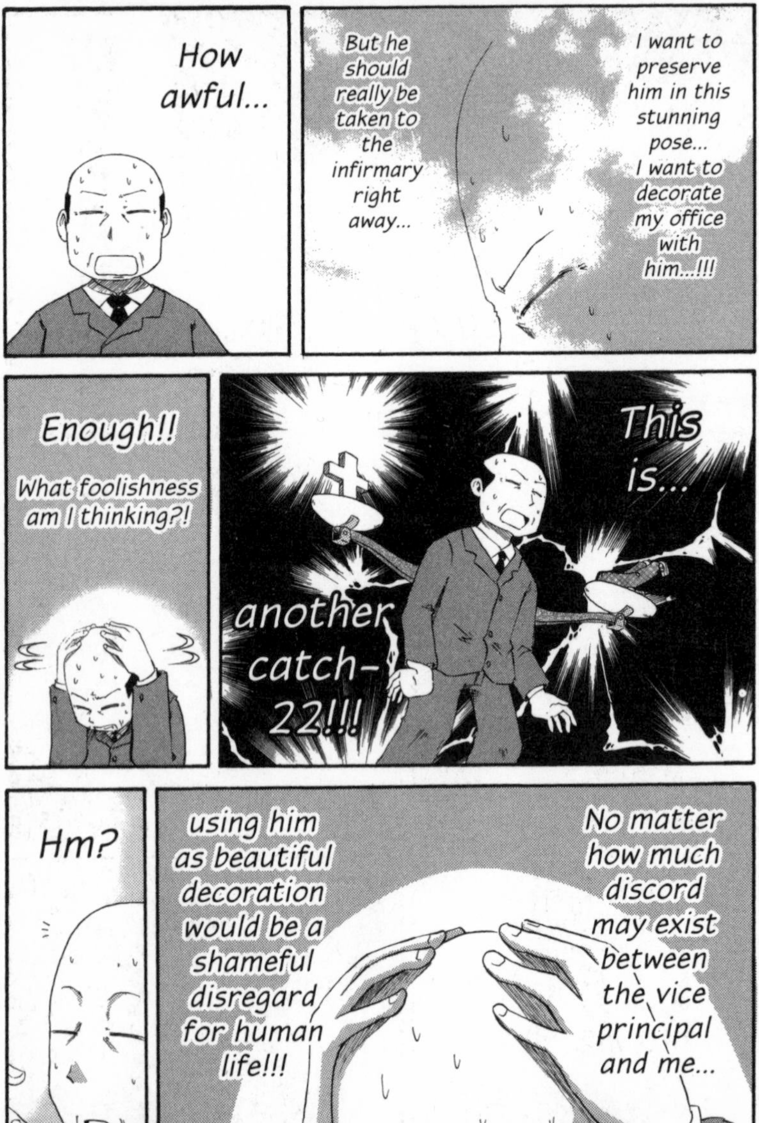
I want to preserve him in this stunning pose... I want to decorate my office with him...!!!
But he should really be taken to the infirmary right away...
How awful...
This is... another catch-22!!!
Enough!!
What foolishness am I thinking?!
No matter how much discord may exist between the vice principal and me...
using him as beautiful decoration would be a shameful disregard for human life!!!
Hm?

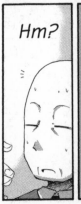

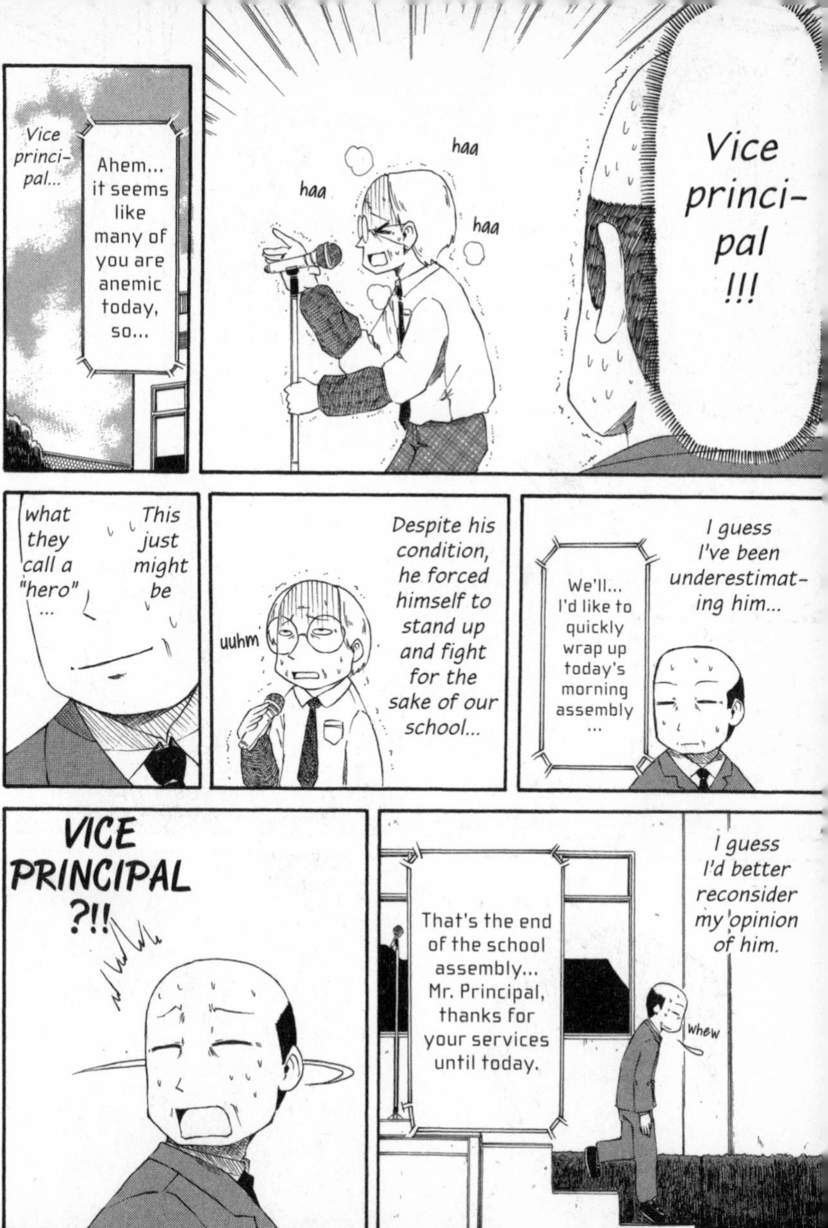

Vice principal !!!
haa
haa
haa
Ahem... it seems like many of you are anemic today, so...
Vice principal...
I guess I've been underestimating him...
We'll... I'd like to quickly wrap up today's morning assembly ...
Despite his condition, he forced himself to stand up and fight for the sake of our school...
uuhm
This just might be
what they call a "hero" ...
I guess I'd better reconsider my opinion of him.
That's the end of the school assembly... Mr. Principal, thanks for your services until today.
whew
VICE PRINCIPAL ?!!

chapter 40: end

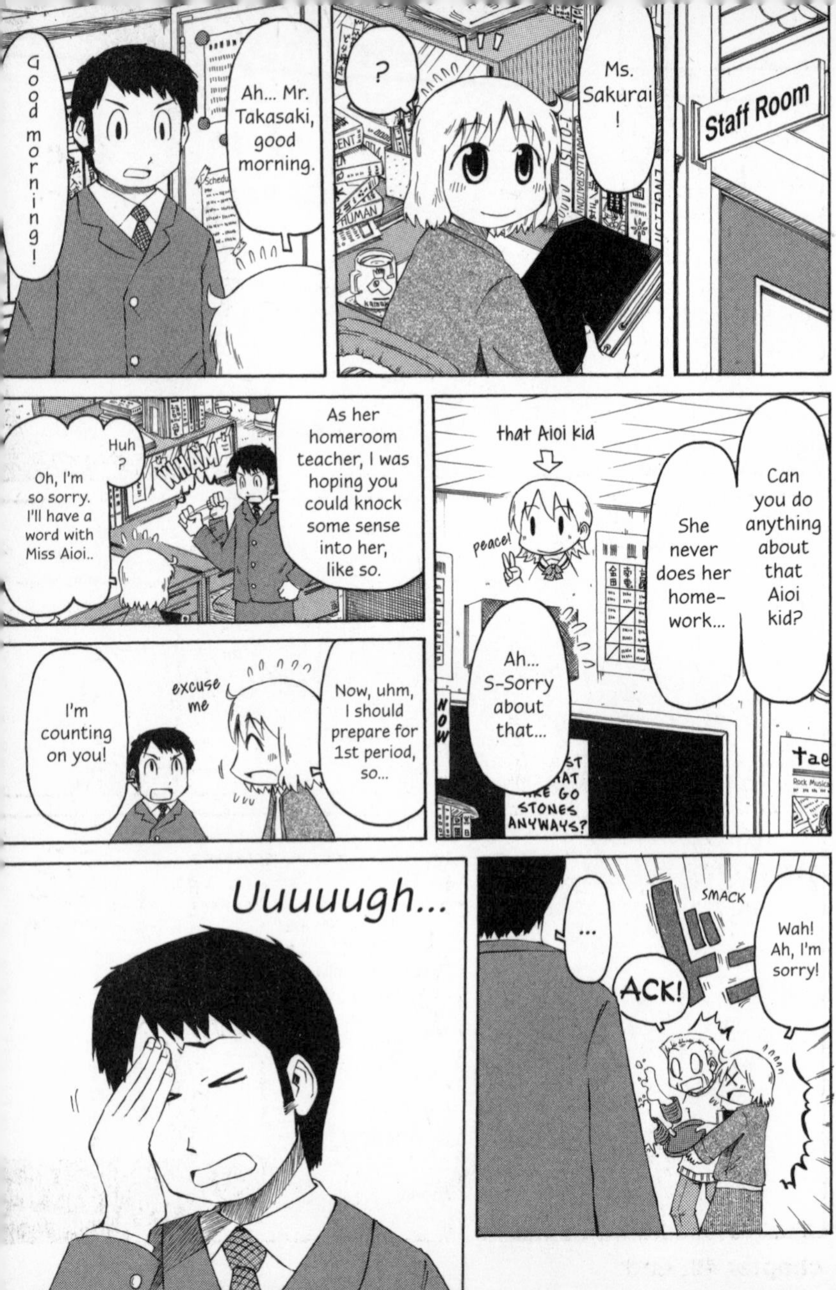

Staff Room
Ms. Sakurai!
?
Ah... Mr. Takasaki, good morning.
Good morning!
Can you do anything about that Aioi kid?
She never does her homework...
that Aioi kid
peace!
Ah... S-Sorry about that...
STONES ANYWAYS?
As her homeroom teacher, I was hoping you could knock some sense into her, like so.
WHAM
Huh?
Oh, I'm so sorry. I'll have a word with Miss Aioi..
Now, uhm, I should prepare for 1st period, so...
excuse me
I'm counting on you!
Wah! Ah, I'm sorry!
SMACK
...
ACK!
Uuuuugh...

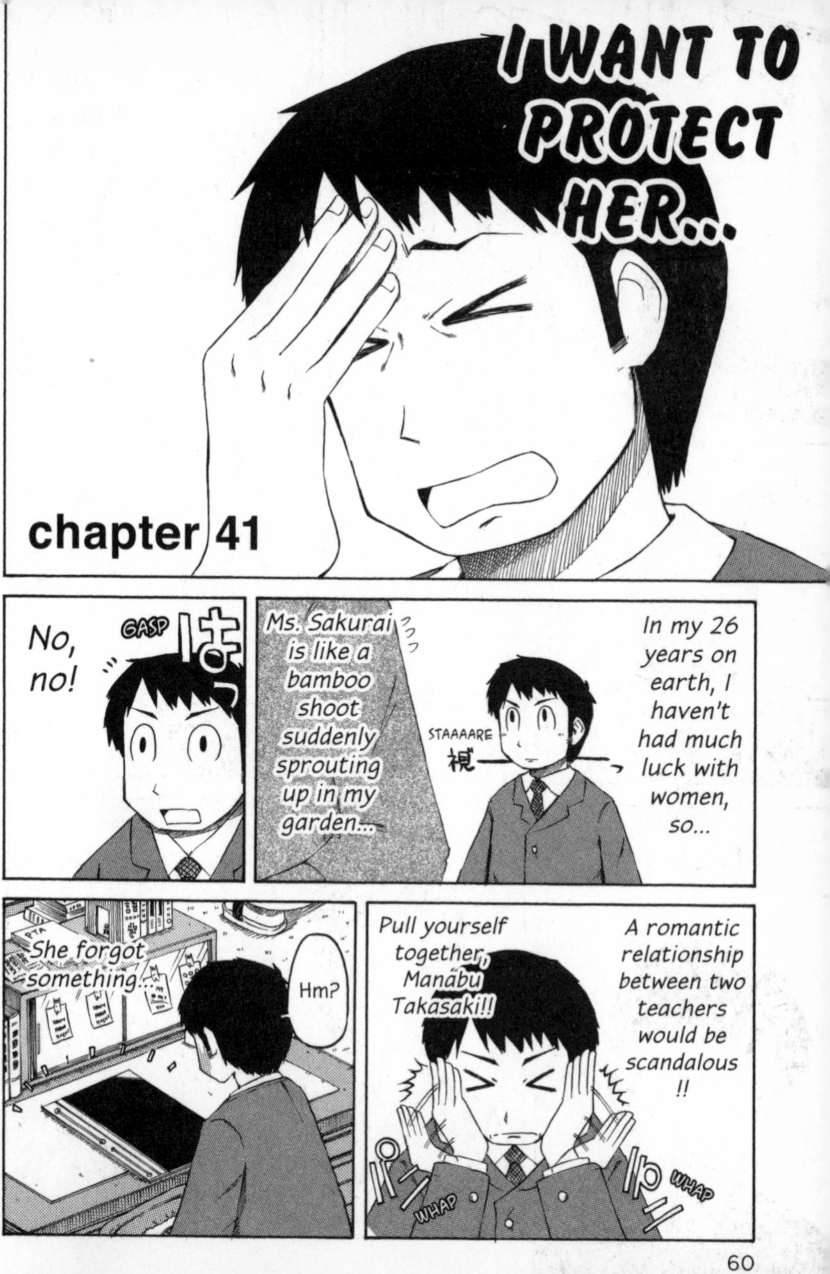
I WANT TO PROTECT HER...
chapter 41
In my 26 years on earth, I haven't had much luck with women, so...
STAAAARE
視
Ms. Sakurai is like a bamboo shoot suddenly sprouting up in my garden...
GASP
No, no!
A romantic relationship between two teachers would be scandalous!!
Pull yourself together, Manābu Takasaki!!
WHAP
WHAP
Hm?
She forgot something...
PTA

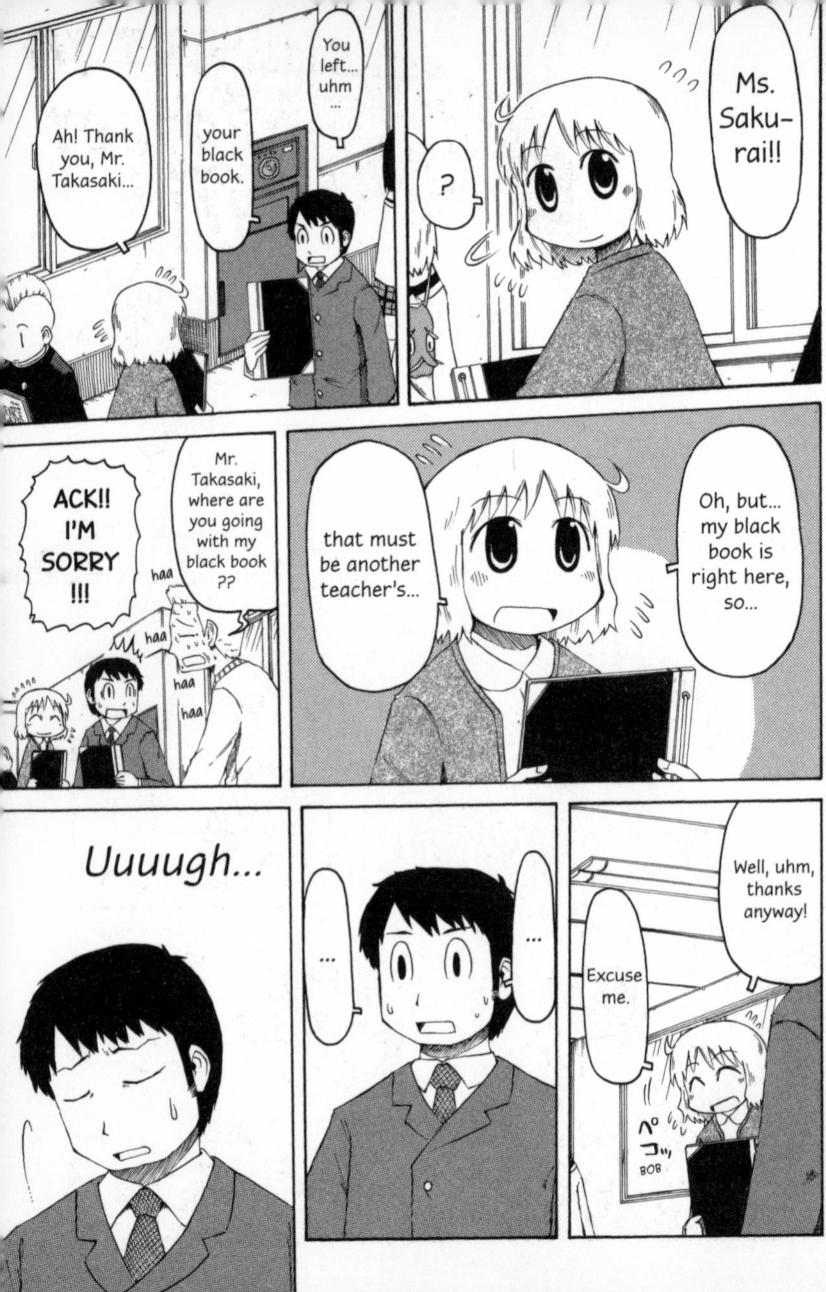

Ms. Saku-rai!!
?
You left... uhm ...
your black book.
Ah! Thank you, Mr. Takasaki...
Oh, but... my black book is right here, so...
that must be another teacher's...
Mr. Takasaki, where are you going with my black book ??
ACK!! I'M SORRY !!!
haa
haa
haa
haa
Well, uhm, thanks anyway!
Excuse me.
ペコッ
BOB
...
...
Uuuugh...

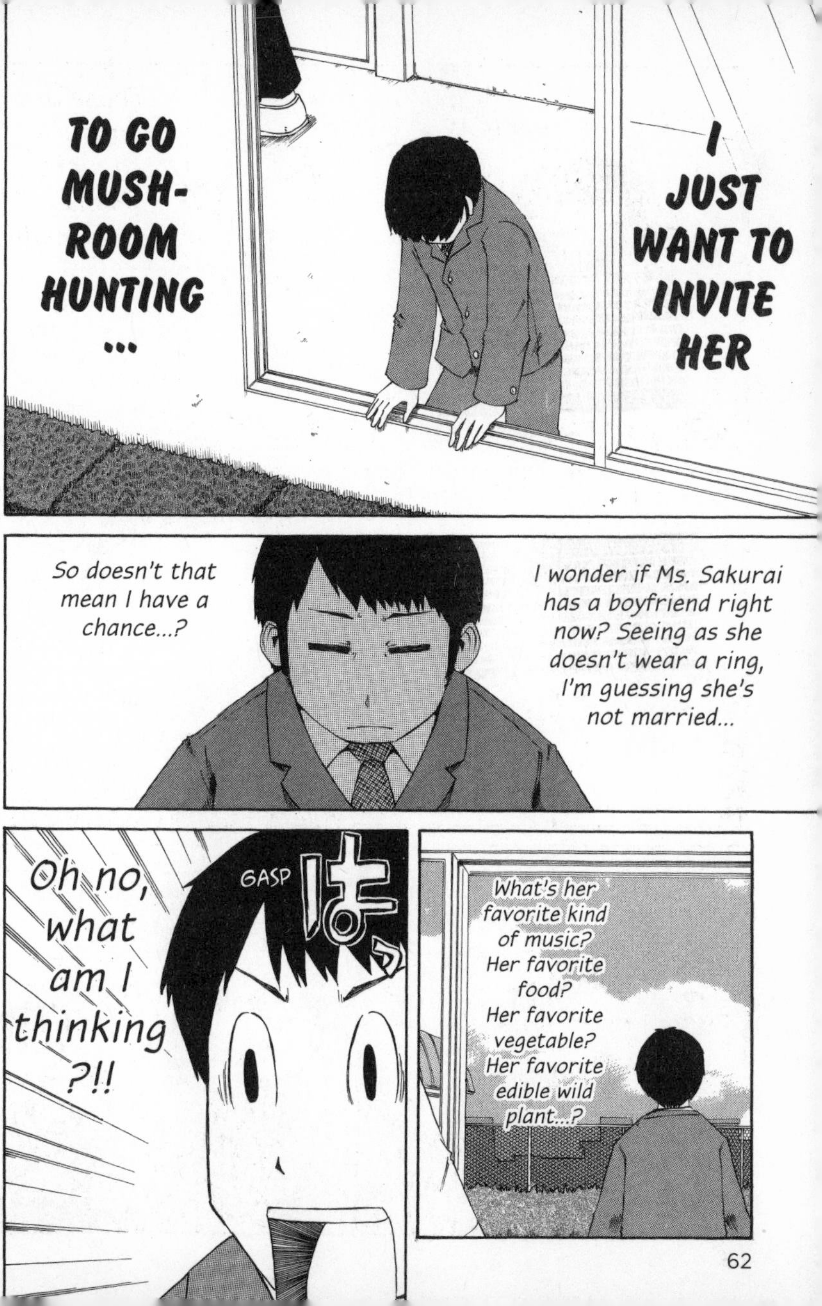
I JUST WANT TO INVITE HER
TO GO MUSH-ROOM HUNTING ...
I wonder if Ms. Sakurai has a boyfriend right now? Seeing as she doesn't wear a ring, I'm guessing she's not married...
So doesn't that mean I have a chance...?
What's her favorite kind of music? Her favorite food? Her favorite vegetable? Her favorite edible wild plant...?
GASP
はっ
Oh no, what am I thinking?!!

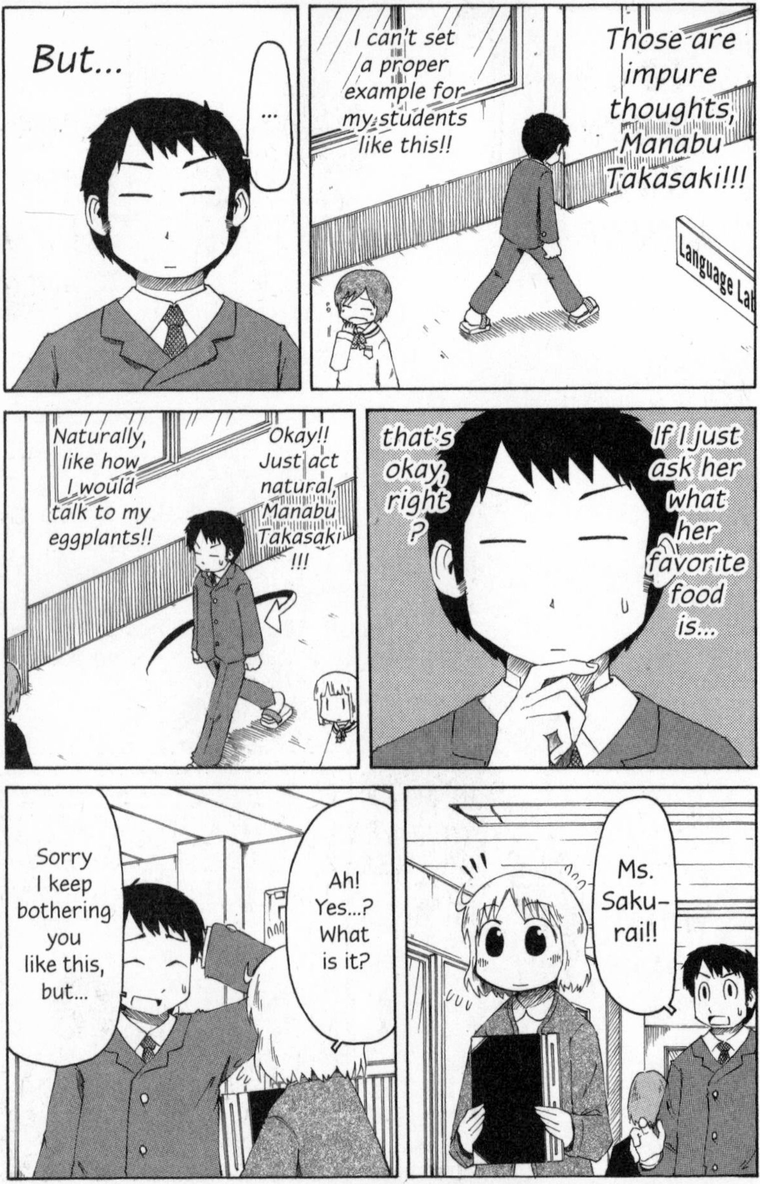
Those are impure thoughts, Manabu Takasaki!!!
I can't set a proper example for my students like this!!
Language La
...
But...
If I just ask her what her favorite food is...
that's okay, right?
Okay!! Just act natural, Manabu Takasaki!!!
Naturally, like how I would talk to my eggplants!!
Ms. Saku-rai!!
Ah! Yes...? What is it?
Sorry I keep bothering you like this, but...

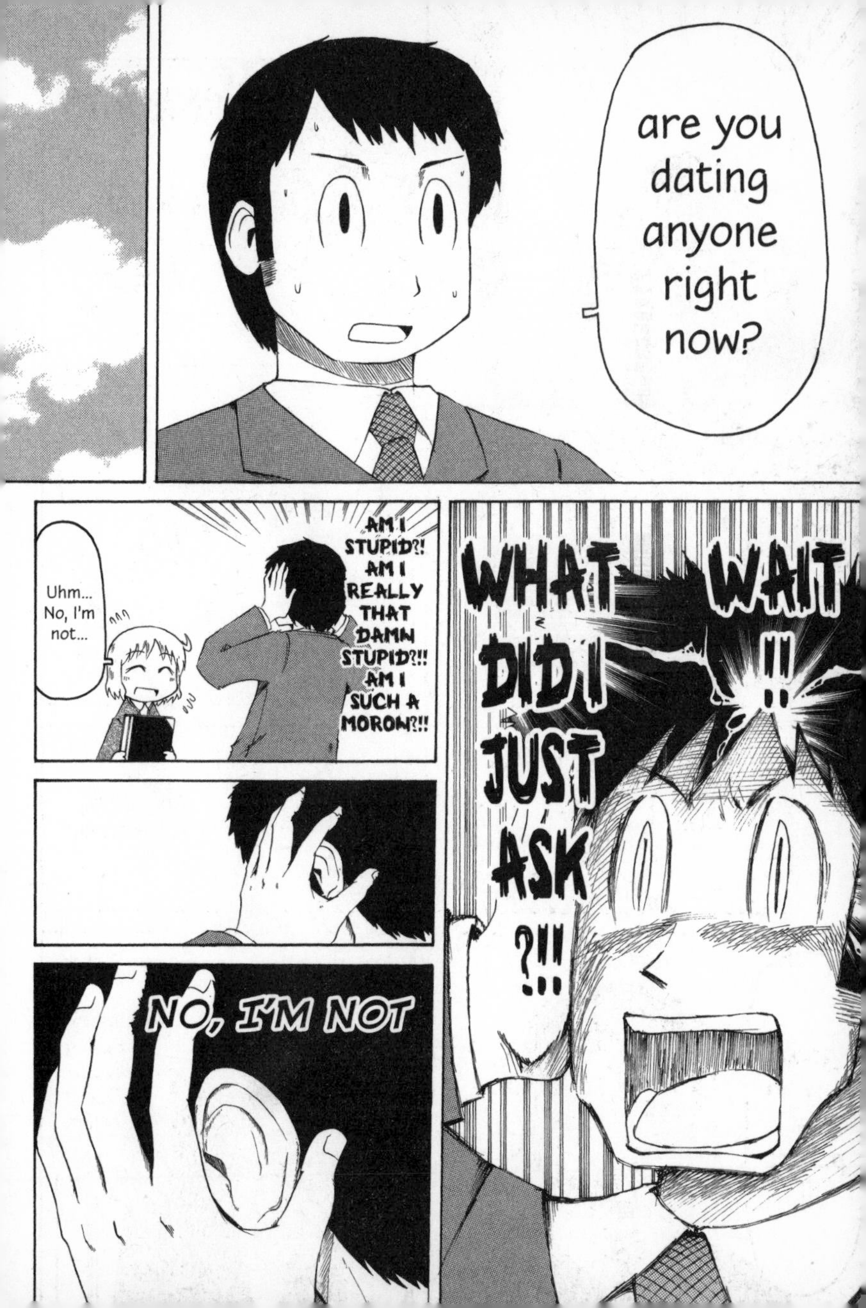
are you dating anyone right now?
WAIT!!
WHAT DID I JUST ASK?!!
AM I STUPID?! AM I REALLY THAT DAMN STUPID?!! AM I SUCH A MORON?!!
Uhm... No, I'm not...
NO, I'M NOT

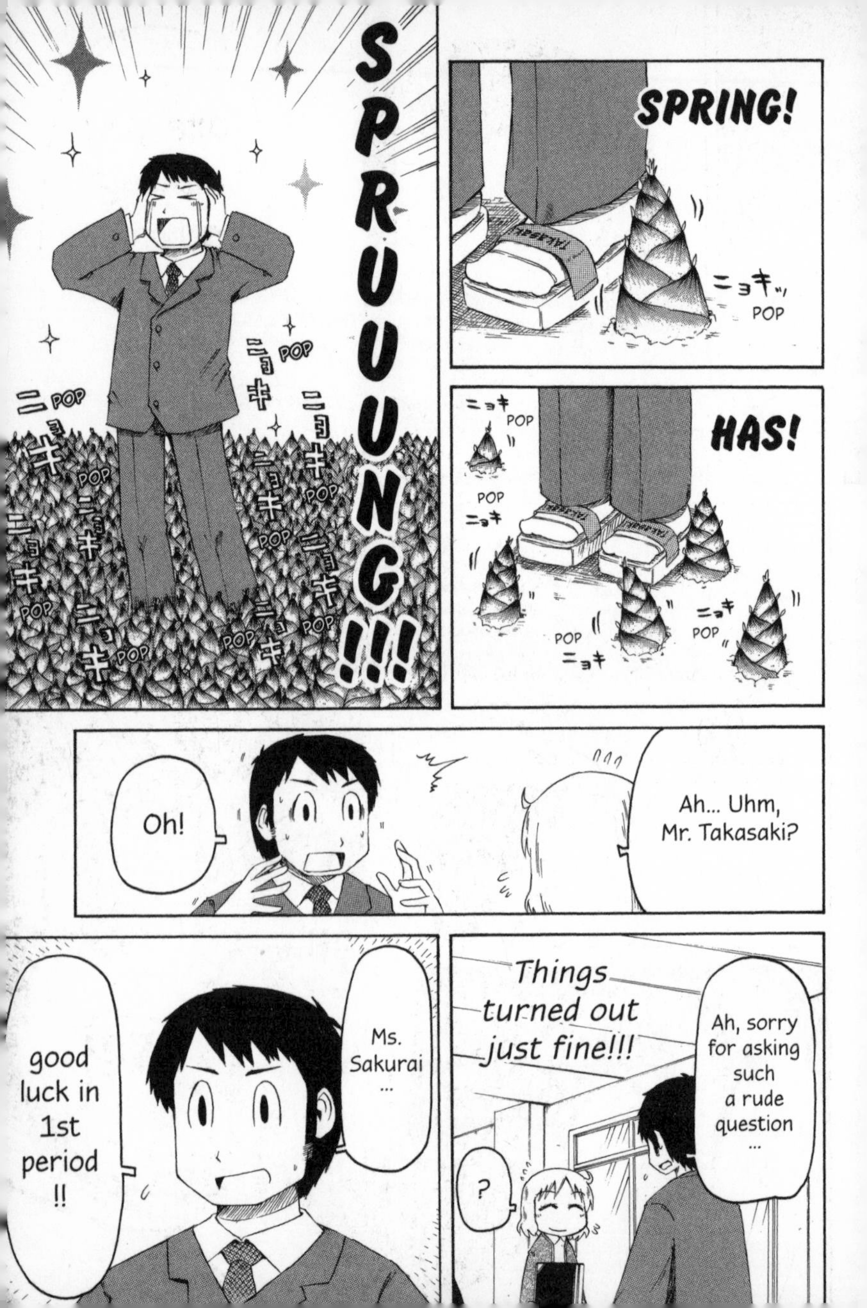
SPRING!
ニョキッ
POP
HAS!
ニョキ
POP
SPRUUUNG!!!
ニョキ
POP
Ah... Uhm, Mr. Takasaki?
Oh!
Things turned out just fine!!!
Ah, sorry for asking such a rude question ...
?
Ms. Sakurai ...
good luck in 1st period !!

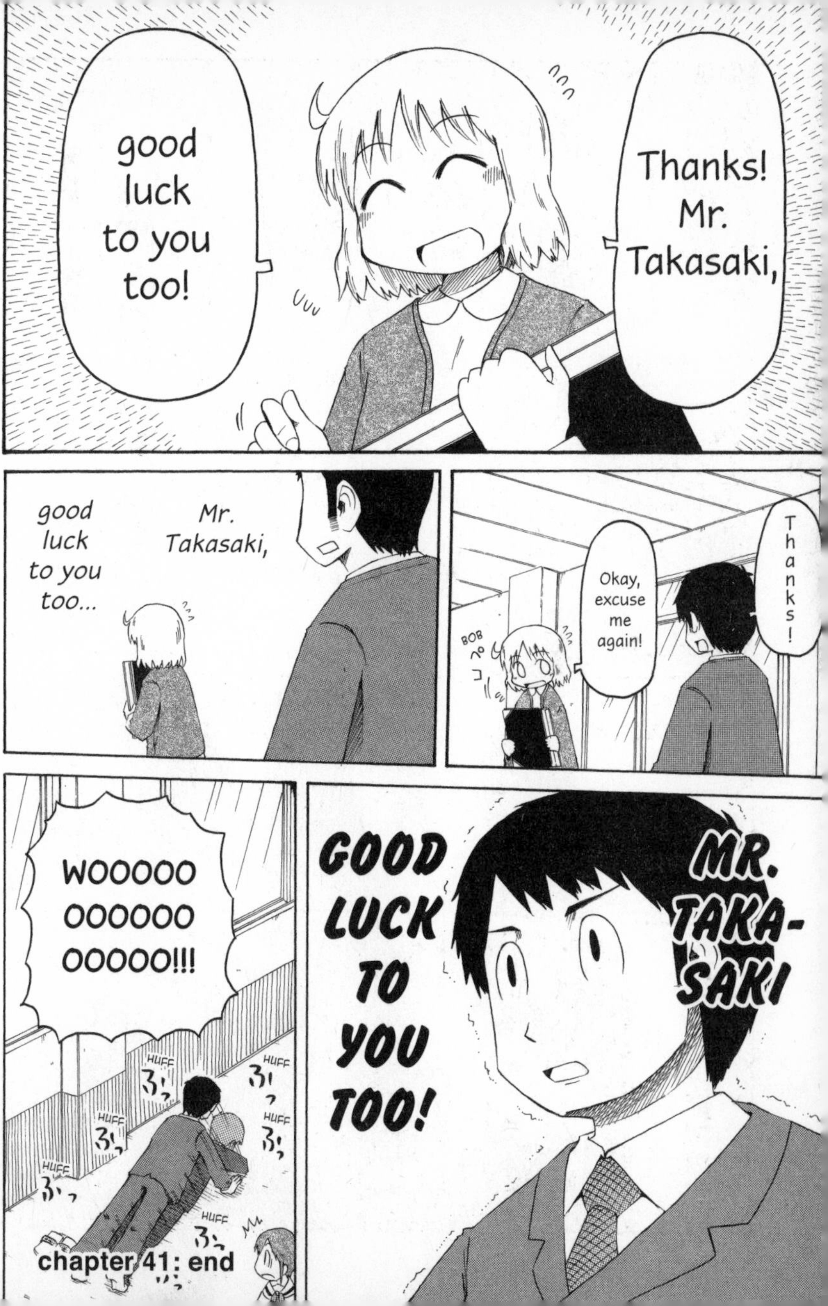
Thanks! Mr. Takasaki,
good luck to you too!
Thanks!
Okay, excuse me again!
BOB
Mr. Takasaki,
good luck to you too...
MR. TAKA-SAKI
GOOD LUCK TO YOU TOO!
WOOOOOOOOOOOOOOOO!!!
HUFF
HUFF
HUFF
HUFF
HUFF
HUFF
chapter 41: end

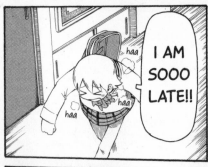

haa haa haa

I AM SOOO LATE!!

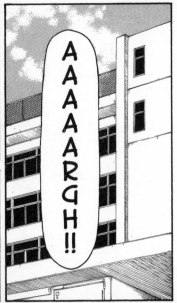

AAAAARGH!!

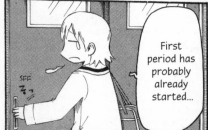

First period has probably already started...

SFF

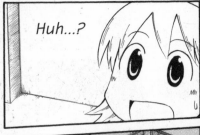

Huh...?

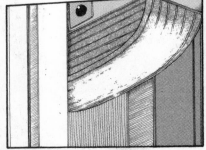

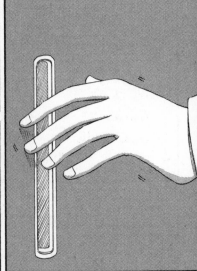

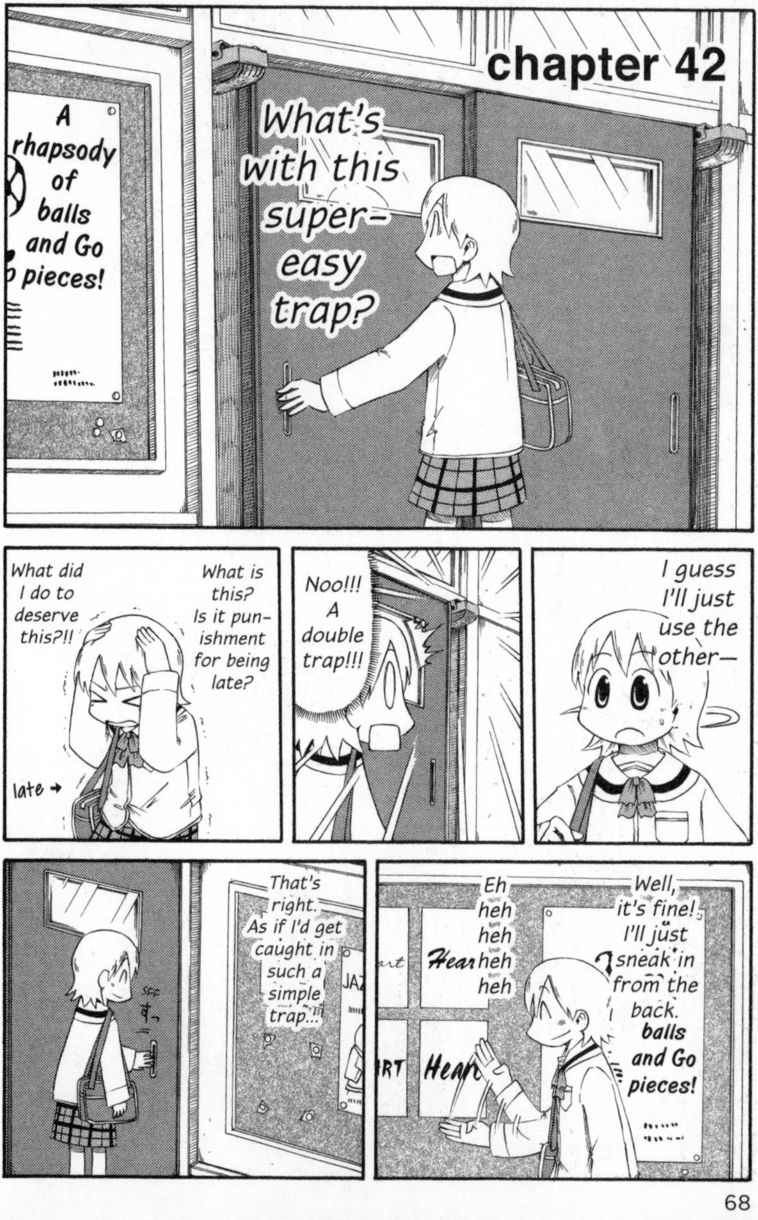
chapter 42
What's with this super-easy trap?
A rhapsody of balls and Go pieces!
I guess I'll just use the other—
Noo!!! A double trap!!!
What is this? Is it punishment for being late?
What did I do to deserve this?!!
late →
Well, it's fine! I'll just sneak in from the back.
balls and Go pieces!
Eh heh heh heh heh
Heart
Heart
That's right. As if I'd get caught in such a simple trap...
すっ

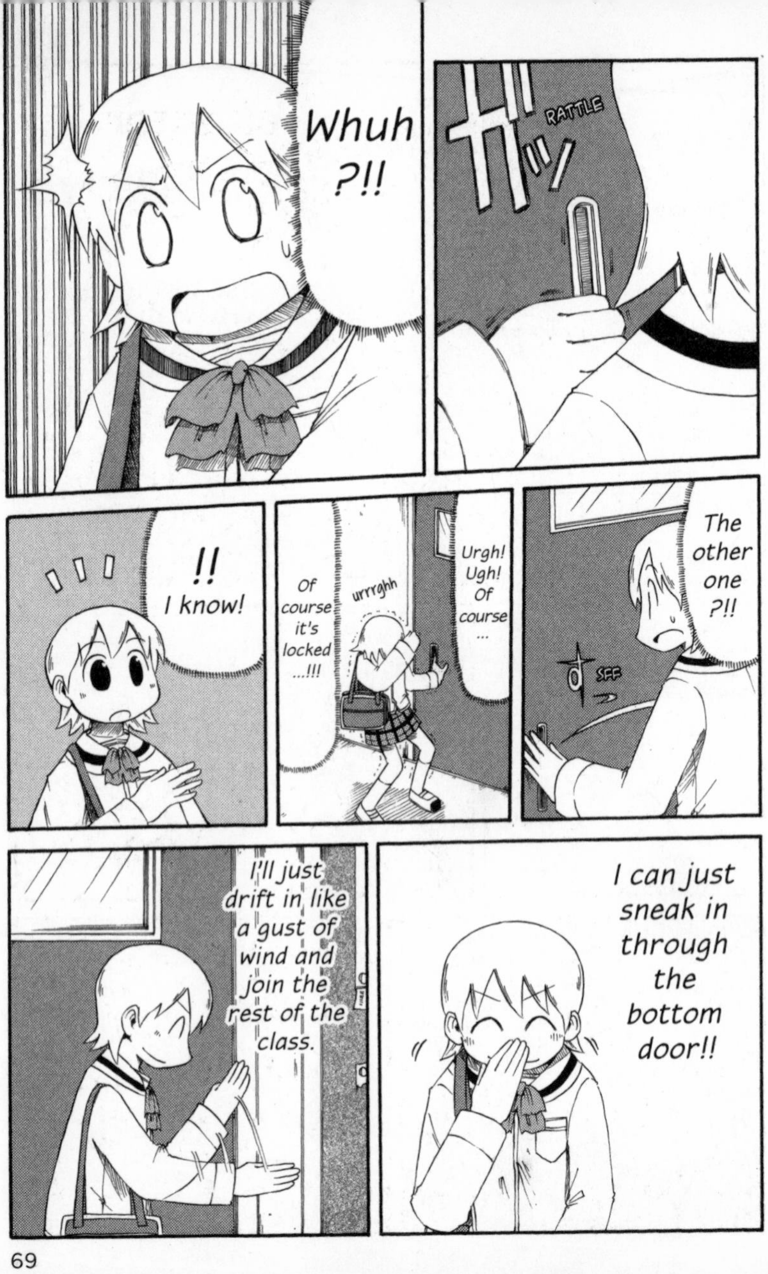
RATTLE
Whuh ?!!
The other one ?!!
SFF
Urgh! Ugh! Of course ...
urrrghh
Of course it's locked ...!!!
!! I know!
I can just sneak in through the bottom door!!
I'll just drift in like a gust of wind and join the rest of the class.

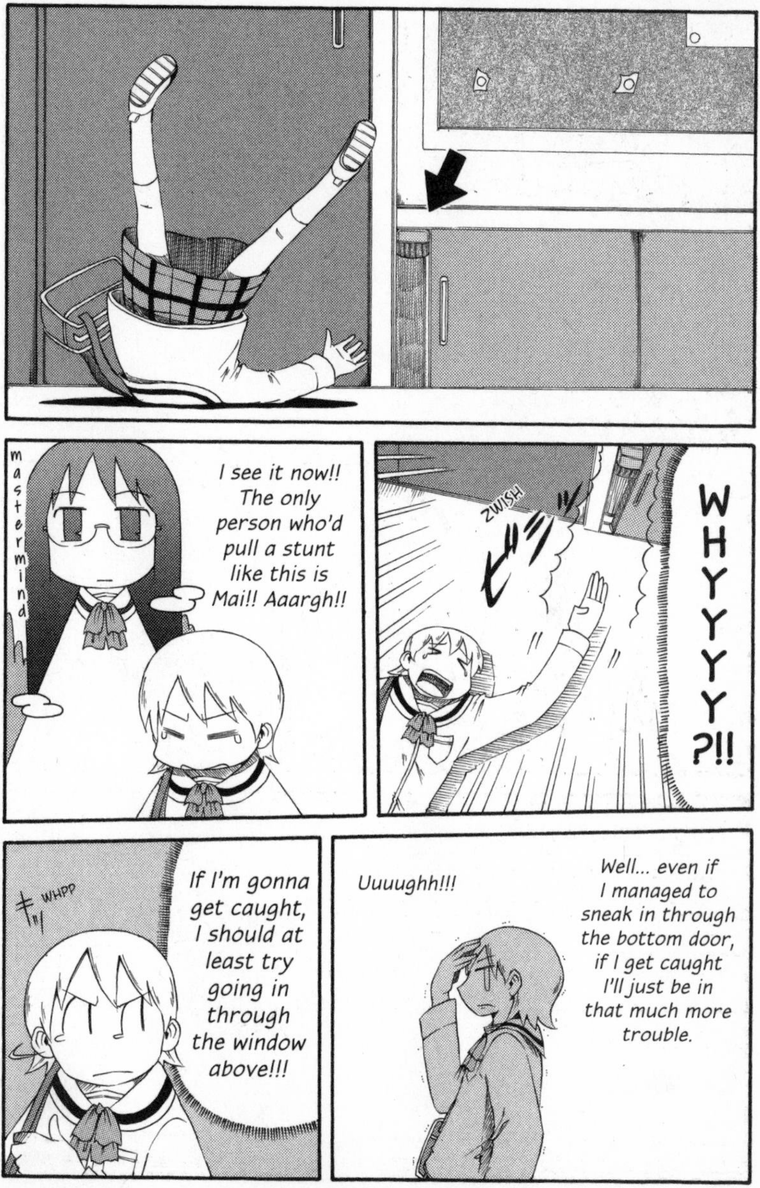
ZWISH
WHYYYY?!!
mastermind
I see it now!! The only person who'd pull a stunt like this is Mai!! Aaargh!!
Well... even if I managed to sneak in through the bottom door, if I get caught I'll just be in that much more trouble.
Uuuughh!!!
WHPP
If I'm gonna get caught, I should at least try going in through the window above!!!

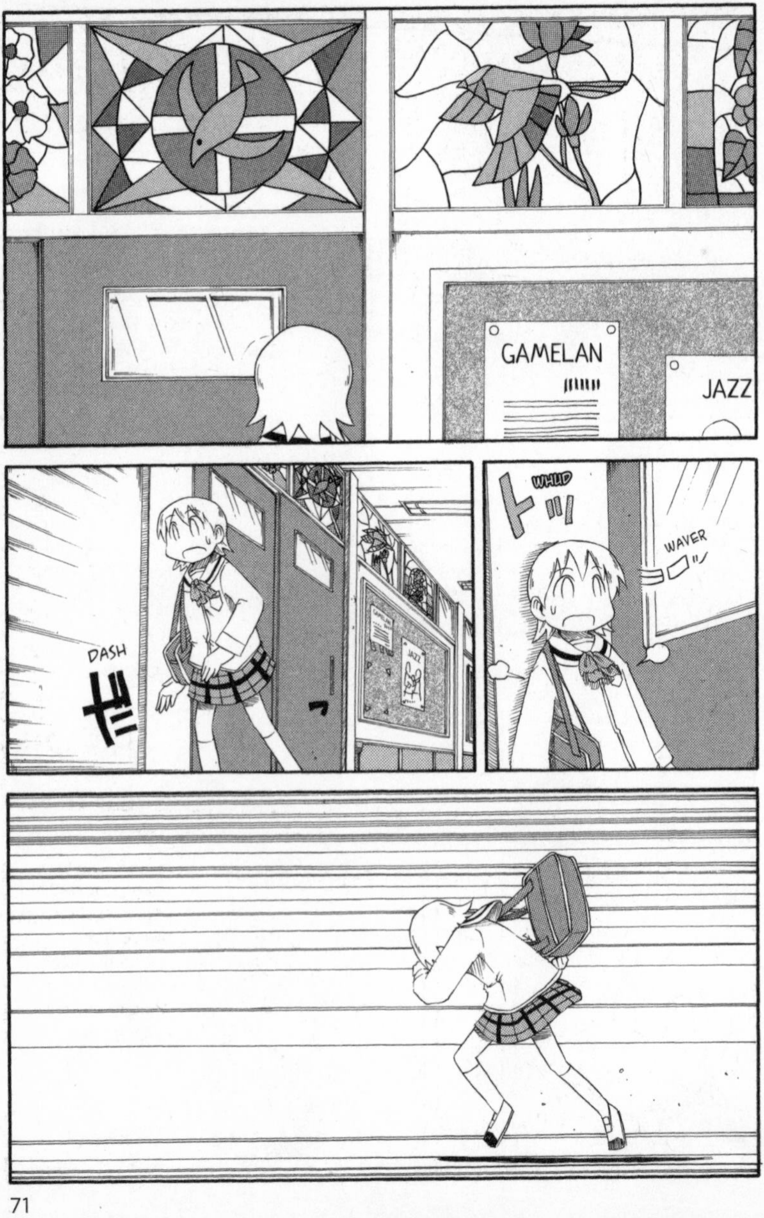
GAMELAN
JAZZ
WHUD
トッ
WAVER
DASH

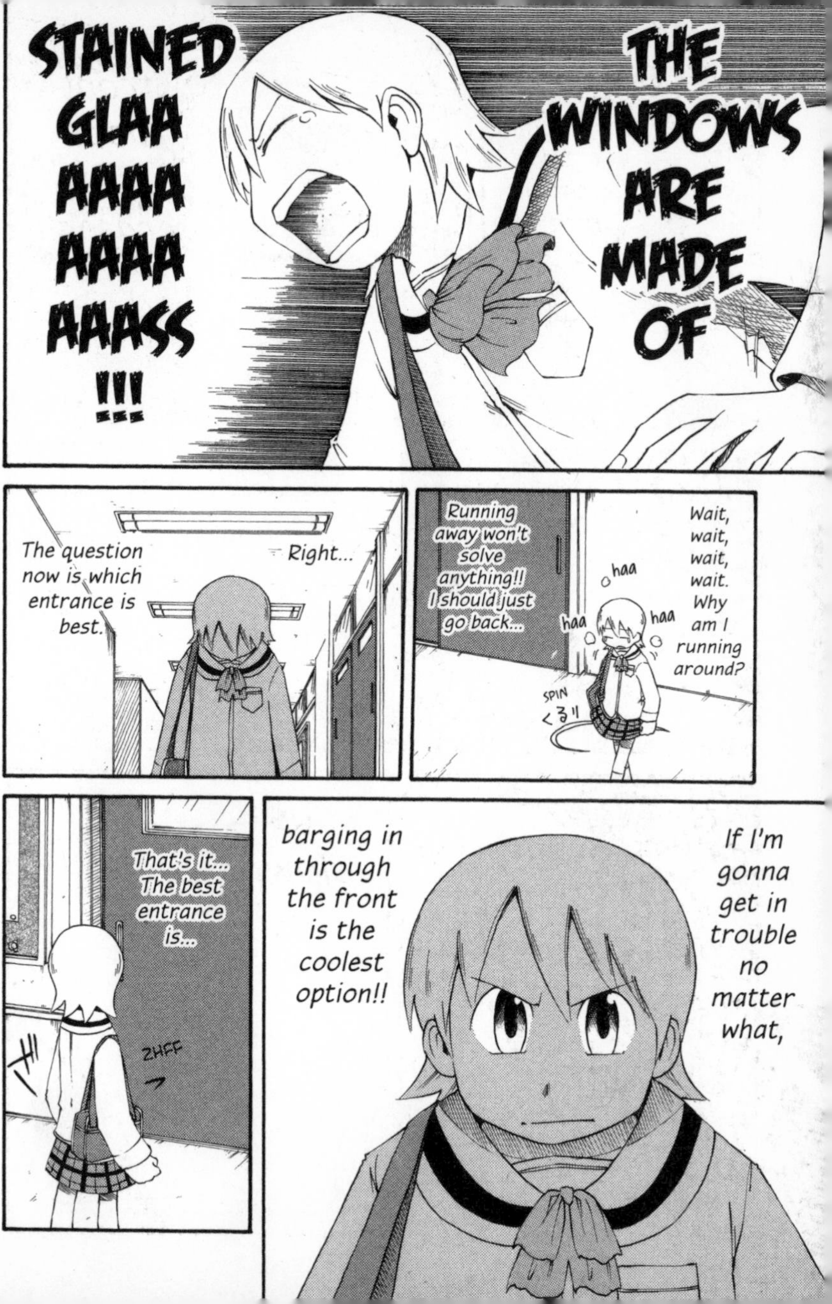
THE WINDOWS ARE MADE OF
STAINED GLAAAAAAAAAAAAAASS!!!
Wait, wait, wait, wait. Why am I running around?
haa
haa
haa
Running away won't solve anything!! I should just go back...
SPIN
くるっ
Right...
The question now is which entrance is best.
If I'm gonna get in trouble no matter what,
barging in through the front is the coolest option!!
That's it... The best entrance is...
ZHFF
ザッ

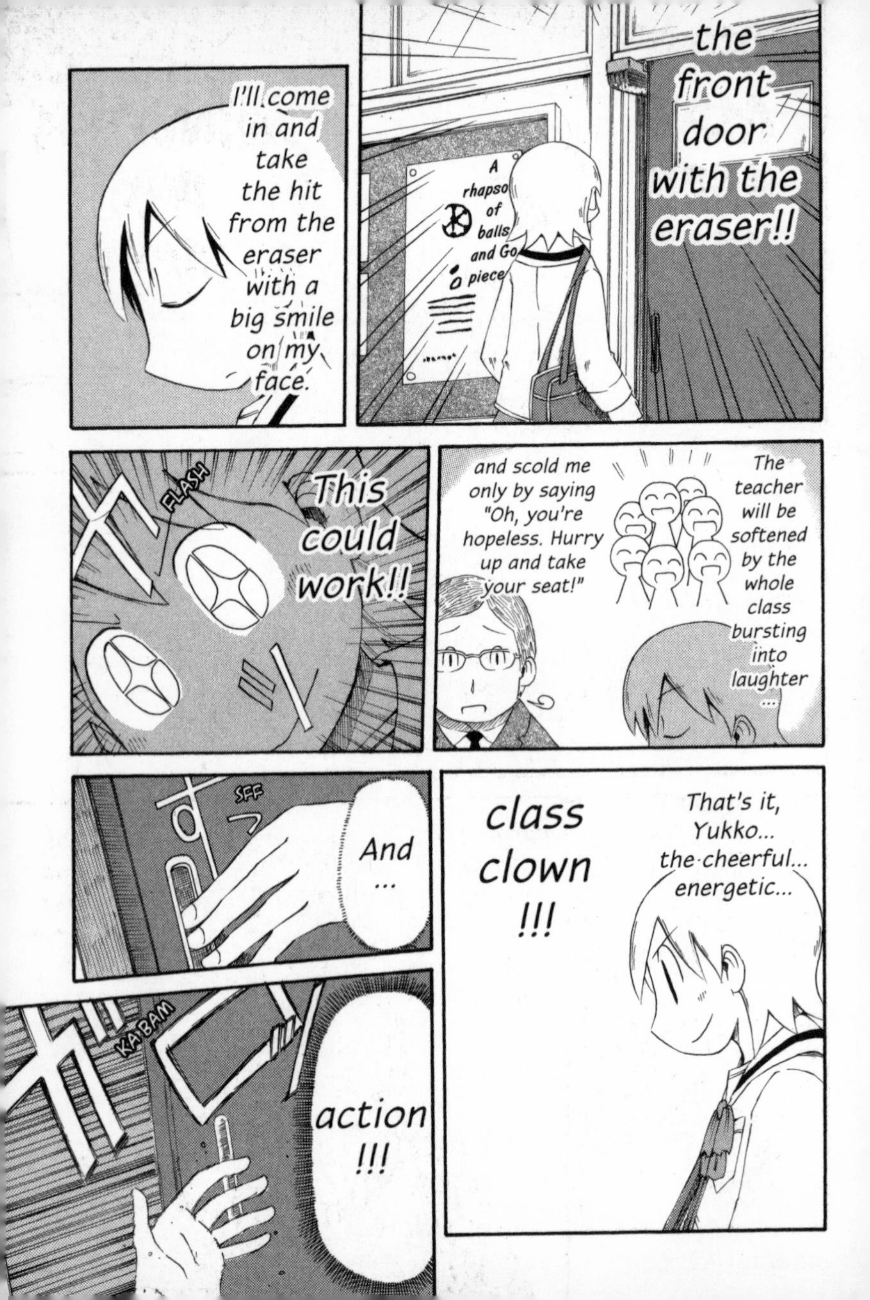
the front door with the eraser!!
A rhapso of balls and Go piece
I'll come in and take the hit from the eraser with a big smile on my face.
The teacher will be softened by the whole class bursting into laughter ...
and scold me only by saying "Oh, you're hopeless. Hurry up and take your seat!"
FLASH
This could work!!
That's it, Yukko... the cheerful... energetic...
class clown !!!
SFF
And ...
KABAM
action !!!

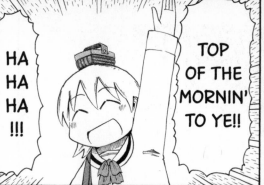

HA HA HA !!!

TOP OF THE MORNIN' TO YE!!

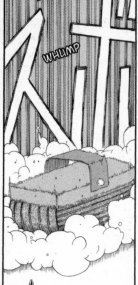

WHUMP

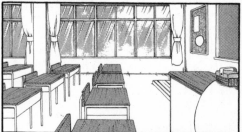

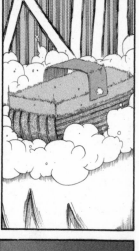

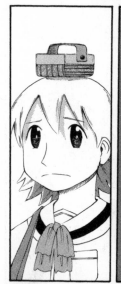

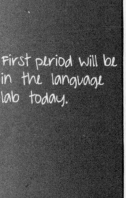

First period will be in the language lab today.

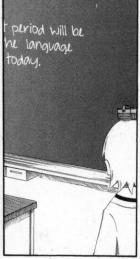

First period will be in the language lab today.

chapter 42: end

chapter 42.5

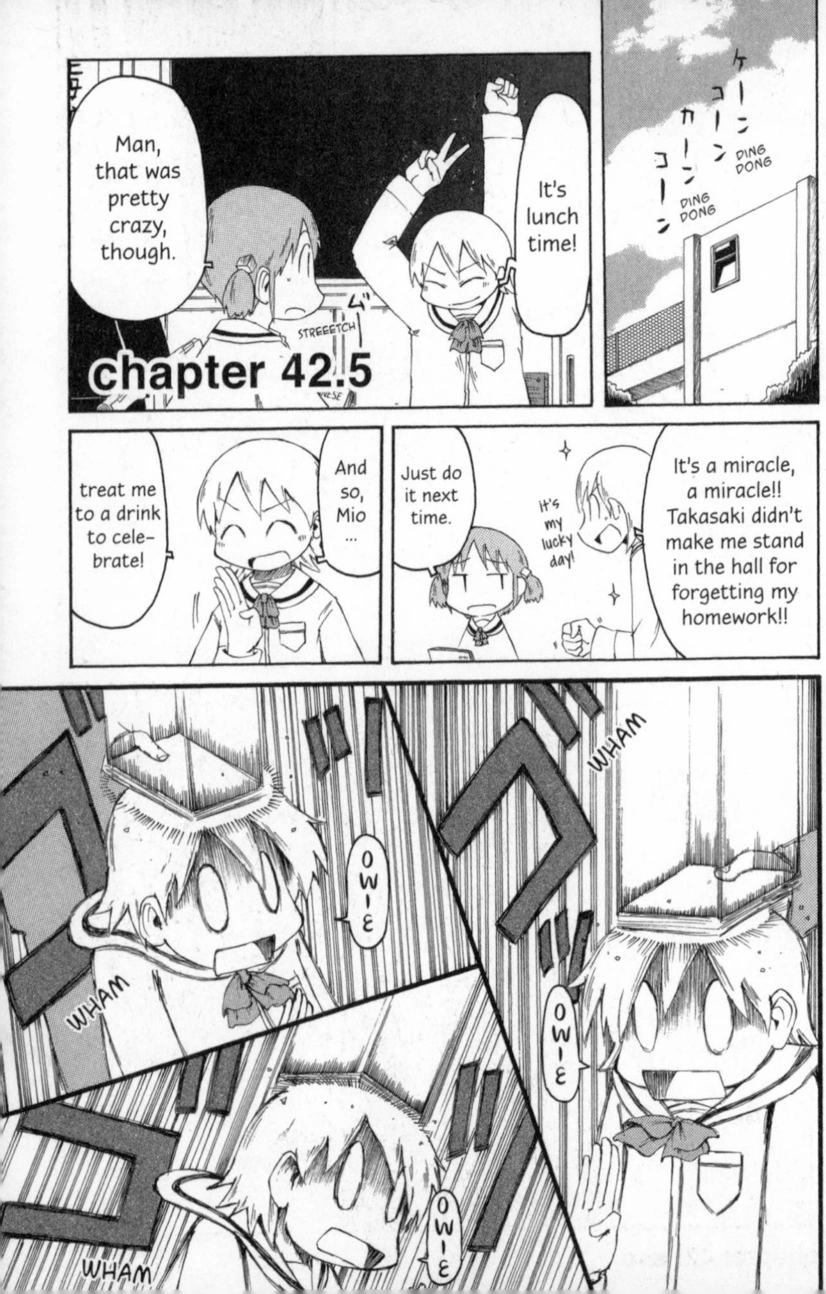
DING DONG
DING DONG
It's lunch time!
STREEETCH
Man, that was pretty crazy, though.
It's a miracle, a miracle!! Takasaki didn't make me stand in the hall for forgetting my homework!!
it's my lucky day!
Just do it next time.
And so, Mio ...
treat me to a drink to cele-brate!
WHAM
OWIE
OWIE
WHAM
OWIE
WHAM

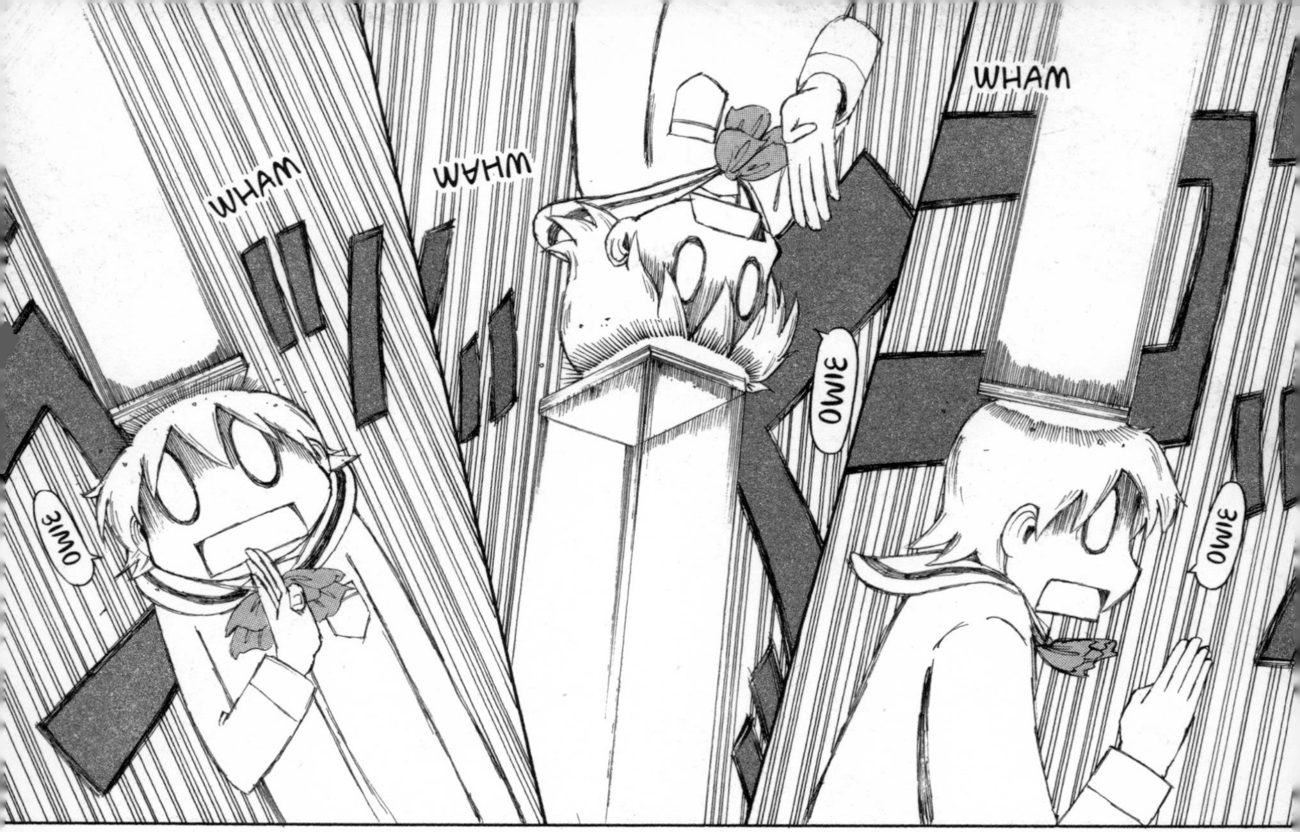
WHAM
OWIE
WHAM
OWIE
WHAM
OWIE

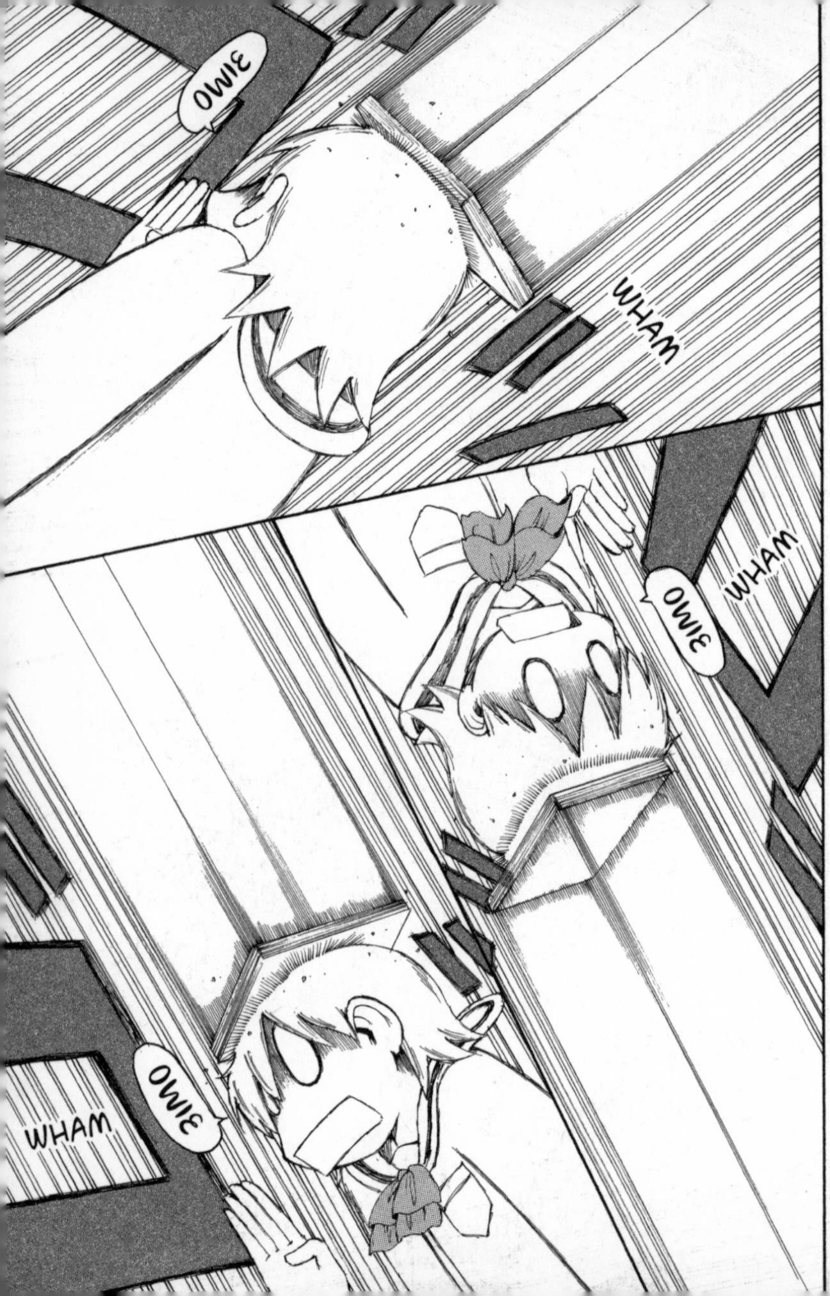

WHAM
OWIE
WHAM
OWIE
OWIE
WHAM

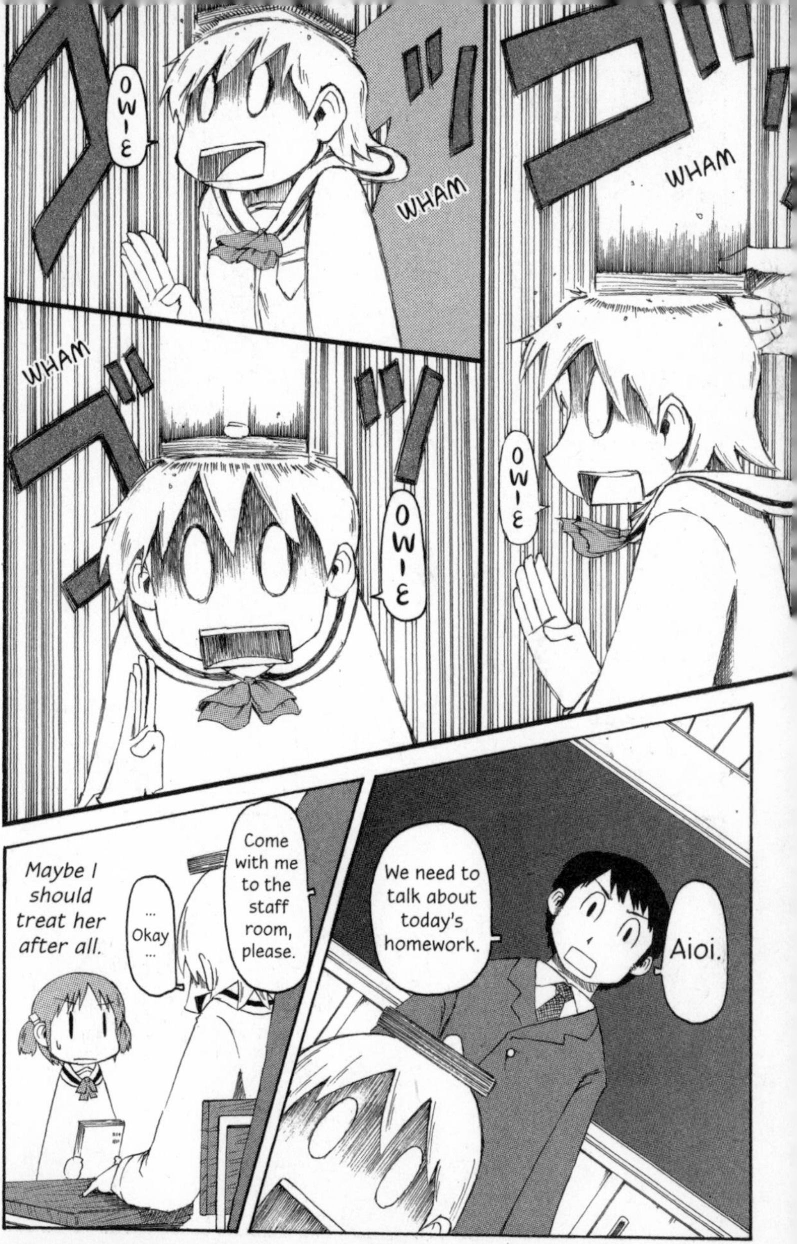
WHAM
OWIE
OWIE
WHAM
WHAM
OWIE
Aioi.
We need to talk about today's homework.
Come with me to the staff room, please.
... Okay ...
Maybe I should treat her after all.

chapter 42.5: end

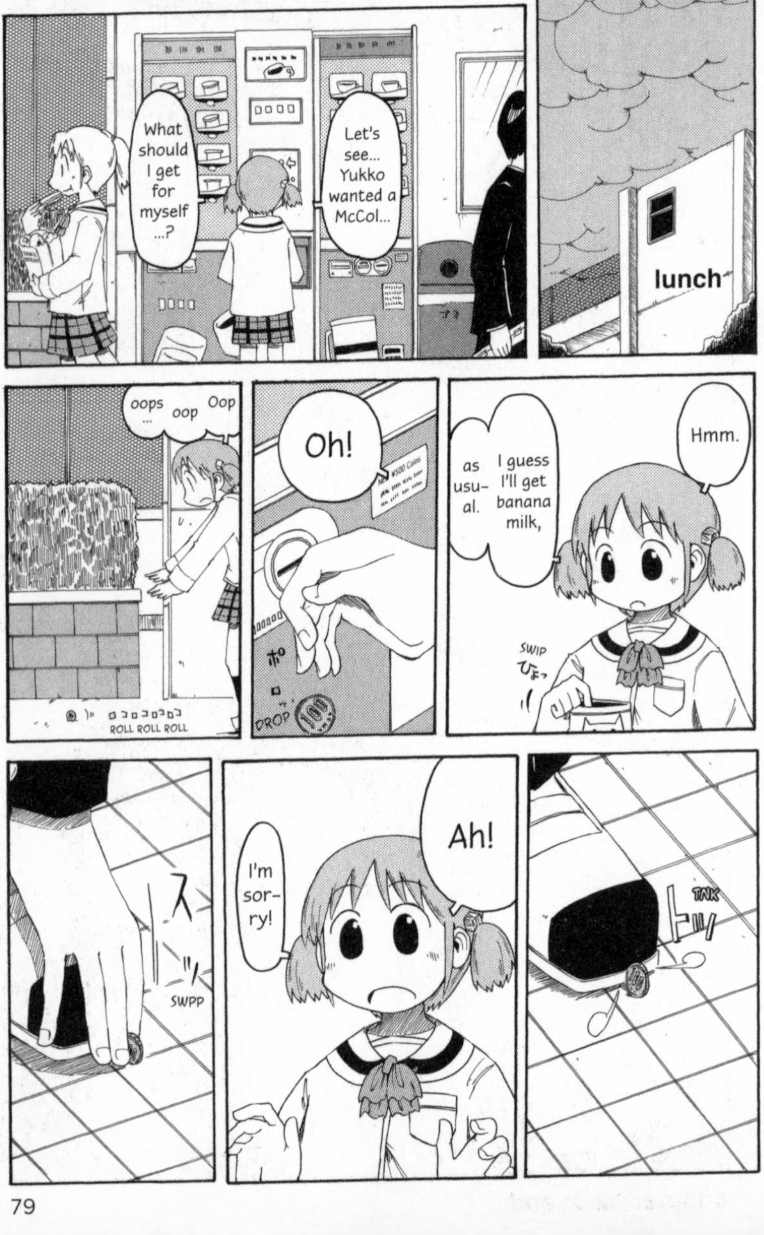
lunch
Let's see... Yukko wanted a McCol...
What should I get for myself ...?
Hmm.
I guess I'll get banana milk,
as usu-al.
SWIP
Oh!
DROP
Oop
oop
oops ...
ROLL ROLL ROLL
TAK
Ah!
I'm sor-ry!
SWPP

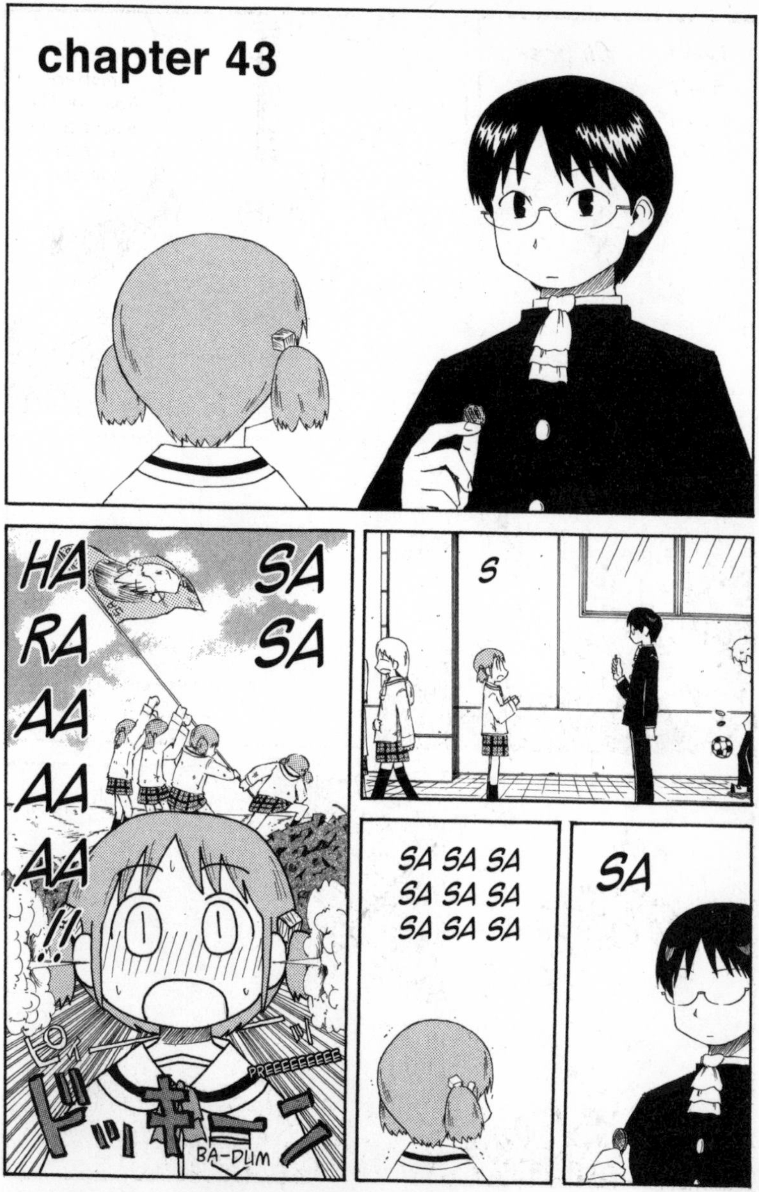
chapter 43
S
SA
SA SA SA
SA SA SA
SA SA SA
SA
SA
HARA
AA
AA
AA!!
PREEEEEEEEEE
ドッキーン
BA-DUM

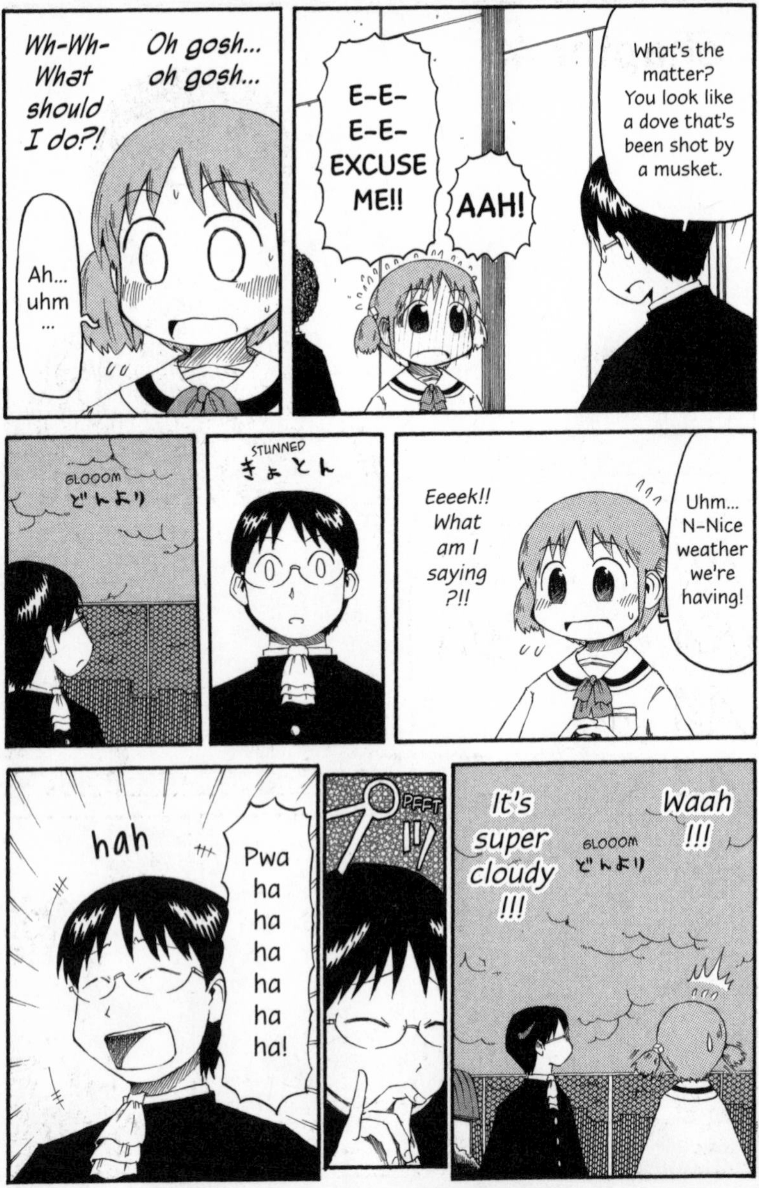
What's the matter? You look like a dove that's been shot by a musket.
AAH!
E-E-E-E-EXCUSE ME!!
Oh gosh... oh gosh...
Wh-Wh-What should I do?!
Ah... uhm ...
Uhm... N-Nice weather we're having!
Eeeek!! What am I saying ?!!
STUNNED
きょとん
GLOOOM
どんより
Waah !!!
GLOOOM
どんより
It's super cloudy !!!
PFFT
Pwa ha ha ha ha ha ha!
hah

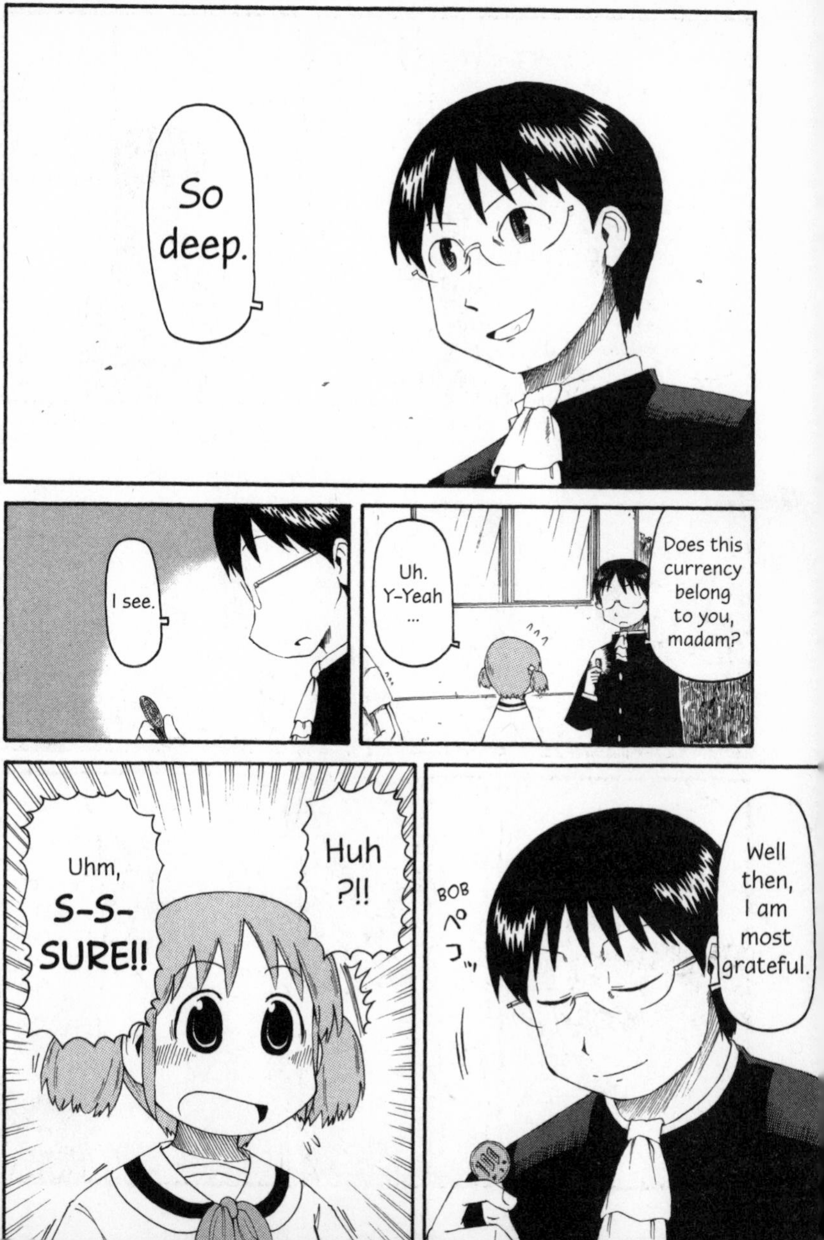
So deep.
Does this currency belong to you, madam?
Uh. Y-Yeah ...
I see.
Well then, I am most grateful.
BOB
ペコ
Huh ?!!
Uhm, S-S-SURE!!

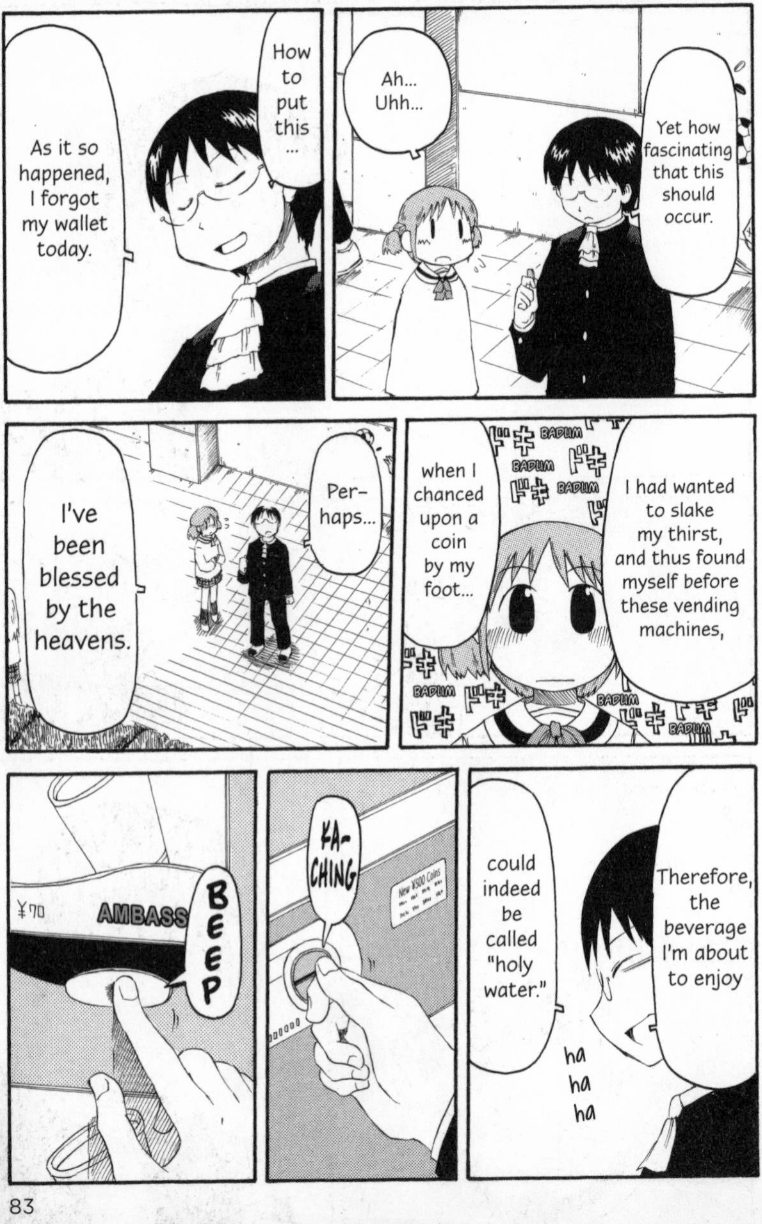
Yet how fascinating that this should occur.
Ah... Uhh...
How to put this ...
As it so happened, I forgot my wallet today.
I had wanted to slake my thirst, and thus found myself before these vending machines,
when I chanced upon a coin by my foot...
BADUM
ドキ
Per-haps...
I've been blessed by the heavens.
Therefore, the beverage I'm about to enjoy
could indeed be called "holy water."
ha ha ha
KA-CHING
New ¥500 Coins
BEEP
¥70
AMBASS

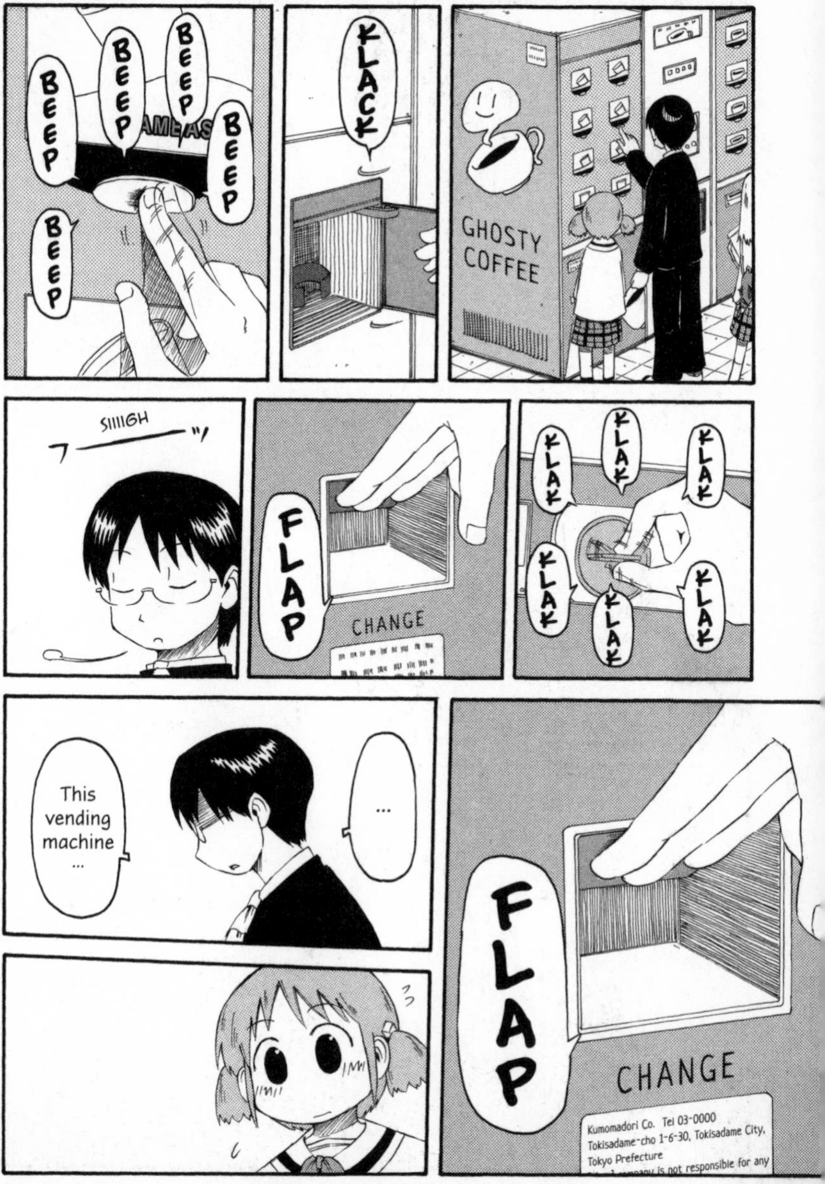
GHOSTY COFFEE
KLACK
BEEP
BEEP
BEEP
BEEP
BEEP
KLAK
KLAK
KLAK
KLAK
KLAK
KLAK
FLAP
CHANGE
SIIIGH
FLAP
CHANGE
Kumomadori Co. Tel 03-0000
Tokisadame-cho 1-6-30, Tokisadame City,
Tokyo Prefecture
company is not responsible for any
...
This vending machine ...

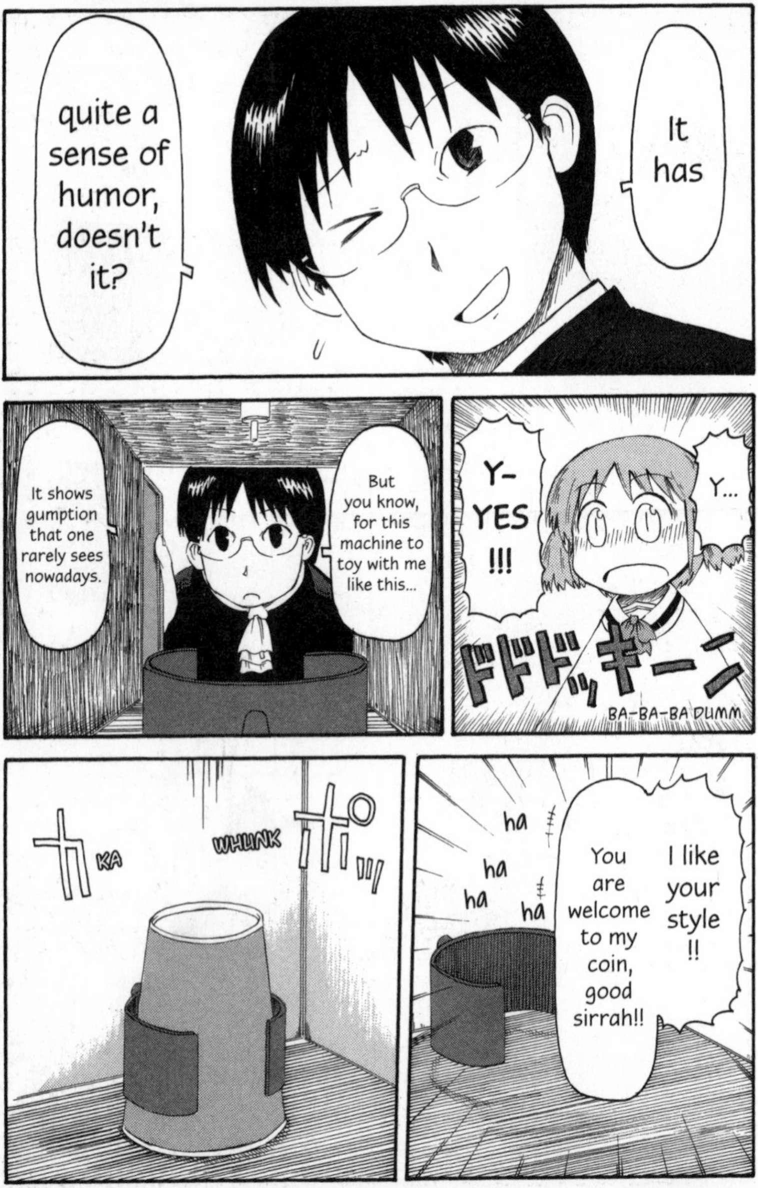
It has
quite a sense of humor, doesn't it?
Y...
Y-YES!!!
ドドドッギーン
BA-BA-BA DUMM
But you know, for this machine to toy with me like this...
It shows gumption that one rarely sees nowadays.
I like your style!!
You are welcome to my coin, good sirrah!!
ha ha ha ha
ポッ
WHUNK
カ
KA

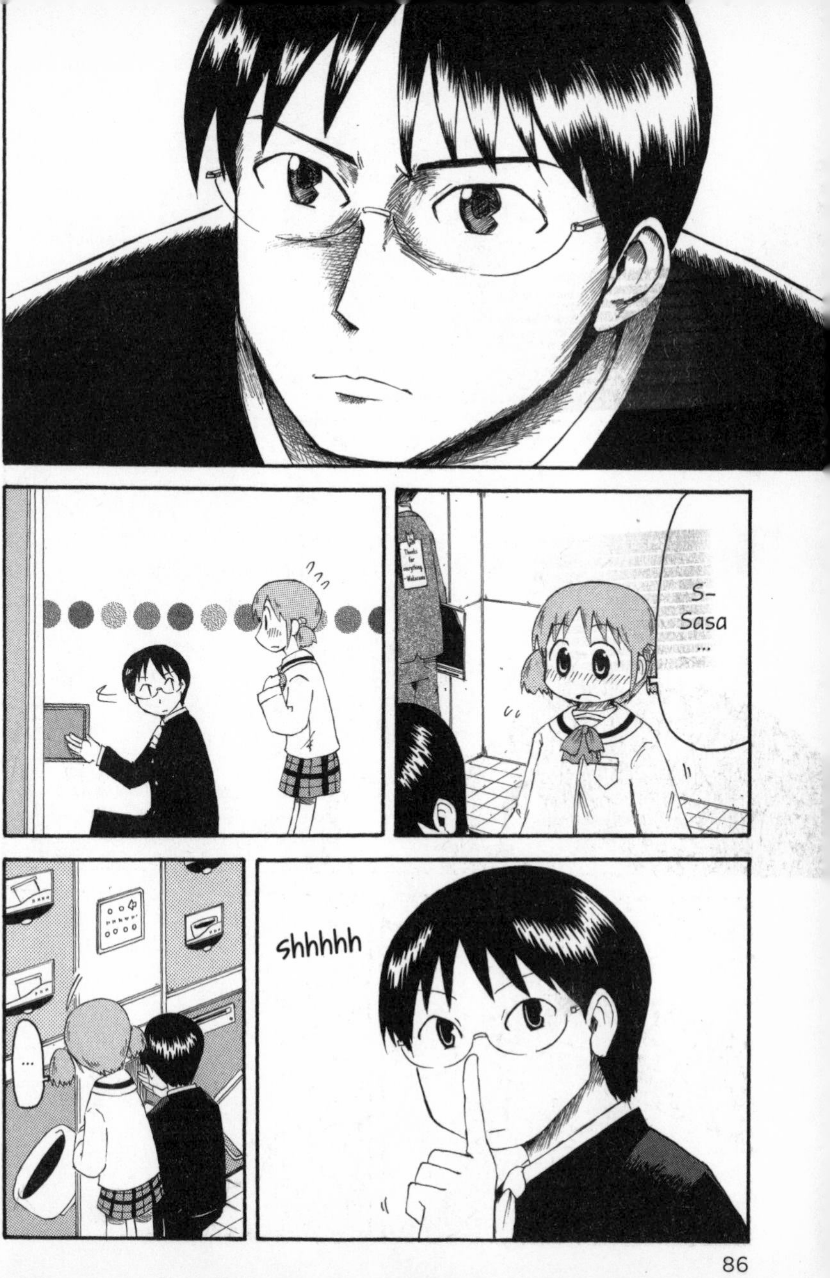
S-
Sasa
...
shhhhh
...

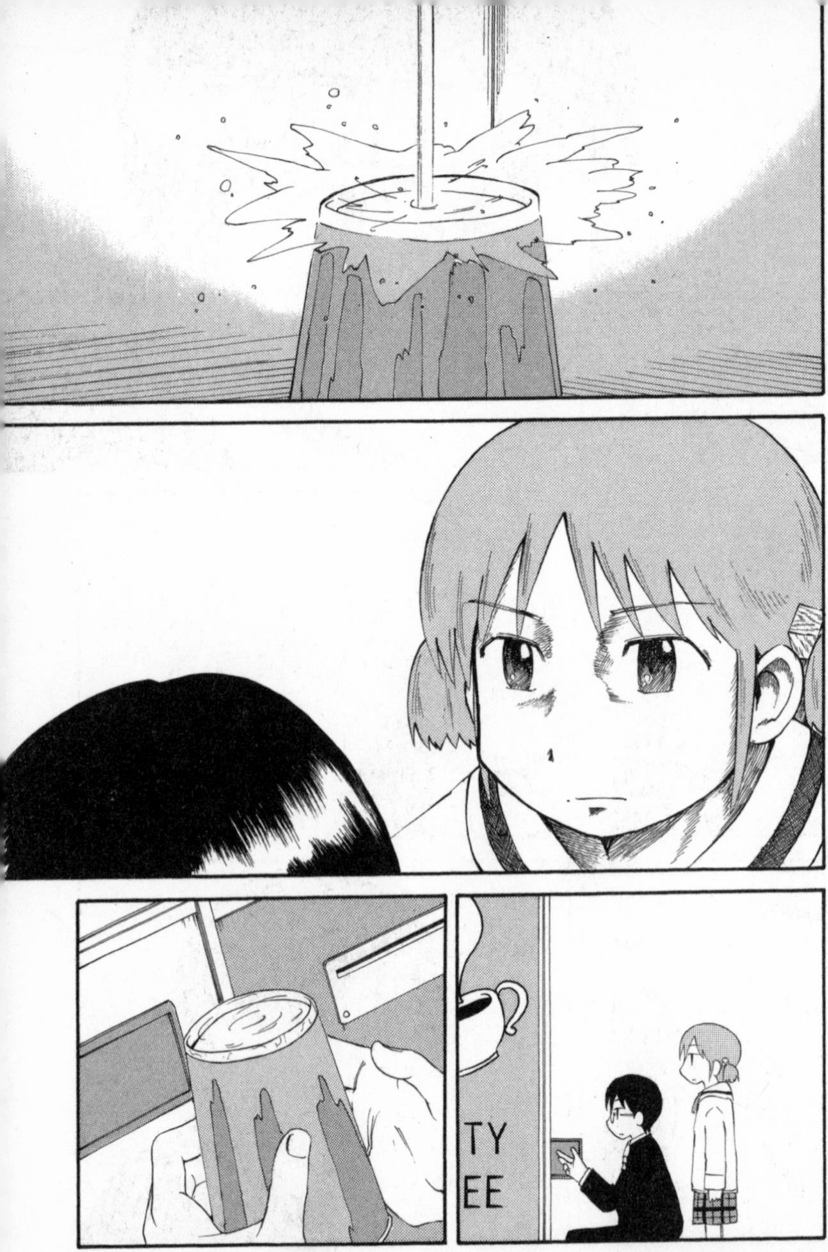
TY
EE

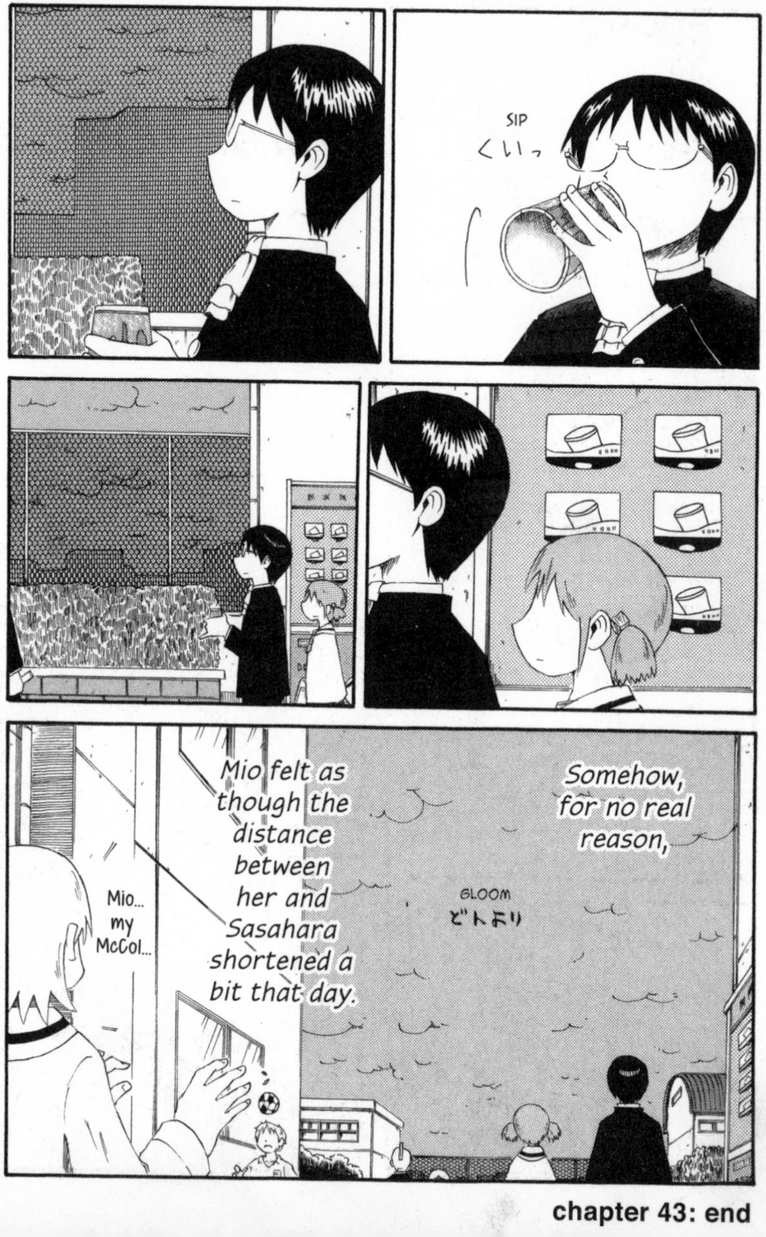
SIP
くいっ
Somehow, for no real reason,
GLOOM
どんより
Mio felt as though the distance between her and Sasahara shortened a bit that day.
Mio... my McCol...

chapter 43: end

ordinary shorts 2

go/soccer club 1

Okay, I'll start us off!
Ready, and...
2!
WHIP
Aaaargh! Sekiguchiiii!! You're not busy, so why do you never play with meeee??
Prez!
Sekiguchi ...!

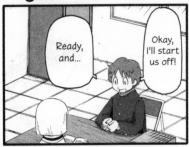

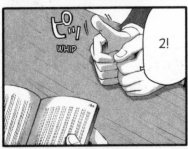

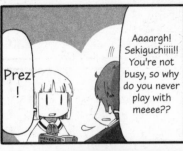

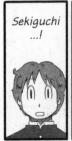

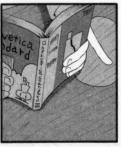

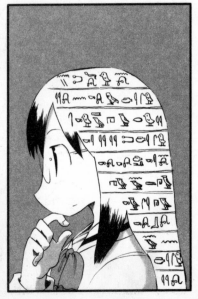

go/soccer club 2

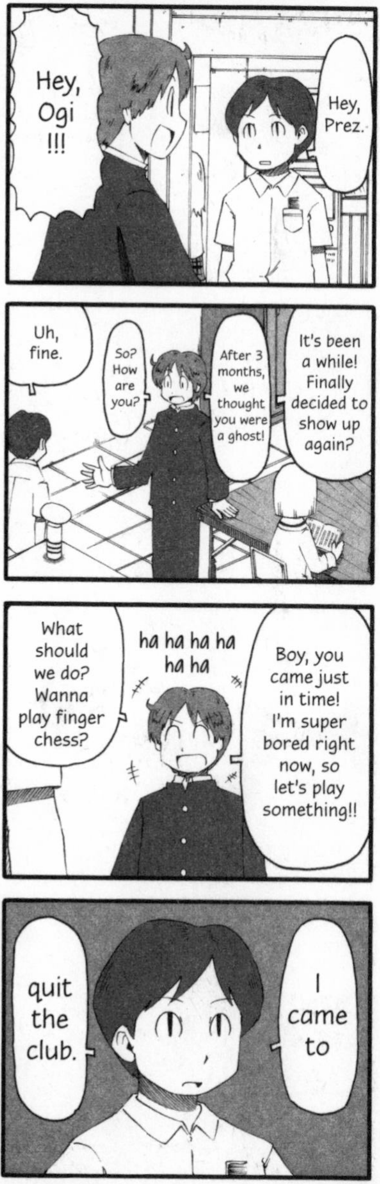
Hey, Prez.
Hey, Ogi!!!
It's been a while! Finally decided to show up again?
After 3 months, we thought you were a ghost!
So? How are you?
Uh, fine.
Boy, you came just in time! I'm super bored right now, so let's play something!!
ha ha ha ha ha ha
What should we do? Wanna play finger chess?
I came to
quit the club.

important business

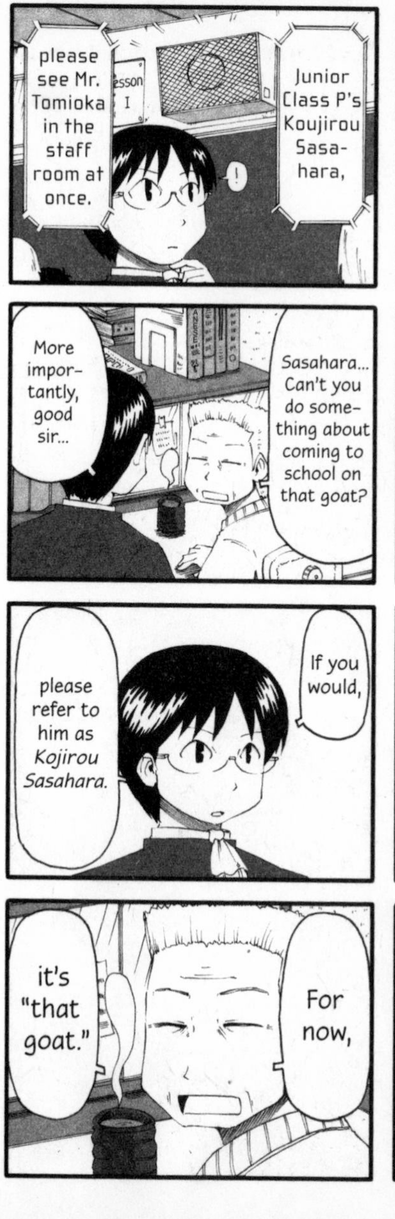
Junior Class P's Koujirou Sasahara,
please see Mr. Tomioka in the staff room at once.
!
Sasahara... Can't you do something about coming to school on that goat?
More importantly, good sir...
If you would,
please refer to him as *Kojirou Sasahara.*
For now,
it's "that goat."

yukko 1

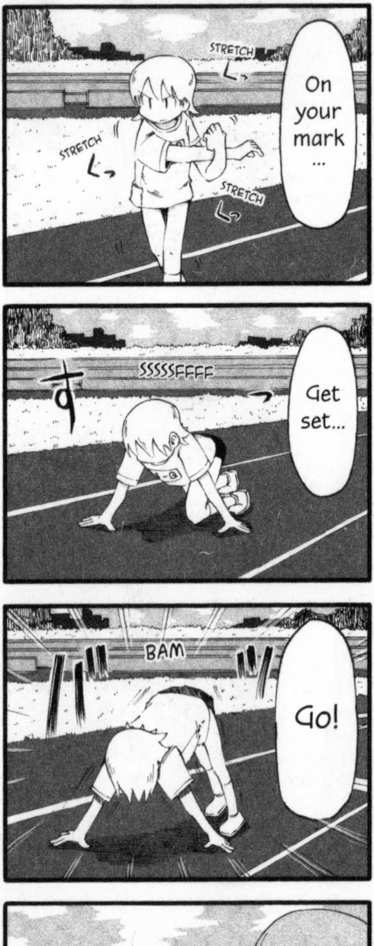
On your mark ...
STRETCH
STRETCH
STRETCH
Get set...
SSSSSFFFF
Go!
BAM

daifuku fair 1

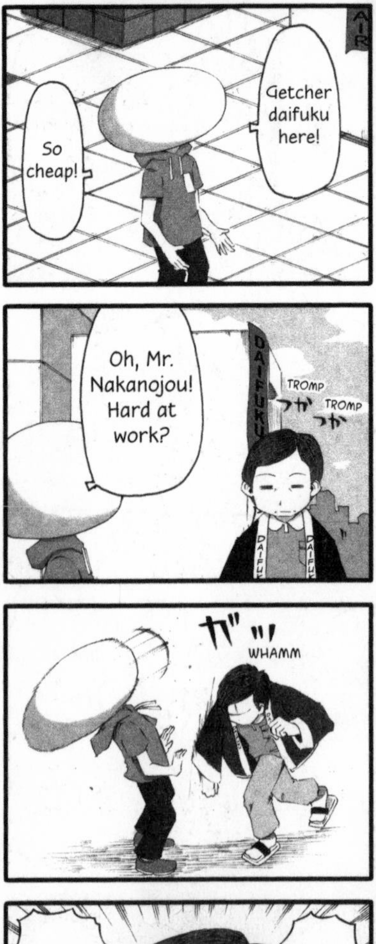
AIR
Getcher daifuku here!
So cheap!
DAIFUKU
TROMP
TROMP
Oh, Mr. Nakanojou! Hard at work?
DAIFUKU
DAIFUKU
WHAMM
DAI-FUKU
DON'T SPEAK !!!

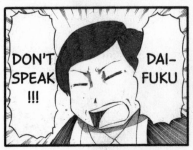

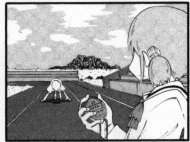

daifuku fair 2

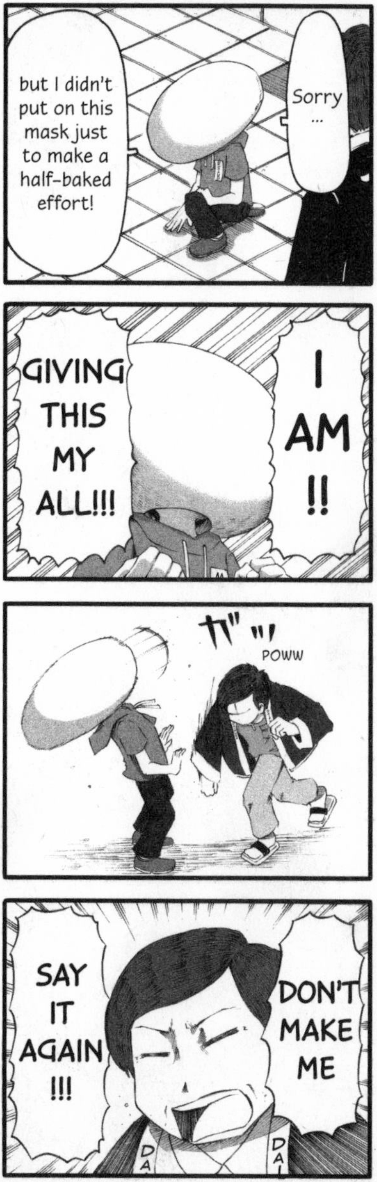
Sorry ...
but I didn't put on this mask just to make a half-baked effort!
I AM !!
GIVING THIS MY ALL!!!
ガッ
POWW
DON'T MAKE ME
SAY IT AGAIN !!!
DAI
DA

guidance counselor

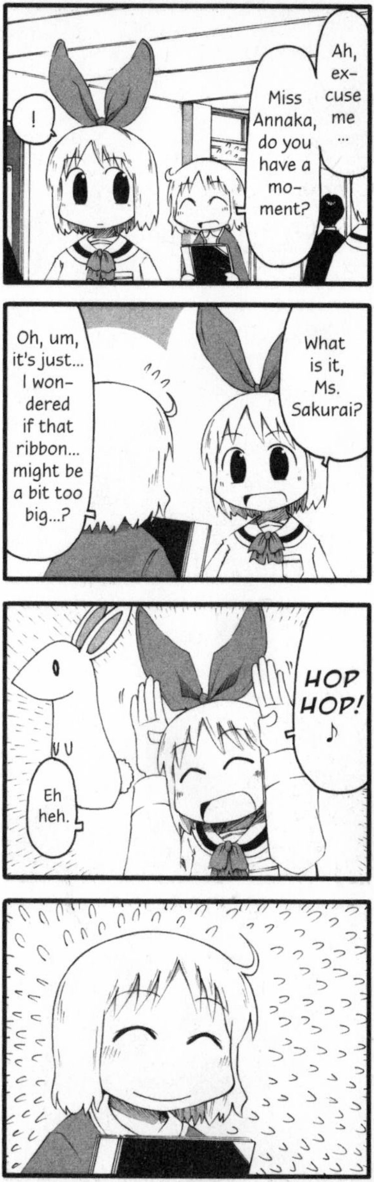
Ah, ex-cuse me ...
Miss Annaka, do you have a mo-ment?
!
What is it, Ms. Sakurai?
Oh, um, it's just... I wondered if that ribbon... might be a bit too big...?
HOP HOP! ♪
Eh heh.

nakanojou

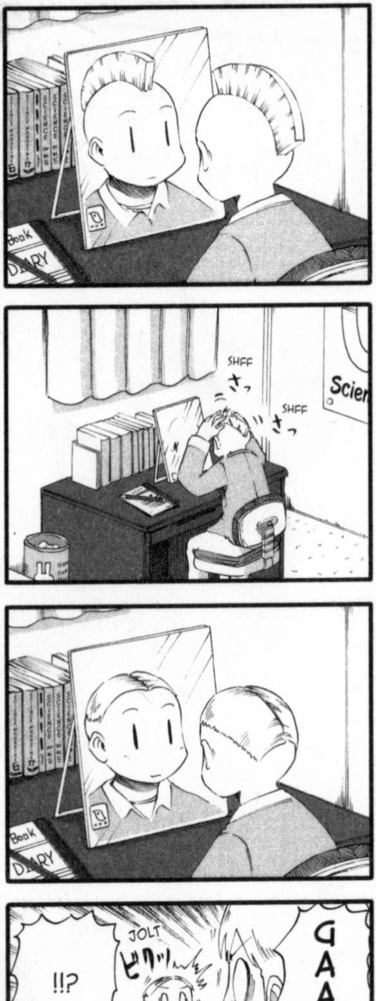

quiz

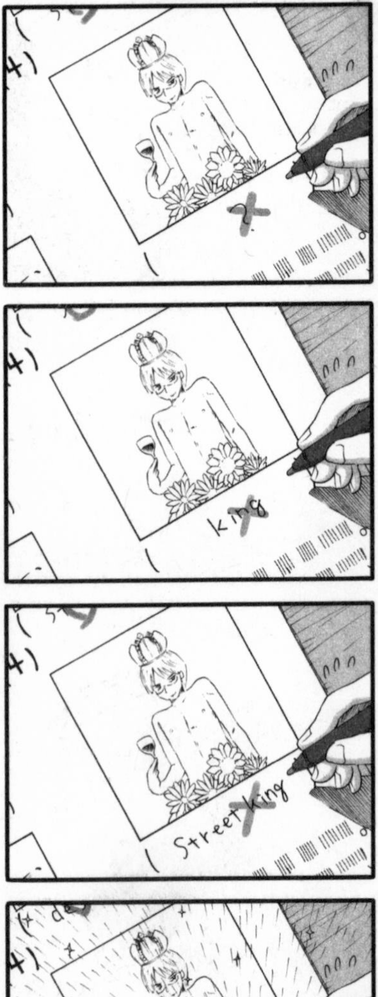

yukko 2

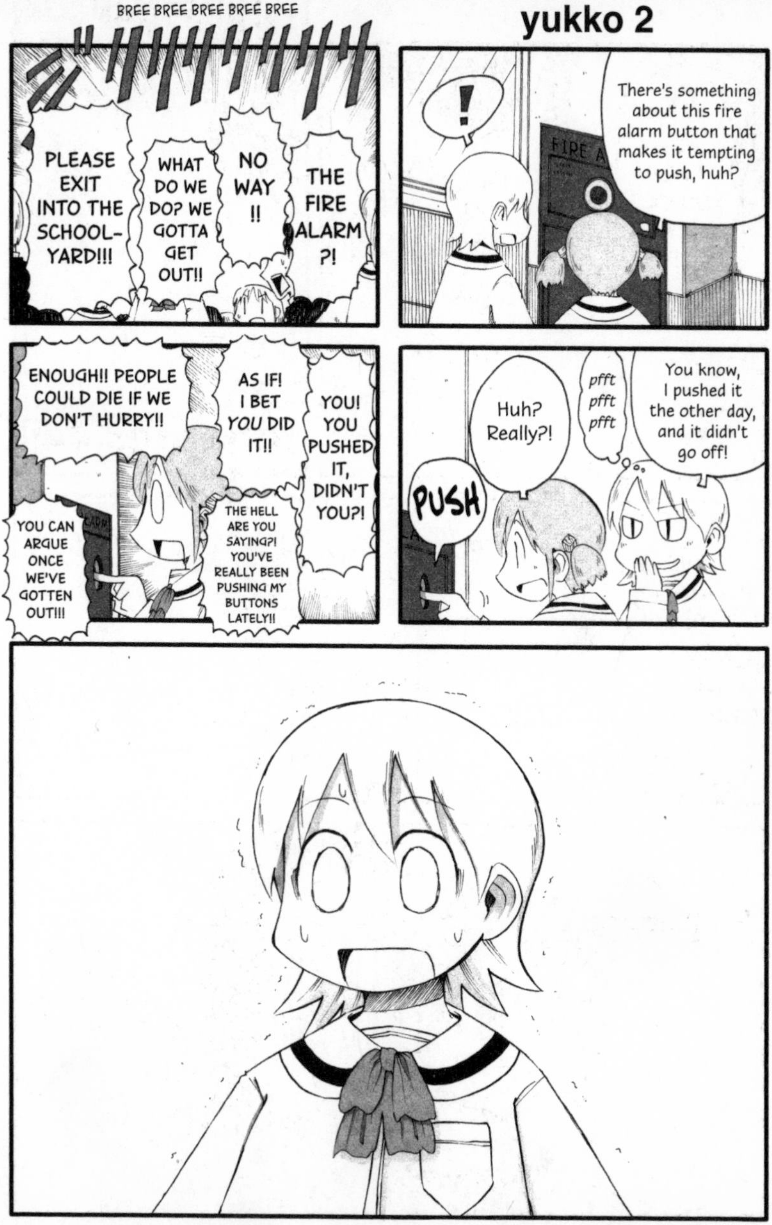
!
There's something about this fire alarm button that makes it tempting to push, huh?
You know, I pushed it the other day, and it didn't go off!
pfft pfft pfft
Huh? Really?!
PUSH
BREE BREE BREE BREE BREE
THE FIRE ALARM?!
NO WAY!!
WHAT DO WE DO? WE GOTTA GET OUT!!
PLEASE EXIT INTO THE SCHOOL-YARD!!!
YOU! YOU PUSHED IT, DIDN'T YOU?!
AS IF! I BET YOU DID IT!!
THE HELL ARE YOU SAYING?! YOU'VE REALLY BEEN PUSHING MY BUTTONS LATELY!!
ENOUGH!! PEOPLE COULD DIE IF WE DON'T HURRY!!
YOU CAN ARGUE ONCE WE'VE GOTTEN OUT!!!

ordinary shorts 2: end

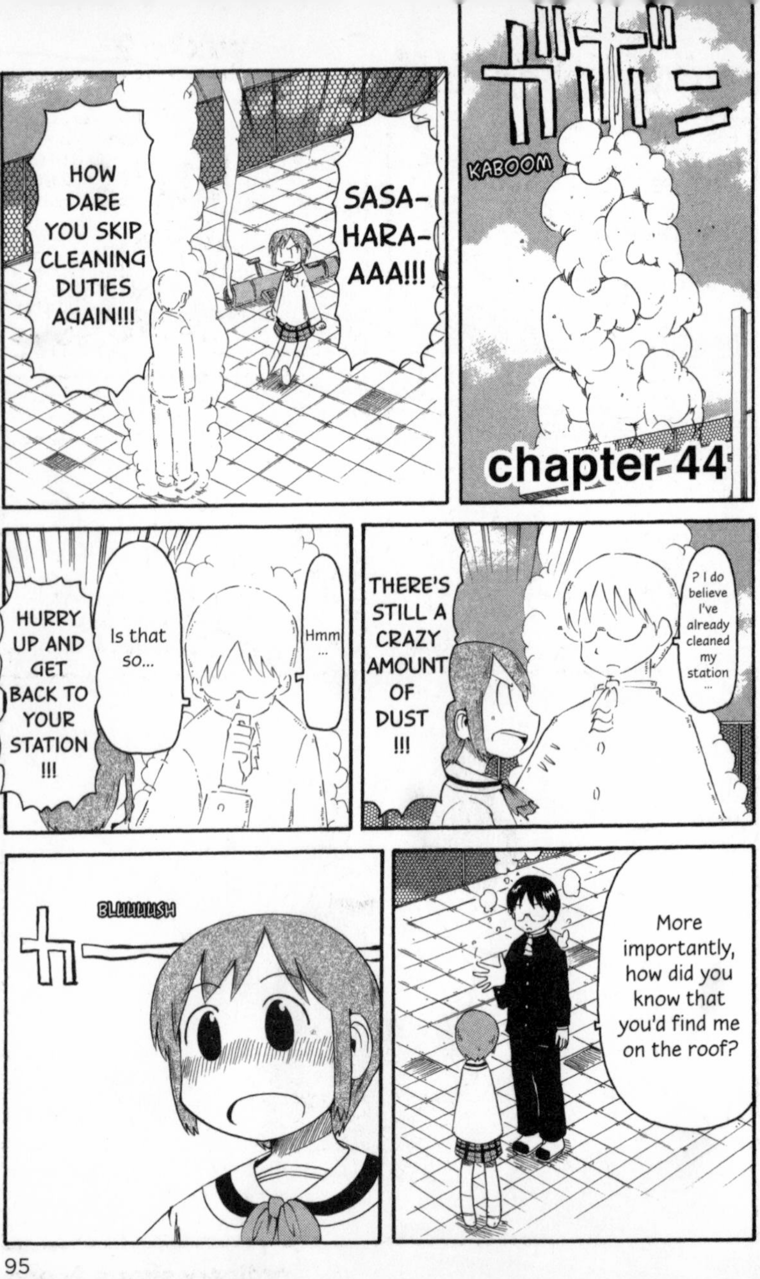
KABOOM
chapter 44
SASA-HARA-AAA!!!
HOW DARE YOU SKIP CLEANING DUTIES AGAIN!!!
? I do believe I've already cleaned my station ...
THERE'S STILL A CRAZY AMOUNT OF DUST !!!
Hmm ...
Is that so...
HURRY UP AND GET BACK TO YOUR STATION !!!
More importantly, how did you know that you'd find me on the roof?
BLUUUUSH

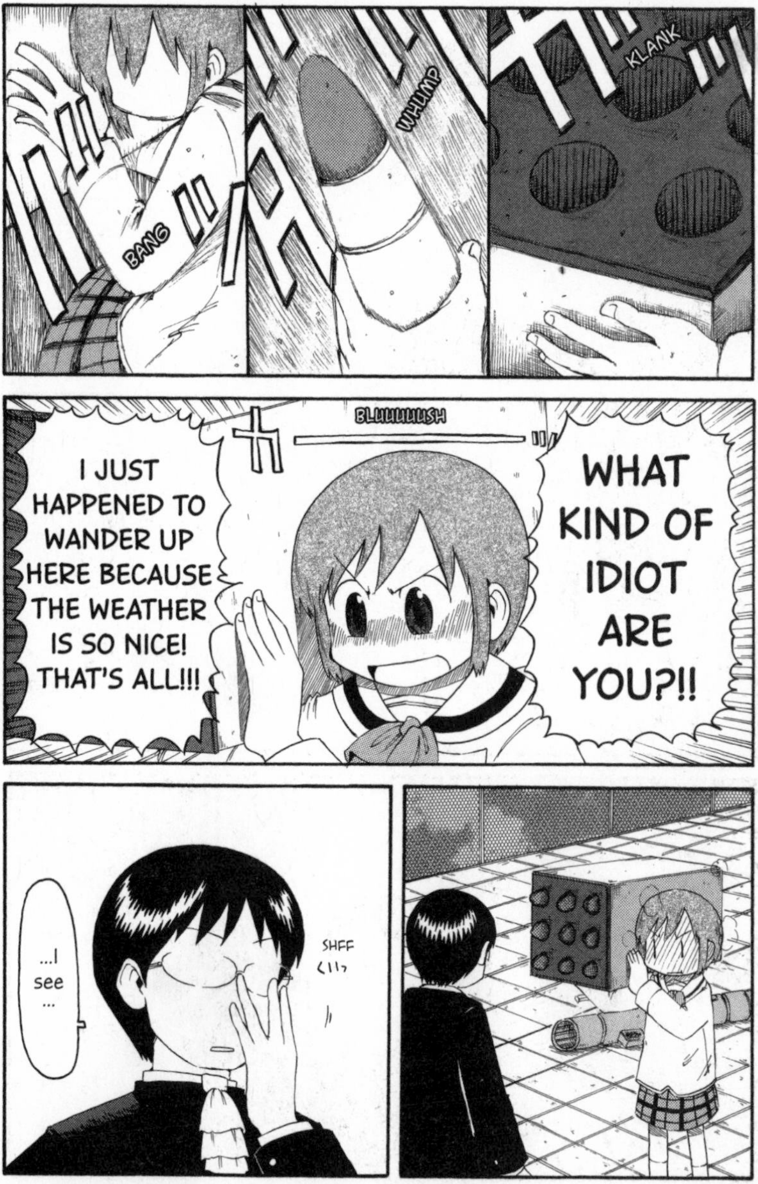
KLANK
WHUMP
BANG
BLUUUUUSH
WHAT KIND OF IDIOT ARE YOU?!!
I JUST HAPPENED TO WANDER UP HERE BECAUSE THE WEATHER IS SO NICE! THAT'S ALL!!!
SHFF
...I see ...

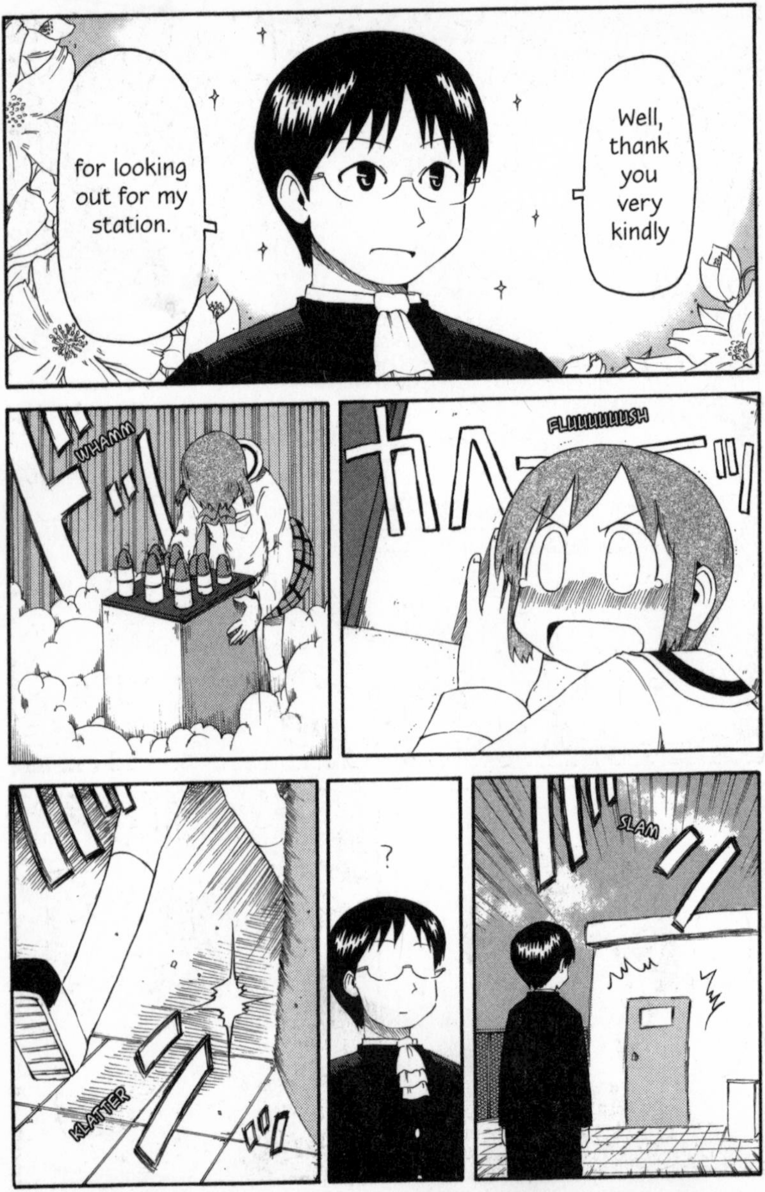
Well, thank you very kindly
for looking out for my station.
FLUUUUUUSH
WHAMM
SLAM
?
KLATTER

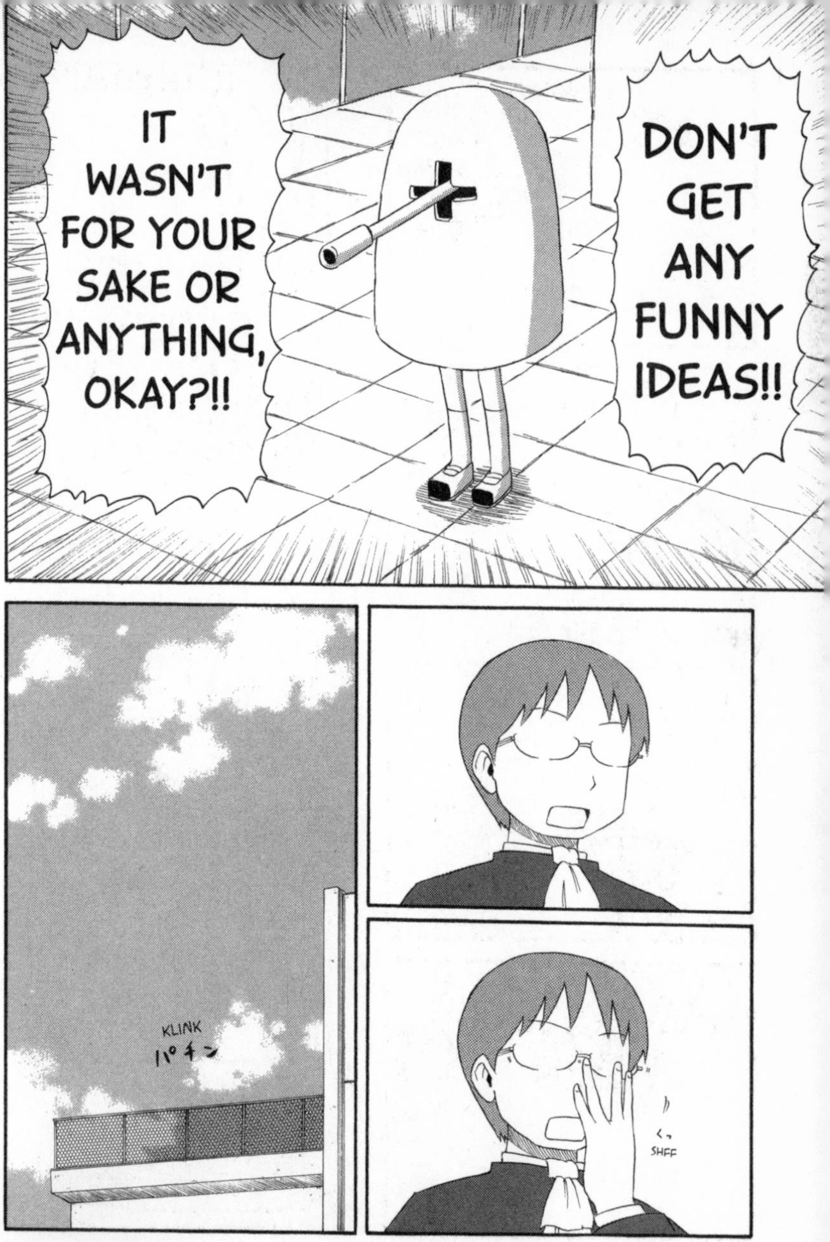
DON'T GET ANY FUNNY IDEAS!!
IT WASN'T FOR YOUR SAKE OR ANYTHING, OKAY?!!
くっ
SHFF
KLINK
パチン

chapter 44: end

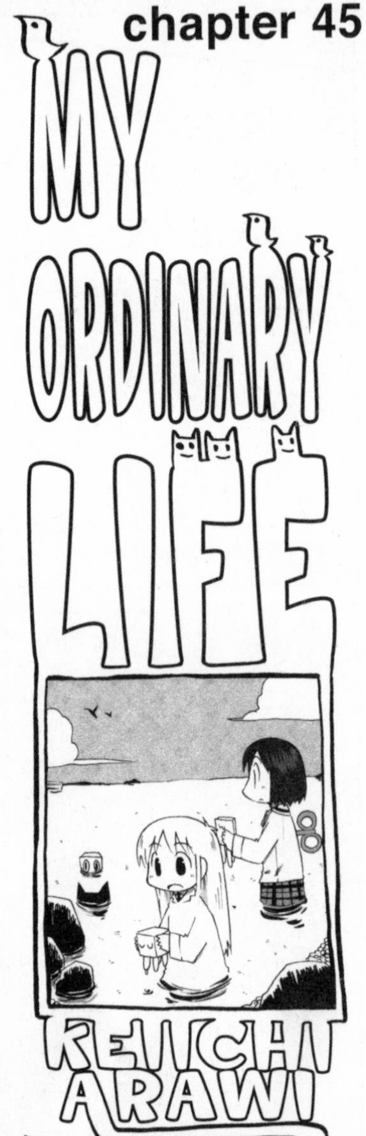
chapter 45
MY ORDINARY LIFE
KEIICHI ARAWI

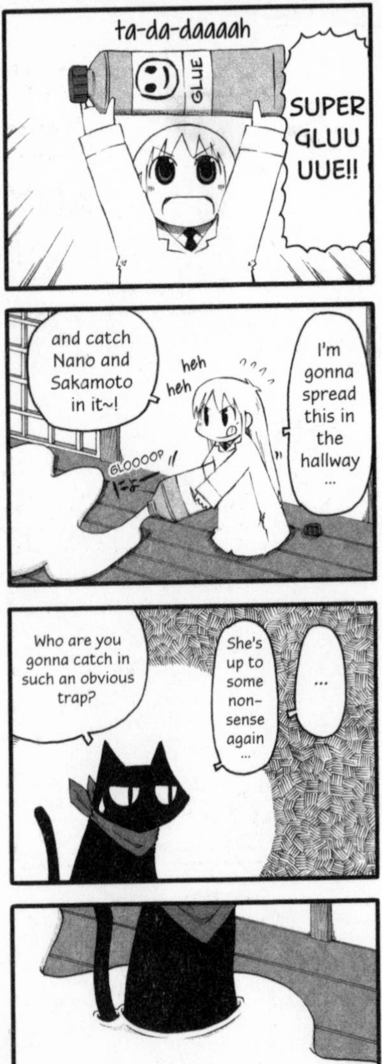
ta-da-daaaah
GLUE
SUPER GLUUUUE!!
I'm gonna spread this in the hallway ...
and catch Nano and Sakamoto in it~!
heh heh
GLOOOOP
にょー
...
She's up to some non-sense again ...
Who are you gonna catch in such an obvious trap?

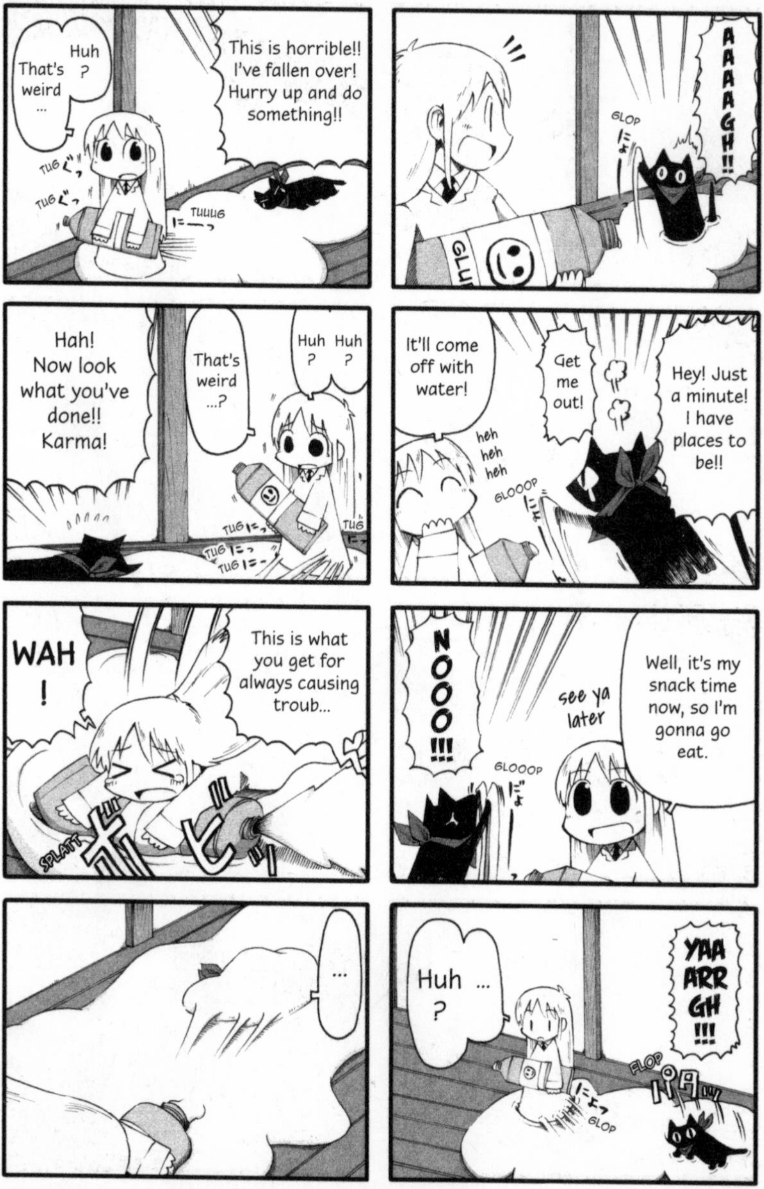
AAAAGH!!
GLOP
This is horrible!! I've fallen over! Hurry up and do something!!
Huh ?
That's weird ...
TUG
TUG
TUUUG
Hey! Just a minute! I have places to be!!
Get me out!
It'll come off with water!
heh heh heh
GLOOOP
Huh ?
Huh ?
That's weird ...?
Hah! Now look what you've done!! Karma!
TUG
TUG
TUG
TUG
Well, it's my snack time now, so I'm gonna go eat.
see ya later
NOOOO!!!
GLOOOP
This is what you get for always causing troub...
WAH !
SPLATT
YAA ARR GH !!!
Huh ... ?
FLOP
GLOP
...

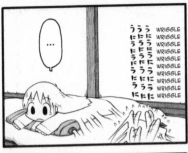

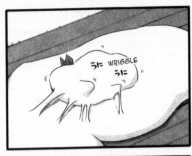

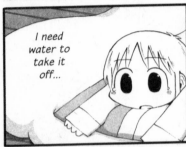

うに WRIGGLE
うに
...
WRIGGLE WRIGGLE WRIGGLE WRIGGLE WRIGGLE WRIGGLE WRIGGLE WRIGGLE WRIGGLE WRIGGLE
うに うに WRIGGLE
うに うに WRIGGLE
うに うに WRIGGLE
I need water to take it off...
うに WRIGGLE WRIGGLE
うに WRIGGLE WRIGGLE
うに WRIGGLE WRIGGLE
うに うに うに WRIGGLE WRIGGLE
じわじわじわ
SNIFFLE SNIFFLE
sob ...
I can't eat my snacks, so I might get hungry...
WRIGGLE WRIGGLE WRIGGLE
WRIGGLE WRIGGLE WRIGGLE
WRIGGLE WRIGGLE WRIGGLE
And then I might diiiie!
WAAAH! WAAAH!
he really might die.
WRIGGLE うにーー
WRIGGLE うにーー

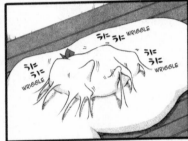

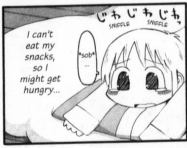

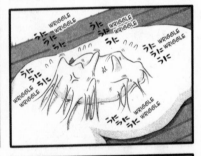

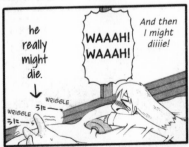

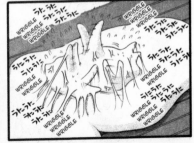

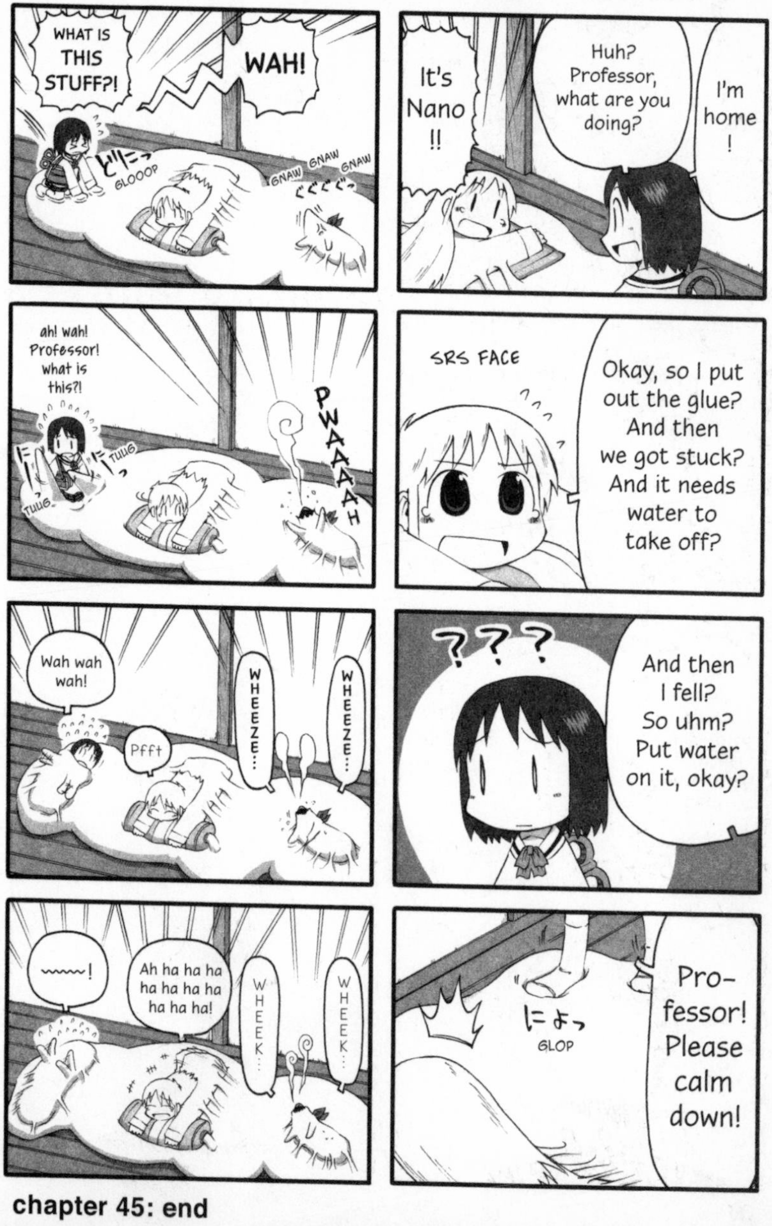
I'm home!
Huh? Professor, what are you doing?
It's Nano!!
WAH!
WHAT IS THIS STUFF?!
GNAW GNAW GNAW
ぐぐぐぐっ
どりにっ
GLOOOP
Okay, so I put out the glue? And then we got stuck? And it needs water to take off?
SRS FACE
PWAAAAH
ah! wah! Professor! what is this?!
TUUG
TUUG
And then I fell? So uhm? Put water on it, okay?
???
WHEEZE...
WHEEZE...
Pfft
Wah wah wah!
Pro-fessor! Please calm down!
にょっ
GLOP
WHEEK...
WHEEK...
Ah ha ha ha ha ha ha ha ha ha ha!
~~~~!

chapter 45: end
~~~~

ordinary shorts 3

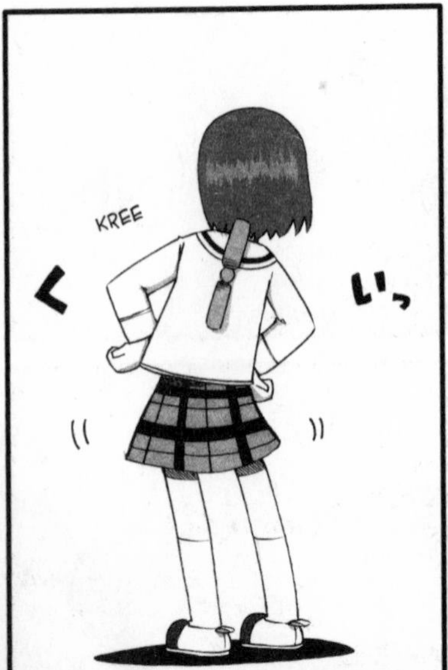
KREE
く
いっ

go/soccer club 1

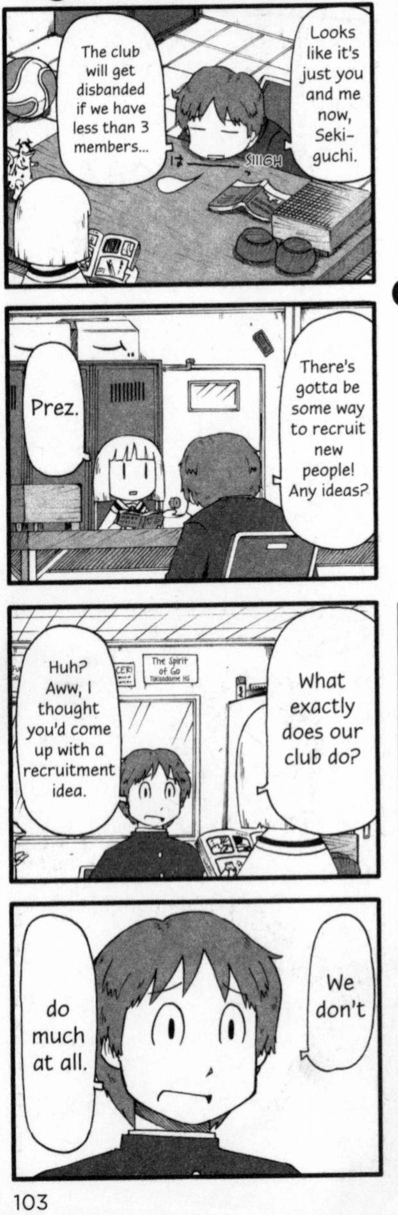
Looks like it's just you and me now, Seki-guchi.
は—
SIIIGH
The club will get disbanded if we have less than 3 members...
There's gotta be some way to recruit new people! Any ideas?
Prez.
What exactly does our club do?
The Spirit of Go Tokisadame HS
Huh? Aww, I thought you'd come up with a recruitment idea.
We don't
do much at all.

go/soccer club 2

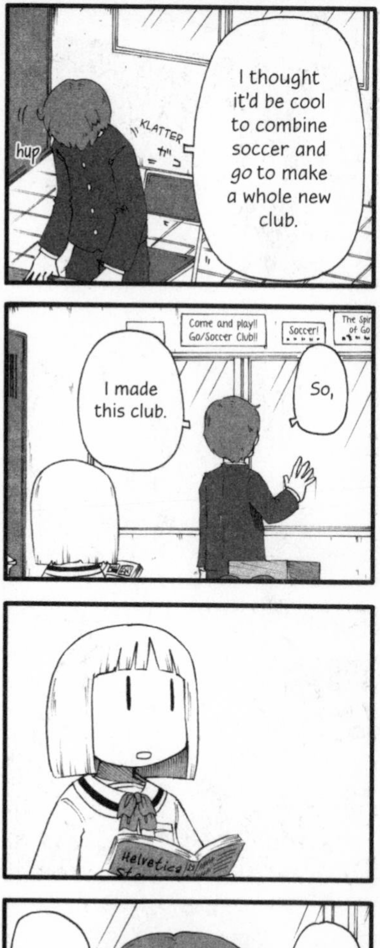
hup
KLATTER
I thought it'd be cool to combine soccer and go to make a whole new club.
Come and play!! Go/Soccer Club!!
Soccer!
So,
I made this club.
Helvetica
But
that's as far as I got.

tanaka

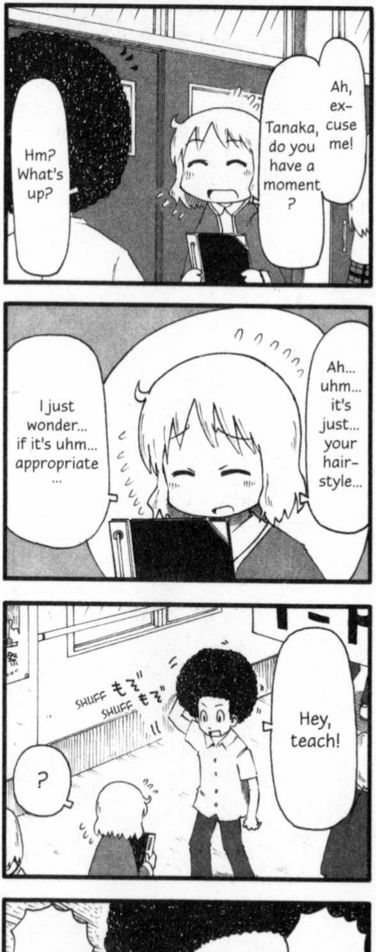
Ah, excuse me!
Tanaka, do you have a moment?
Hm? What's up?
Ah... uhm... it's just... your hair-style...
I just wonder... if it's uhm... appropriate ...
Hey, teach!
SHUFF
SHUFF
?
How 'bout some
dora-yaki?*
Station Plaza

*azuki bean jam-filled pancakes

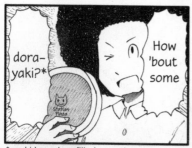

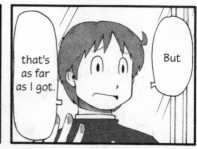

fortune telling

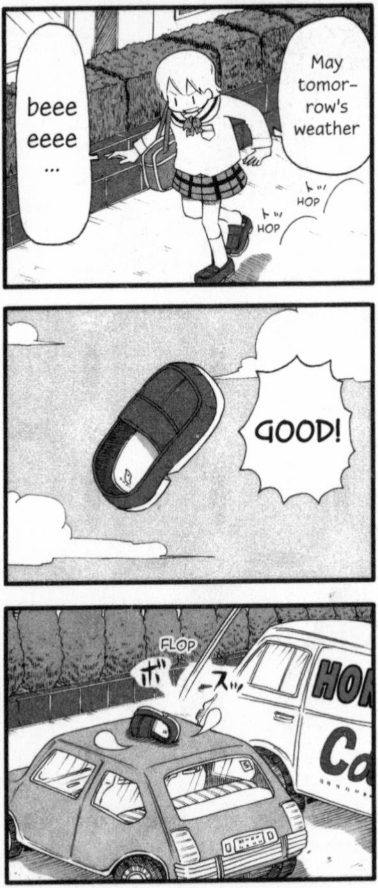
May tomorrow's weather
beeee eeee ...
トッ HOP
トッ HOP
GOOD!
FLOP
ボーズッ

the vice principal's doll

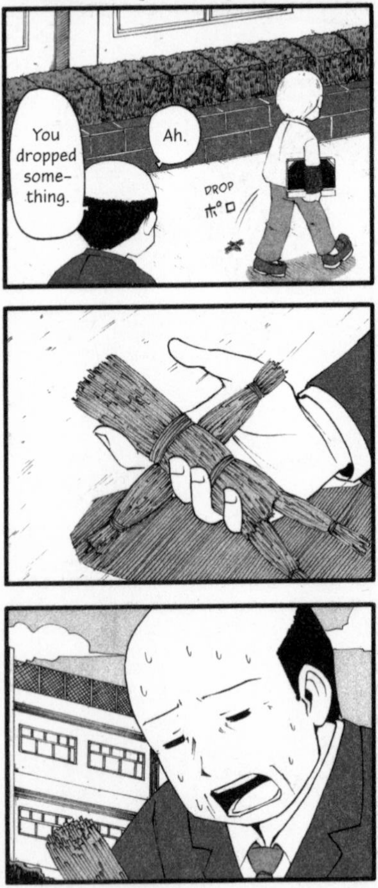
Ah.
You dropped something.
DROP
ポロ

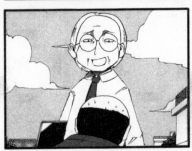

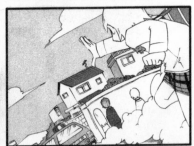

mr. takasaki

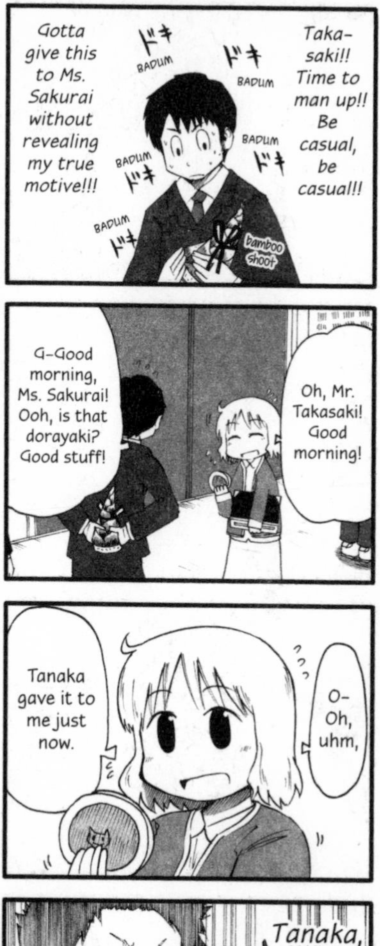

Taka-saki!! Time to man up!! Be casual, be casual!!
ドキ BADUM
ドキ BADUM
ドキ BADUM
ドキ BADUM
Gotta give this to Ms. Sakurai without revealing my true motive!!!
bamboo shoot
Oh, Mr. Takasaki! Good morning!
G-Good morning, Ms. Sakurai! Ooh, is that dorayaki? Good stuff!
O- Oh, uhm,
Tanaka gave it to me just now.
Tanaka, you bastard!

big money

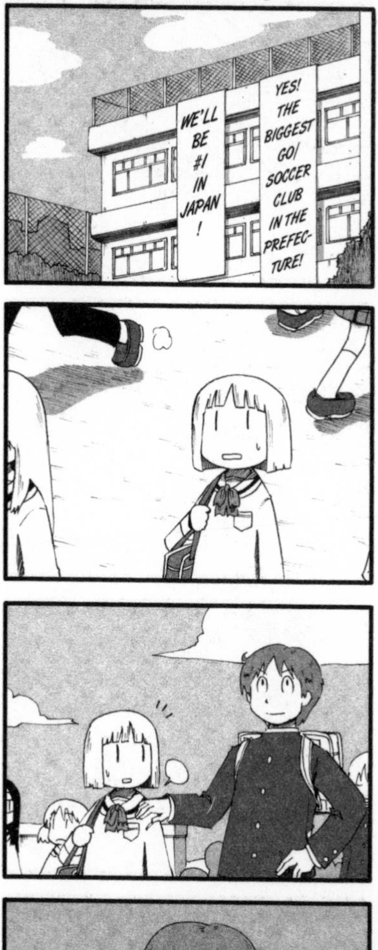

YES! THE BIGGEST GO/ SOCCER CLUB IN THE PREFEC-TURE!
WE'LL BE #1 IN JAPAN!
NAILED IT

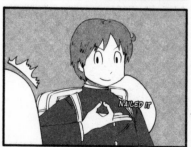

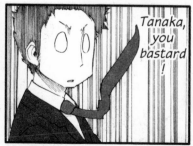

shoes

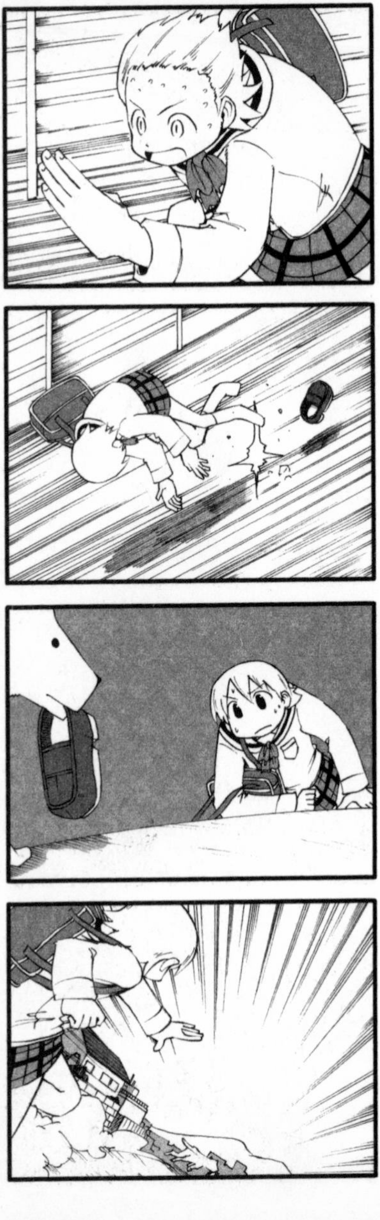

the vice principal's natto

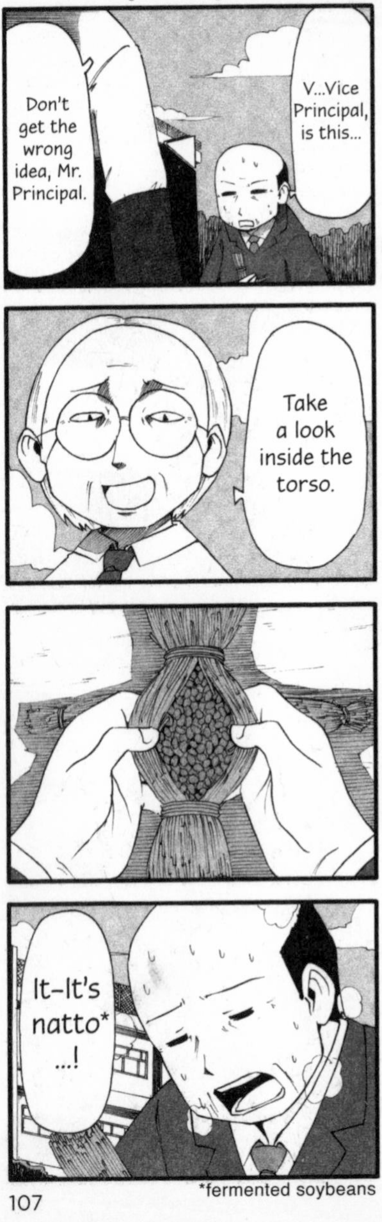
V...Vice Principal, is this...
Don't get the wrong idea, Mr. Principal.
Take a look inside the torso.
It-It's natto* ...!

*fermented soybeans

buddy

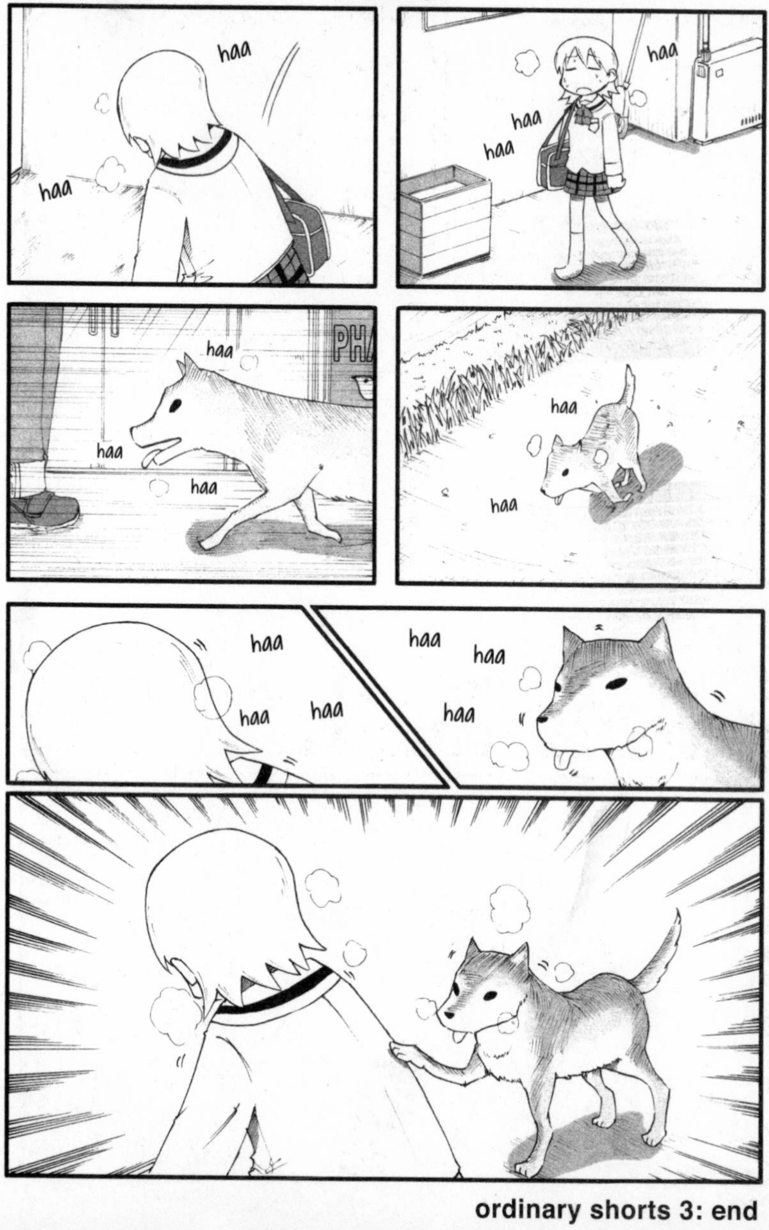
haa
haa
haa
haa
haa
haa
haa
haa
haa
haa
haa
haa
haa
haa
haa
haa

ordinary shorts 3: end

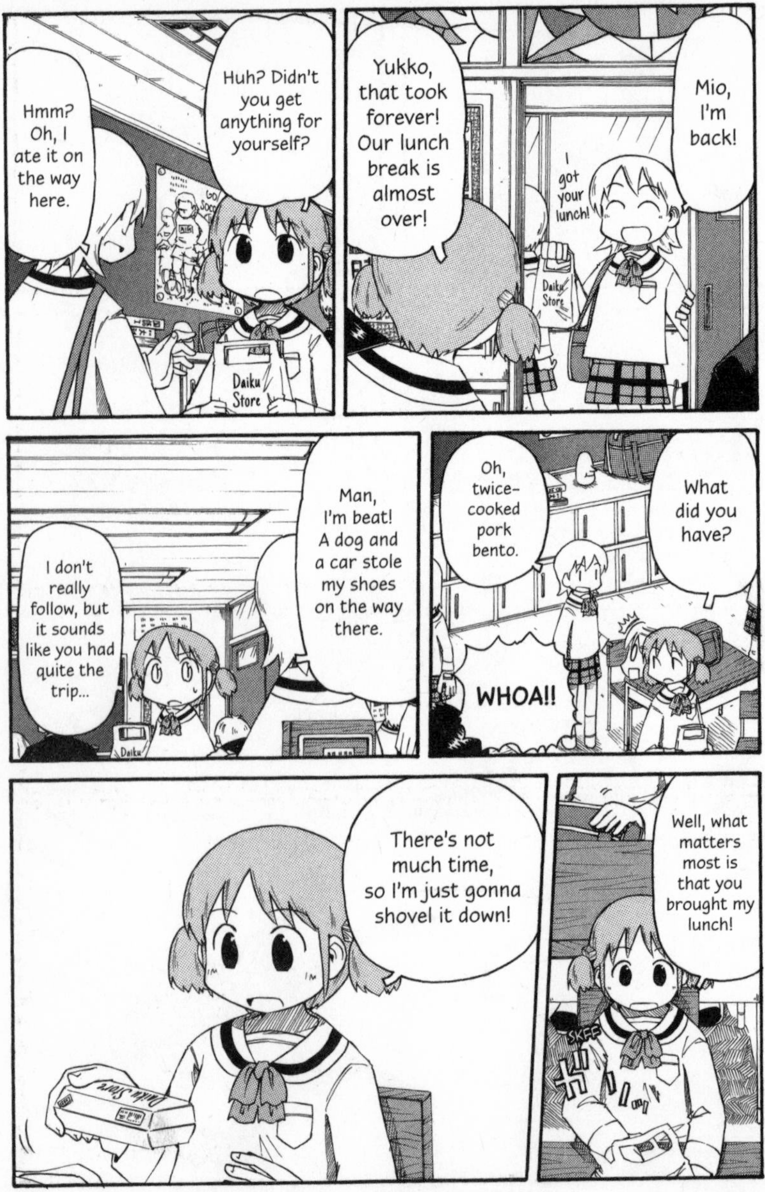

Mio, I'm back!
I got your lunch!
Daiku Store
Yukko, that took forever! Our lunch break is almost over!
Huh? Didn't you get anything for yourself?
Daiku Store
Hmm? Oh, I ate it on the way here.
What did you have?
Oh, twice-cooked pork bento.
WHOA!!
Man, I'm beat! A dog and a car stole my shoes on the way there.
I don't really follow, but it sounds like you had quite the trip...
Daiku
Well, what matters most is that you brought my lunch!
SKFF
There's not much time, so I'm just gonna shovel it down!
Daiku Store

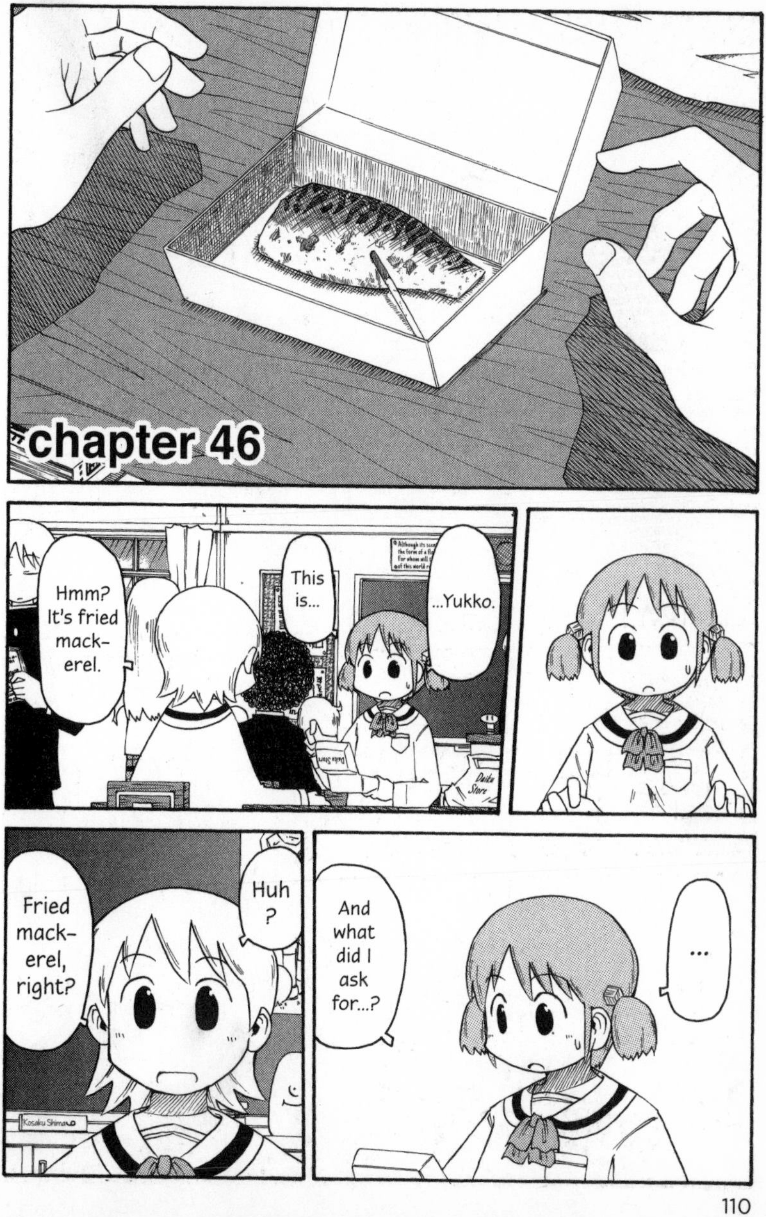
chapter 46
...Yukko.
This is...
Hmm? It's fried mack-erel.
Daiku Store
...
And what did I ask for...?
Huh?
Fried mack-erel, right?
Kosaku Shima

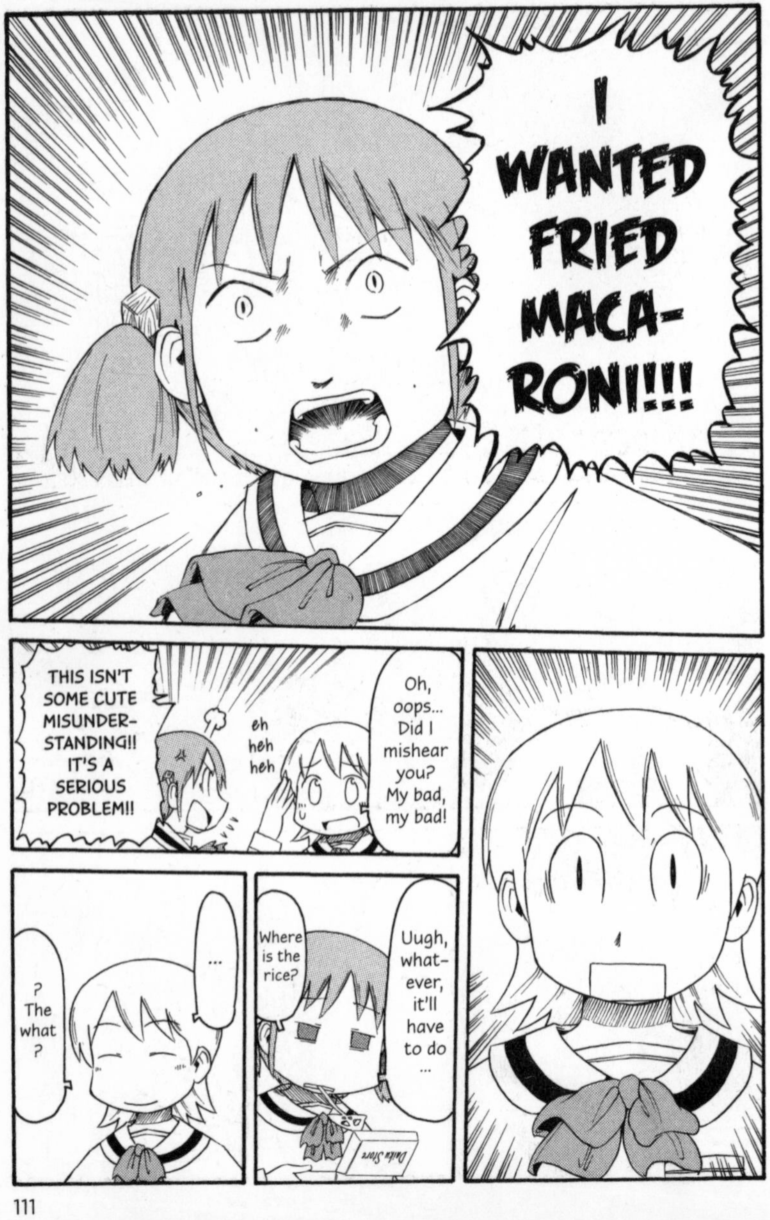
I WANTED FRIED MACA-RONI!!!
Oh, oops... Did I mishear you? My bad, my bad!
eh heh heh
THIS ISN'T SOME CUTE MISUNDER-STANDING!! IT'S A SERIOUS PROBLEM!!
Uugh, what-ever, it'll have to do ...
Where is the rice?
Daiku Store
...
? The what ?

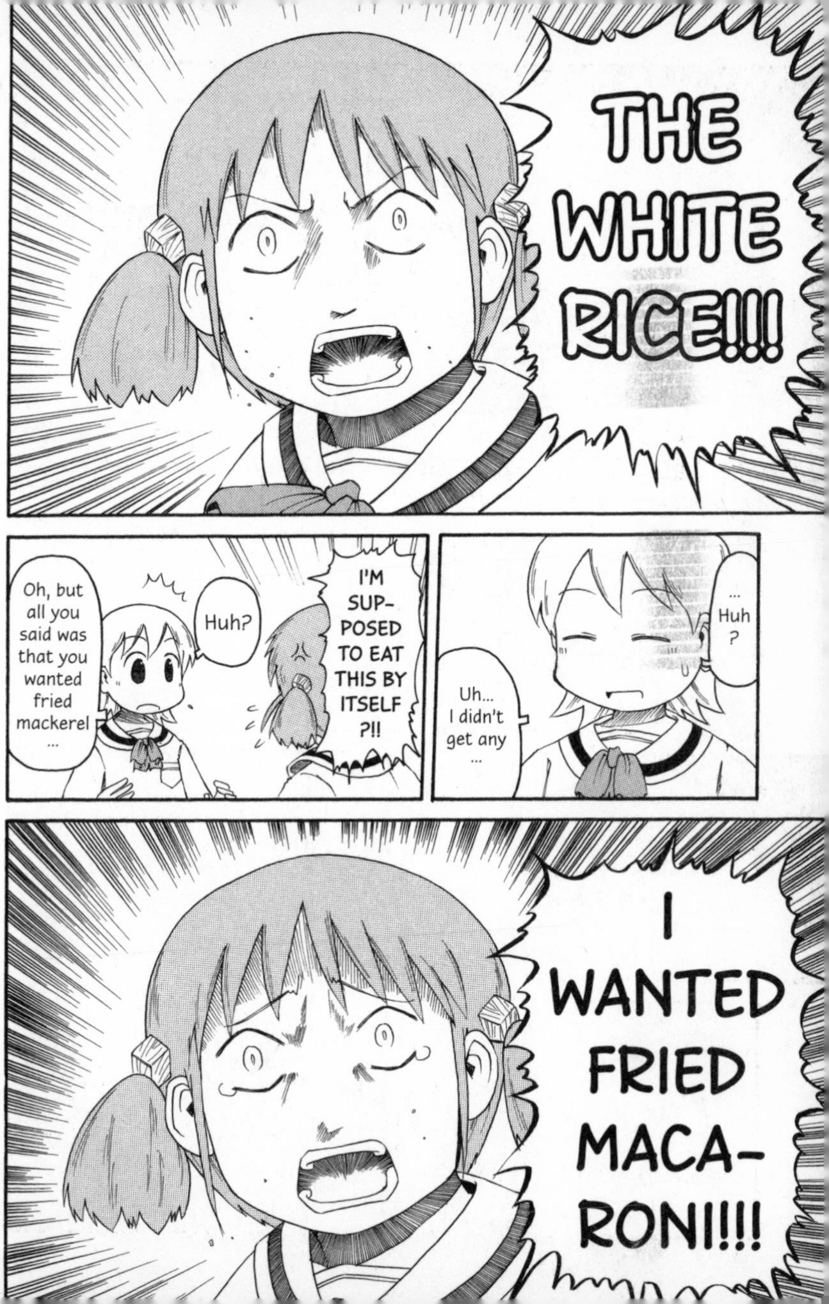
THE WHITE RICE!!!
... Huh?
Uh... I didn't get any ...
I'M SUP-POSED TO EAT THIS BY ITSELF ?!!
Huh?
Oh, but all you said was that you wanted fried mackerel ...
I WANTED FRIED MACA-RONI!!!

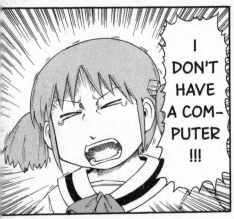

Fried! Macaroni!!!
W-Well, at least this will make a funny story for your blog, right ...?
Gol Soccer Club
I DON'T HAVE A COMPUTER!!!
Geez, no need to get so mad. I was pointing out its potential...
I'll go back, okay? Gimme some cash.
WHY DO I HAVE TO PAY TWICE?!!
Ugh, fine! Just hurry up and get it!
Lunch break is almost over!
OK, OK.
all I have ...
?

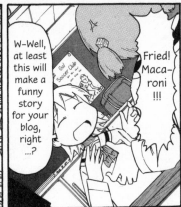

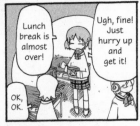

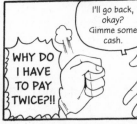

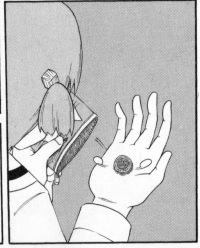

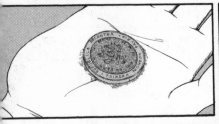

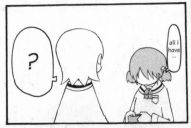

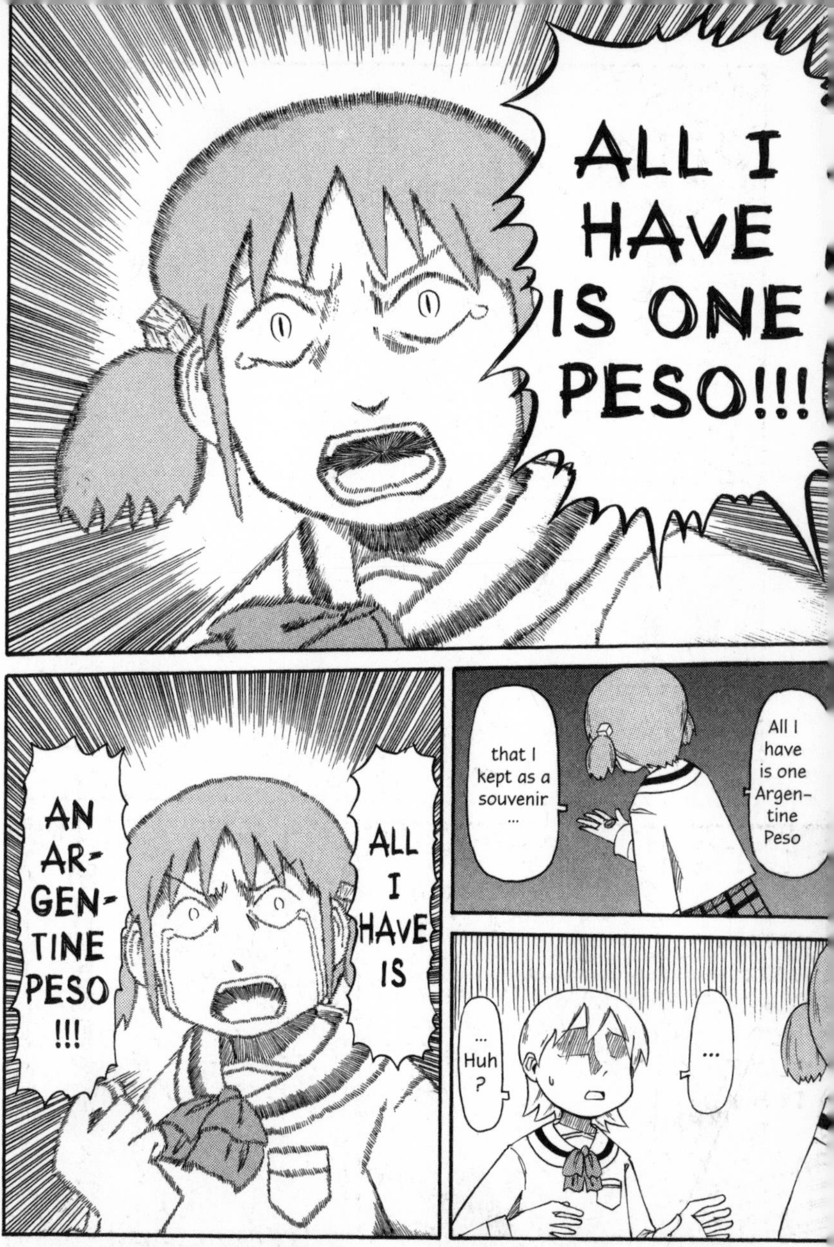
ALL I HAVE IS ONE PESO!!!
All I have is one Argen-tine Peso
that I kept as a souvenir ...
...
... Huh?
ALL I HAVE IS
AN AR-GEN-TINE PESO!!!

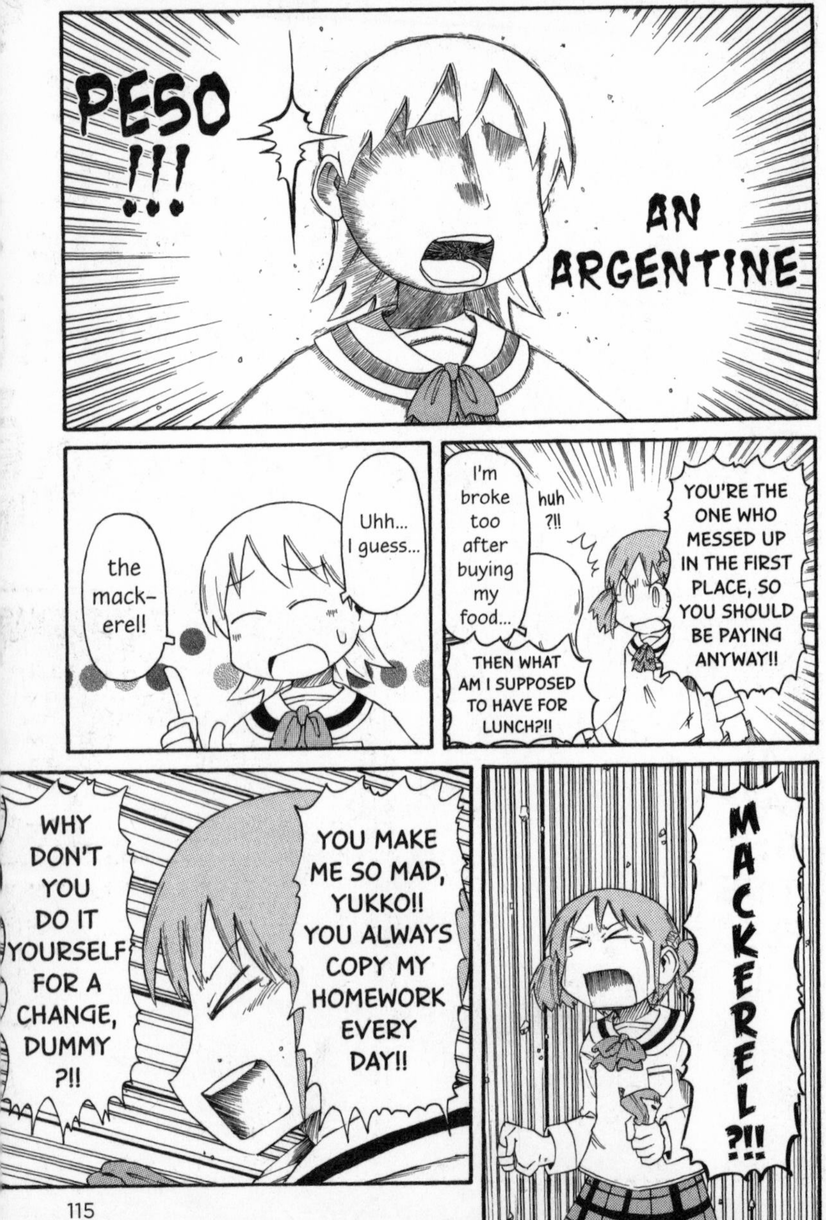
AN ARGENTINE
PESO!!!
YOU'RE THE ONE WHO MESSED UP IN THE FIRST PLACE, SO YOU SHOULD BE PAYING ANYWAY!!
huh ?!!
I'm broke too after buying my food...
THEN WHAT AM I SUPPOSED TO HAVE FOR LUNCH?!!
Uhh... I guess...
the mackerel!
MACKEREL?!!
YOU MAKE ME SO MAD, YUKKO!! YOU ALWAYS COPY MY HOMEWORK EVERY DAY!!
WHY DON'T YOU DO IT YOURSELF FOR A CHANGE, DUMMY?!!

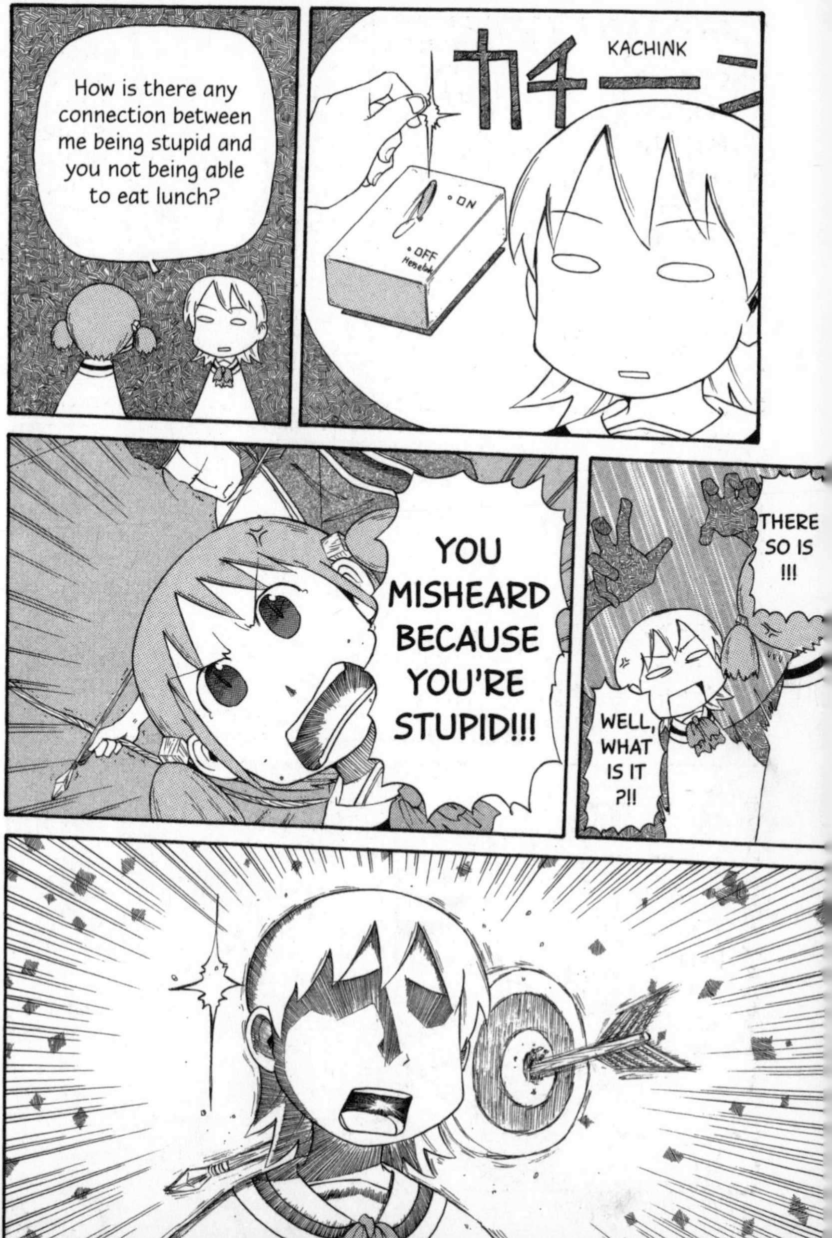
KACHINK
How is there any connection between me being stupid and you not being able to eat lunch?
THERE SO IS !!!
WELL, WHAT IS IT ?!!
YOU MISHEARD BECAUSE YOU'RE STUPID!!!

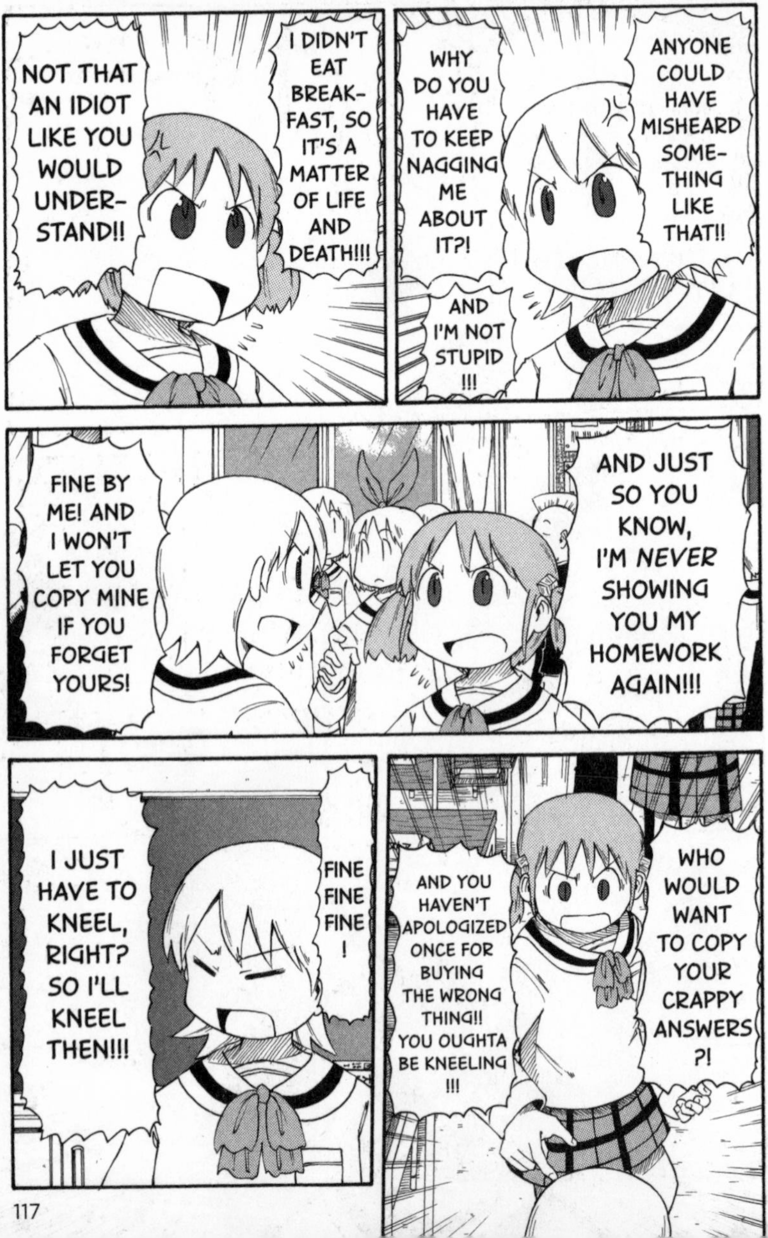
ANYONE COULD HAVE MISHEARD SOMETHING LIKE THAT!!
WHY DO YOU HAVE TO KEEP NAGGING ME ABOUT IT?!
AND I'M NOT STUPID !!!
I DIDN'T EAT BREAKFAST, SO IT'S A MATTER OF LIFE AND DEATH!!!
NOT THAT AN IDIOT LIKE YOU WOULD UNDERSTAND!!
AND JUST SO YOU KNOW, I'M *NEVER* SHOWING YOU MY HOMEWORK AGAIN!!!
FINE BY ME! AND I WON'T LET YOU COPY MINE IF YOU FORGET YOURS!
WHO WOULD WANT TO COPY YOUR CRAPPY ANSWERS ?!
AND YOU HAVEN'T APOLOGIZED ONCE FOR BUYING THE WRONG THING!! YOU OUGHTA BE KNEELING !!!
FINE FINE FINE !
I JUST HAVE TO KNEEL, RIGHT? SO I'LL KNEEL THEN!!!

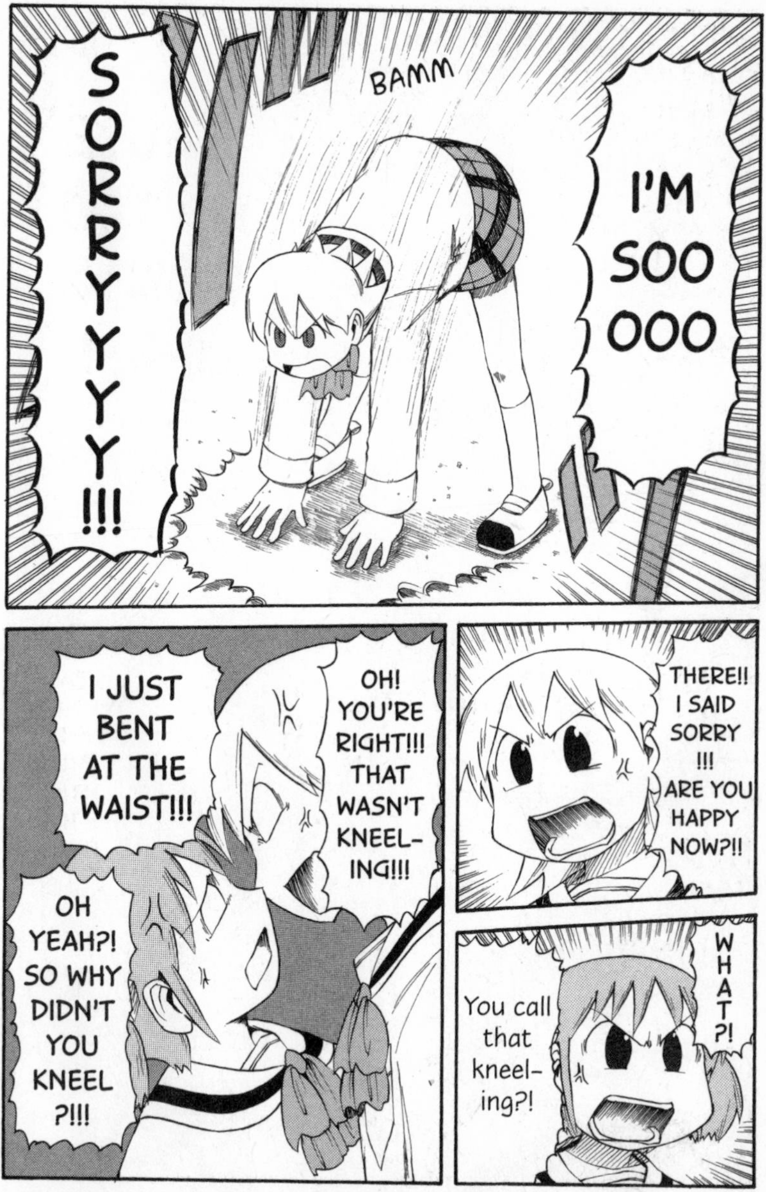
BAMM
I'M SOO OOO
SORRYYYY!!!
THERE!! I SAID SORRY!!! ARE YOU HAPPY NOW?!!
WHAT?!
You call that kneel-ing?!
OH! YOU'RE RIGHT!!! THAT WASN'T KNEEL-ING!!!
I JUST BENT AT THE WAIST!!!
OH YEAH?! SO WHY DIDN'T YOU KNEEL?!!!

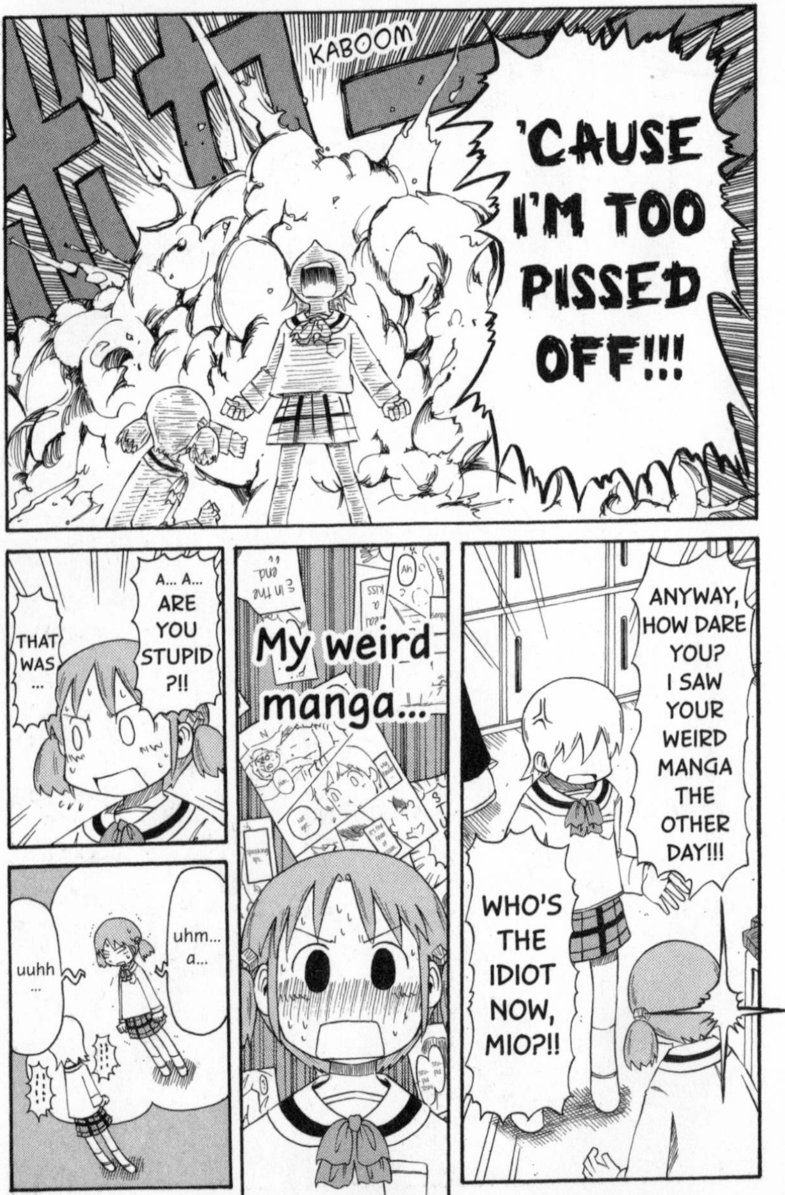
KABOOM
'CAUSE I'M TOO PISSED OFF!!!
ANYWAY, HOW DARE YOU? I SAW YOUR WEIRD MANGA THE OTHER DAY!!!
WHO'S THE IDIOT NOW, MIO?!!
My weird manga...
A... A... ARE YOU STUPID ?!!
THAT WAS ...
uhm... a...
uuhh ...

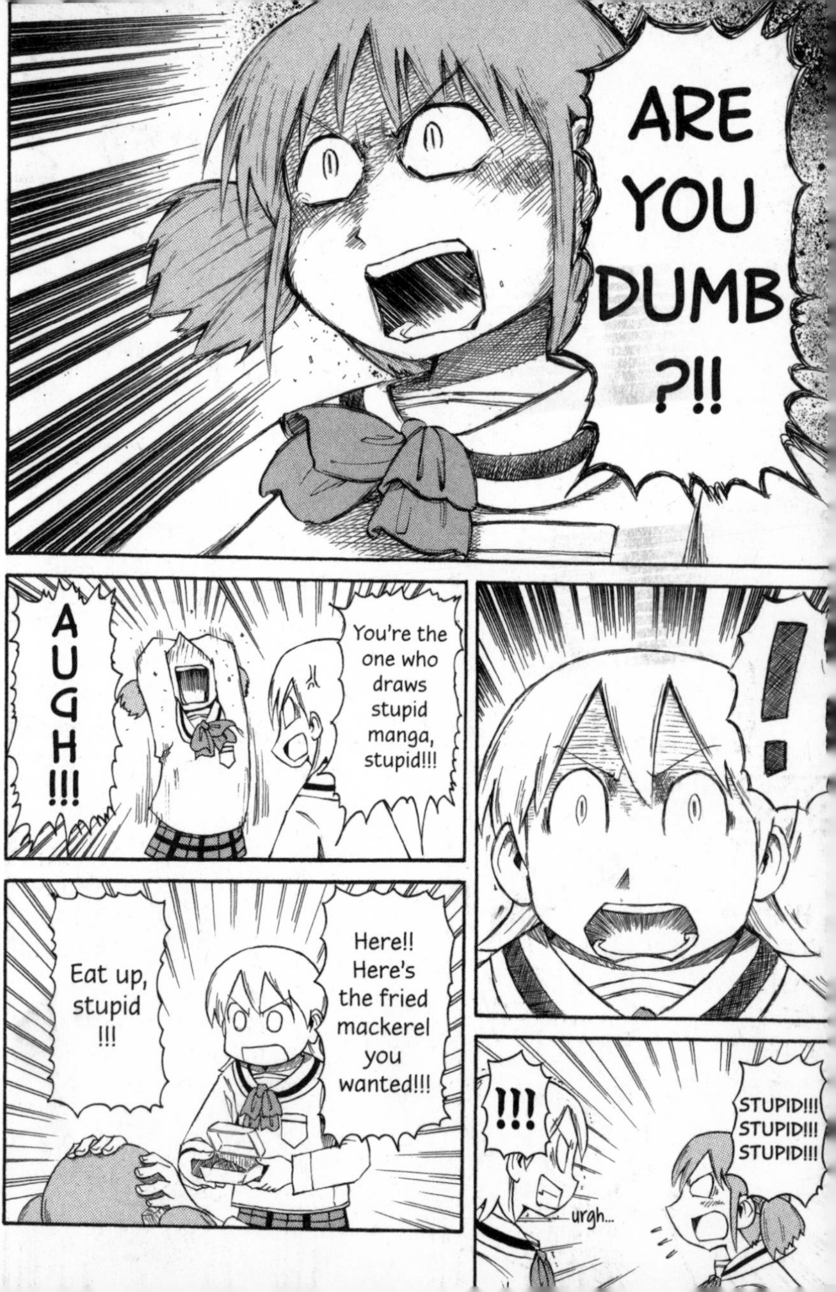
ARE YOU DUMB ?!!
!
You're the one who draws stupid manga, stupid!!!
AUGH!!!
Here!! Here's the fried mackerel you wanted!!!
Eat up, stupid !!!
STUPID!!! STUPID!!! STUPID!!!
!!!
urgh...

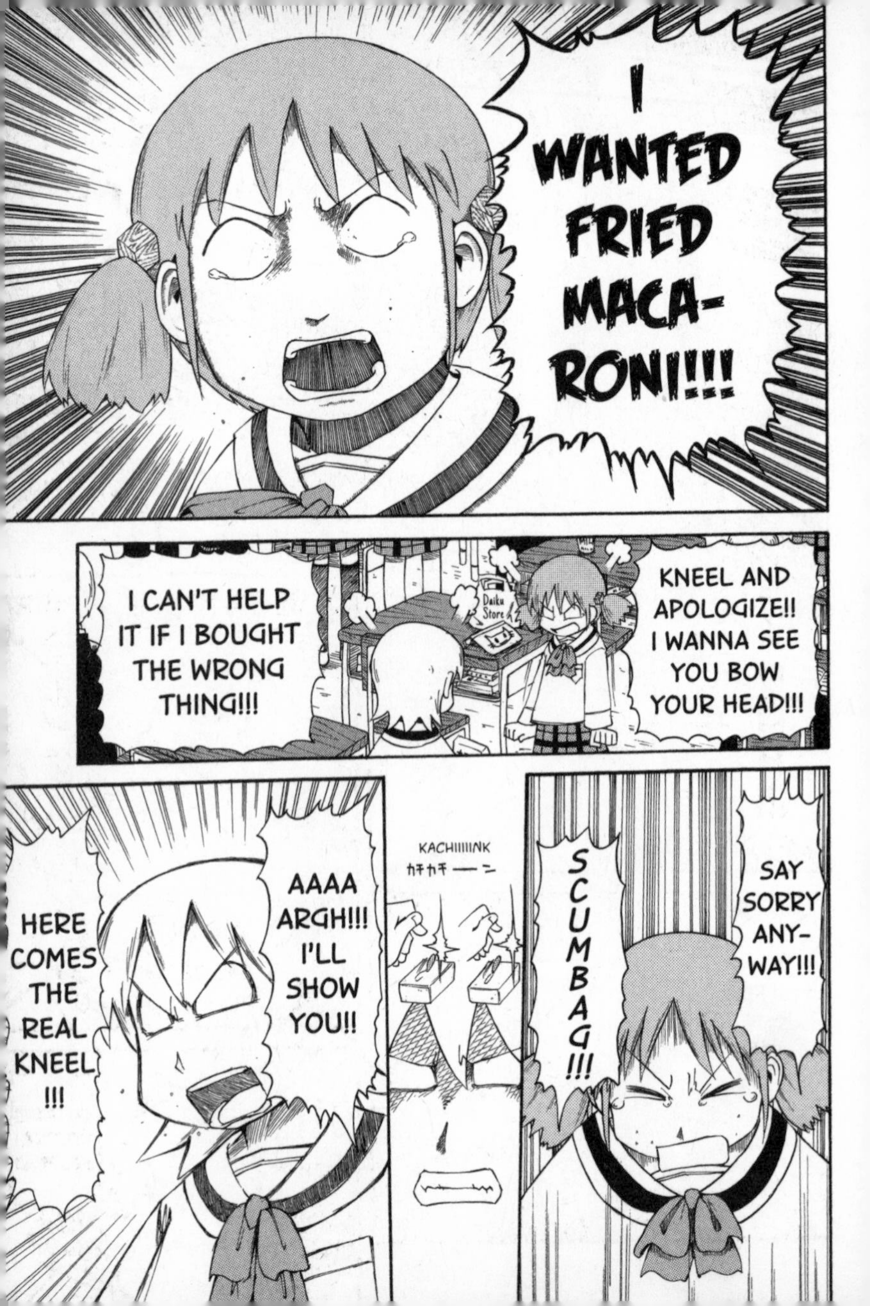
I WANTED FRIED MACA-RONI!!!
KNEEL AND APOLOGIZE!! I WANNA SEE YOU BOW YOUR HEAD!!!
Daiku Store
I CAN'T HELP IT IF I BOUGHT THE WRONG THING!!!
SAY SORRY ANY-WAY!!!
SCUMBAG!!!
KACHIIIIINK
カチカチーーン
AAAA ARGH!!! I'LL SHOW YOU!!
HERE COMES THE REAL KNEEL!!!

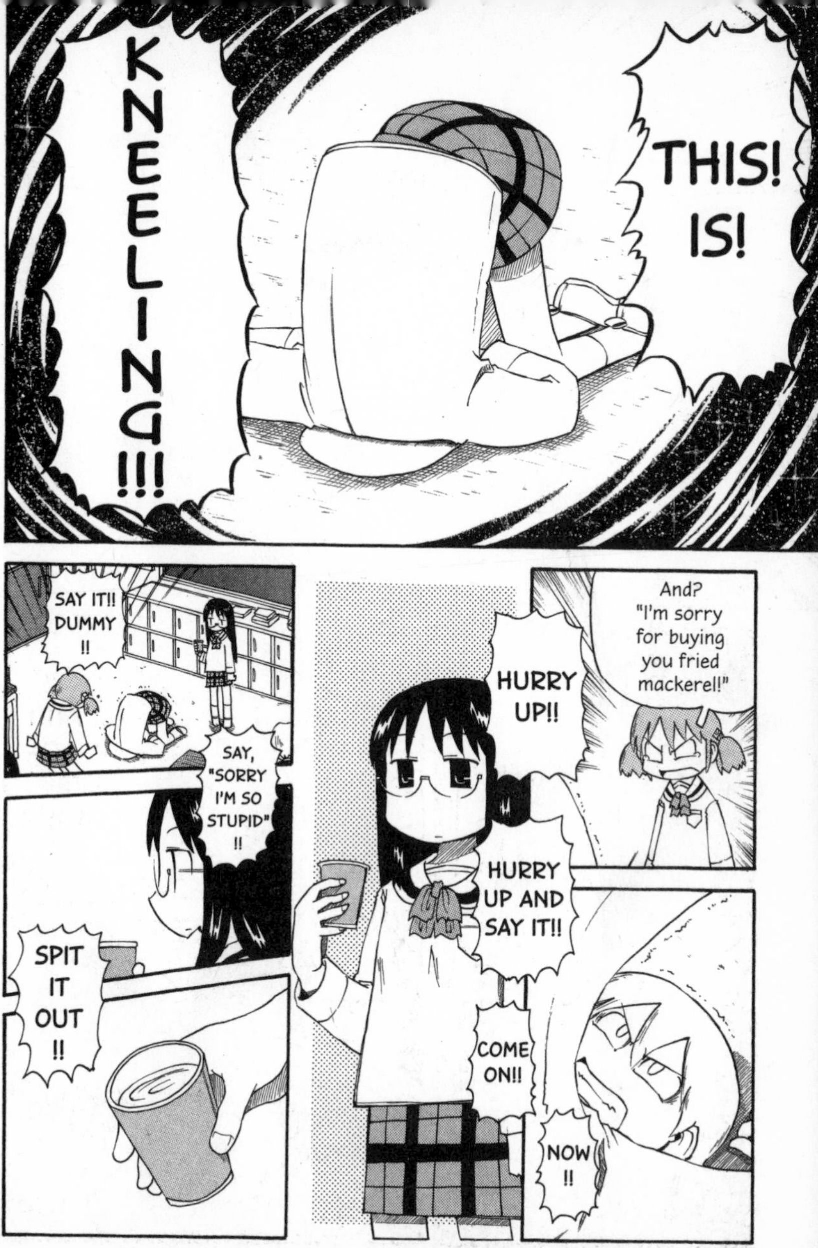
THIS! IS!
KNEELING!!!
And? "I'm sorry for buying you fried mackerel!"
NOW !!
HURRY UP!!
HURRY UP AND SAY IT!!
COME ON!!
SAY IT!! DUMMY !!
SAY, "SORRY I'M SO STUPID" !!
SPIT IT OUT !!

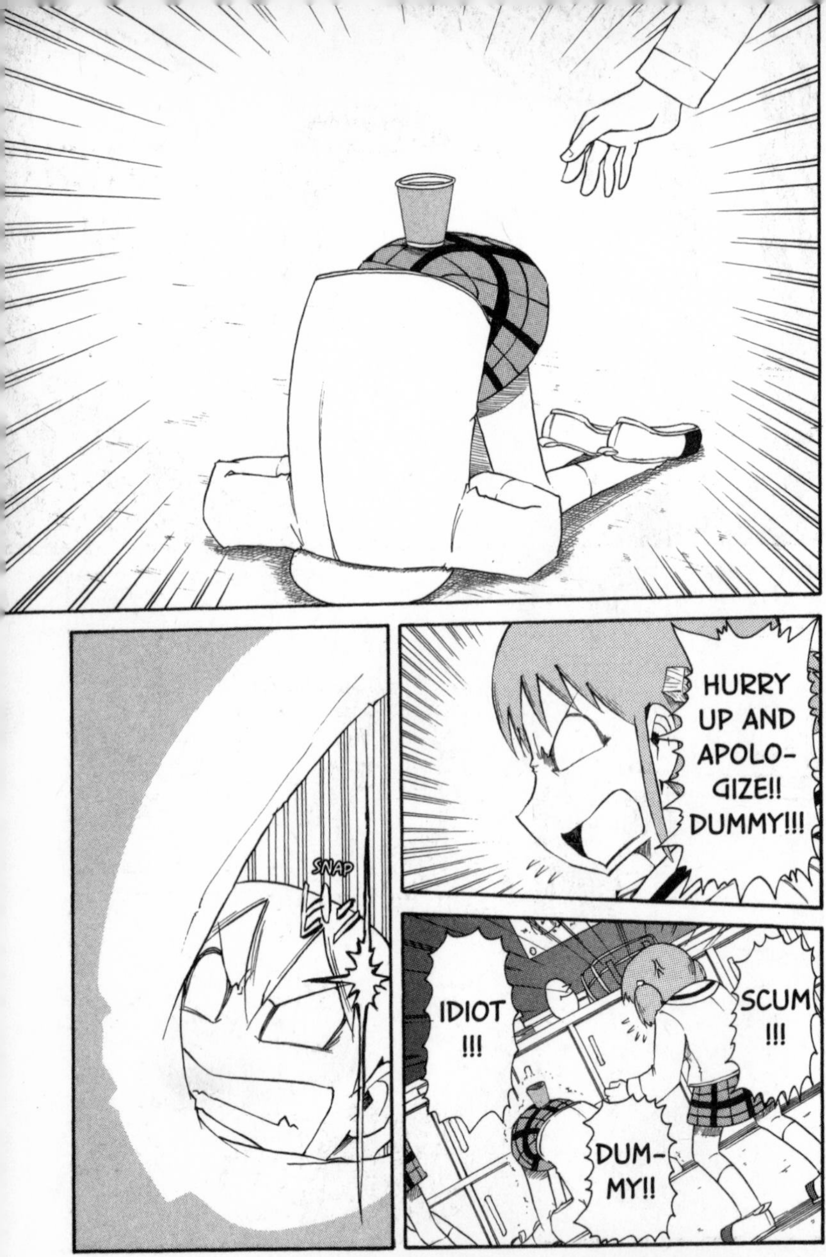
HURRY UP AND APOLO-GIZE!! DUMMY!!!
SNAP
SCUM !!!
IDIOT !!!
DUM-MY!!

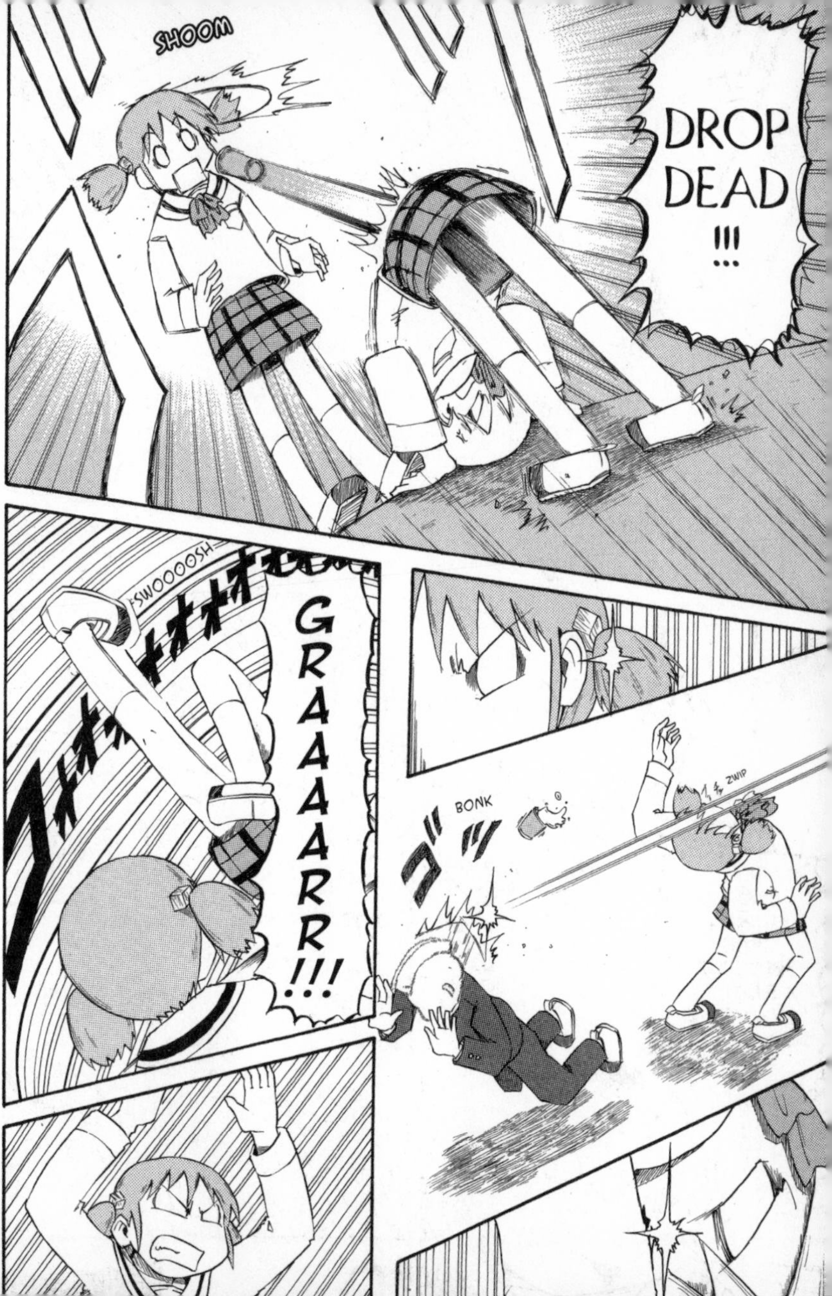
SHOOM
DROP DEAD !!! ...
BONK
ZWIP
SWOOOOSH
GRAAAAARRR!!!

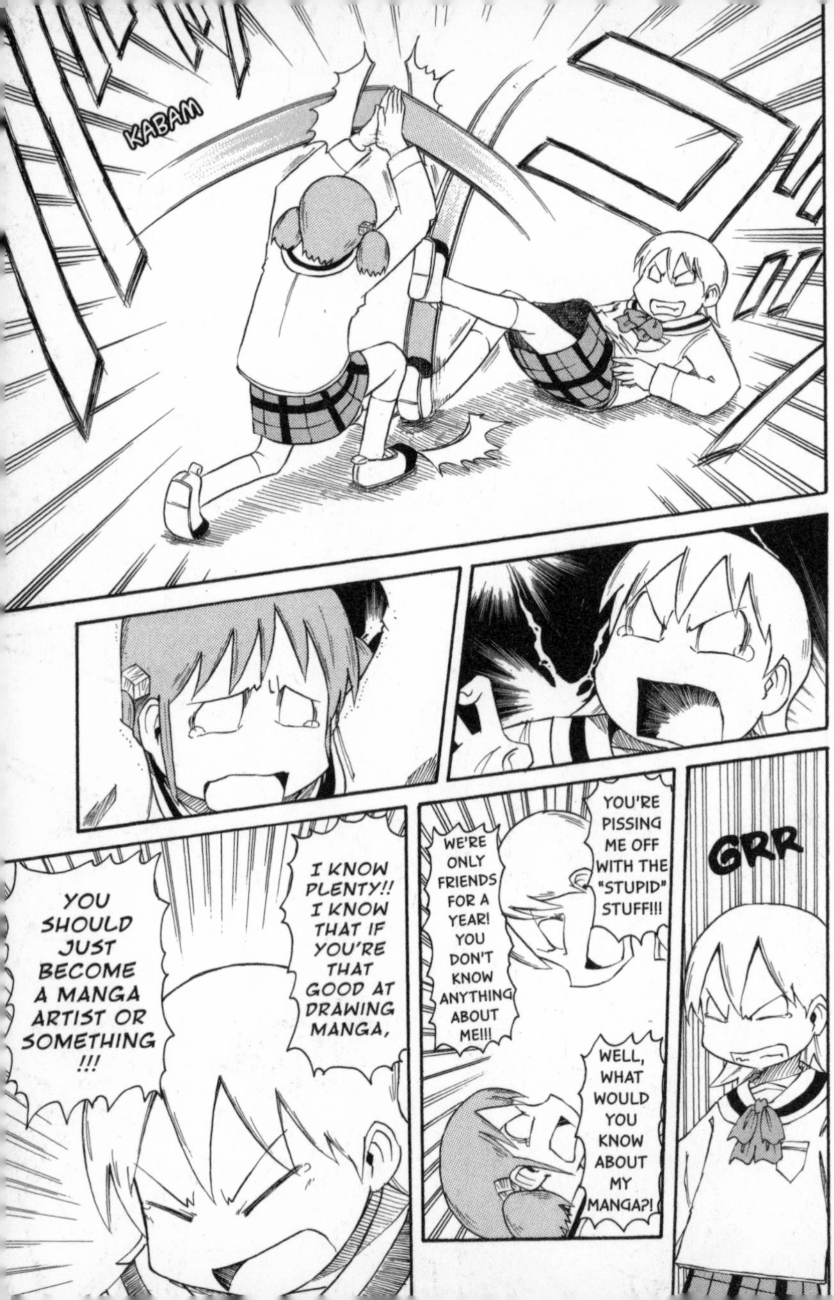
KABAM
GRR
YOU'RE PISSING ME OFF WITH THE "STUPID" STUFF!!!
WELL, WHAT WOULD YOU KNOW ABOUT MY MANGA?!
WE'RE ONLY FRIENDS FOR A YEAR! YOU DON'T KNOW ANYTHING ABOUT ME!!!
I KNOW PLENTY!!! I KNOW THAT IF YOU'RE THAT GOOD AT DRAWING MANGA,
YOU SHOULD JUST BECOME A MANGA ARTIST OR SOMETHING !!!

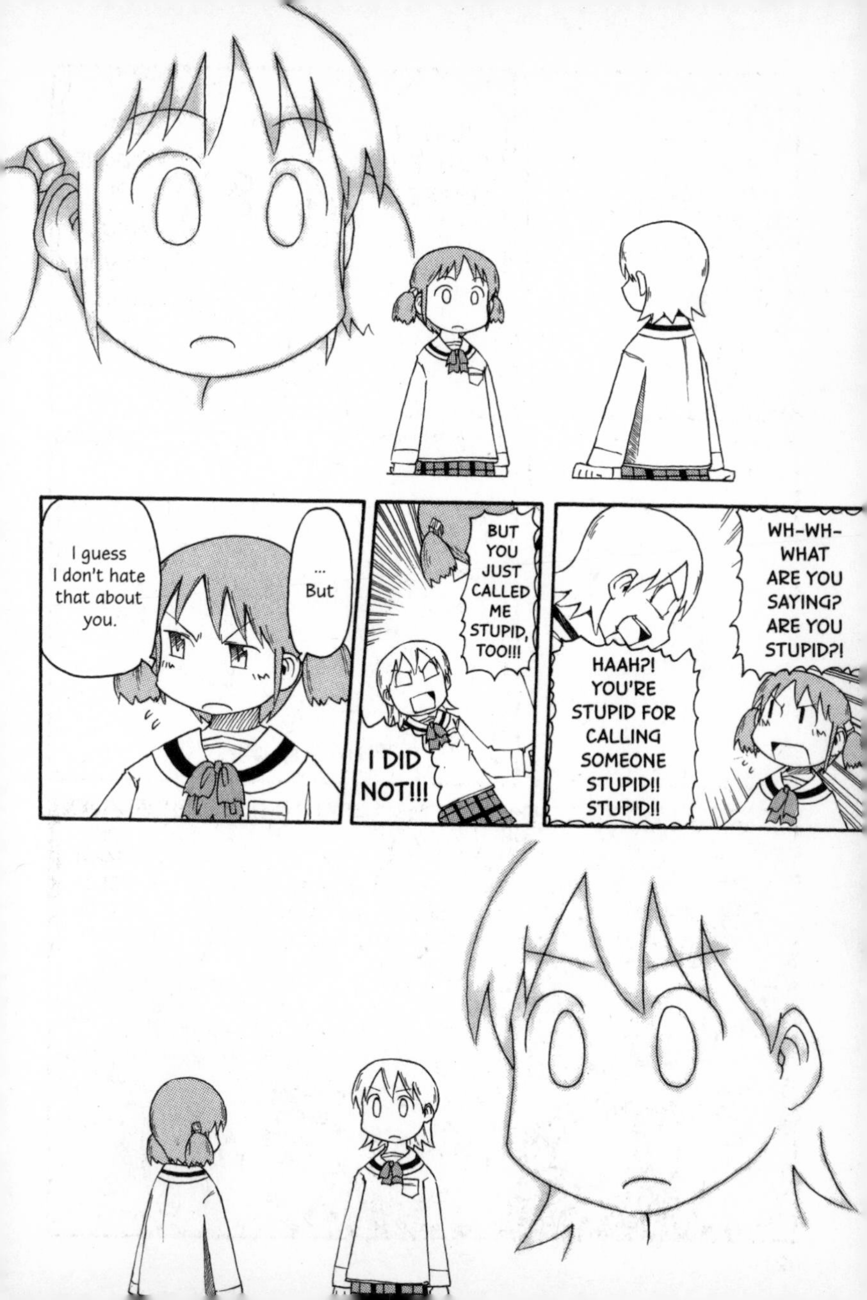

WH-WH-WHAT ARE YOU SAYING? ARE YOU STUPID?!
HAAH?! YOU'RE STUPID FOR CALLING SOMEONE STUPID!! STUPID!!
BUT YOU JUST CALLED ME STUPID, TOO!!!
I DID NOT!!!
... But
I guess I don't hate that about you.

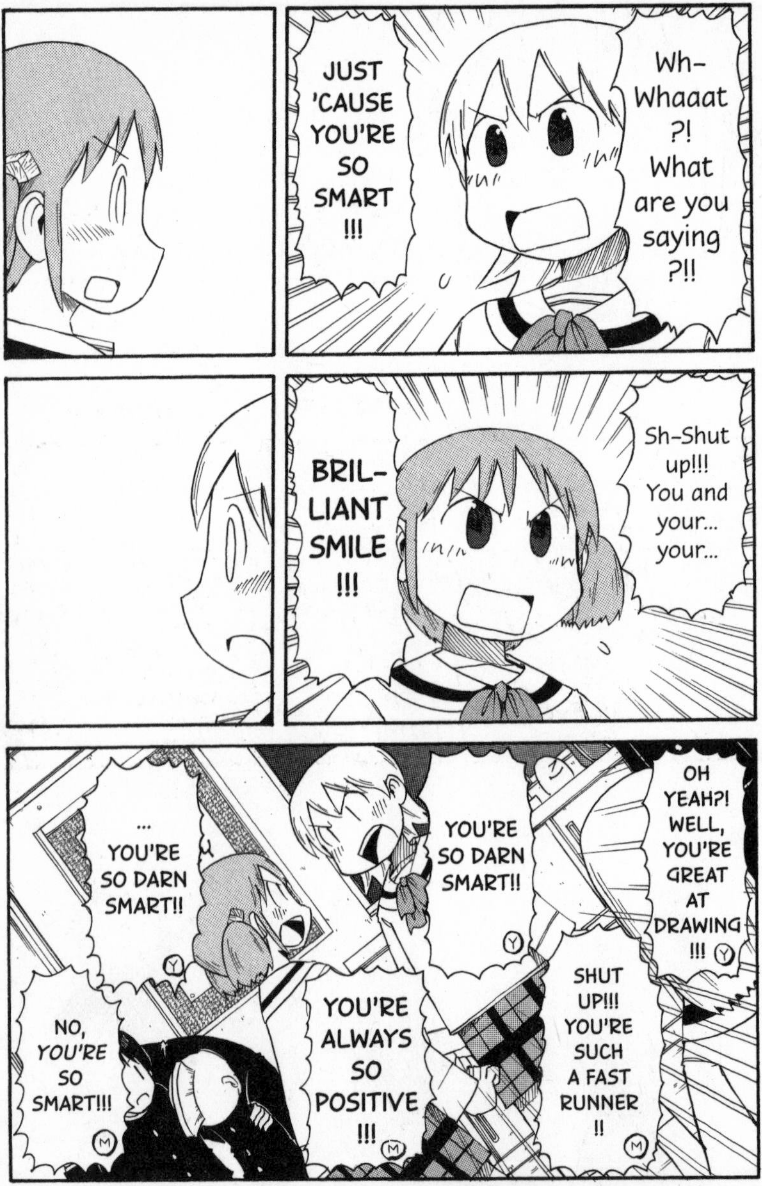
Wh-Whaaat?! What are you saying?!!
JUST 'CAUSE YOU'RE SO SMART!!!
Sh-Shut up!!! You and your... your...
BRIL-LIANT SMILE!!!
OH YEAH?! WELL, YOU'RE GREAT AT DRAWING!!!
YOU'RE SO DARN SMART!!
... YOU'RE SO DARN SMART!!
SHUT UP!!! YOU'RE SUCH A FAST RUNNER!!
YOU'RE ALWAYS SO POSITIVE!!!
NO, *YOU'RE* SO SMART!!!

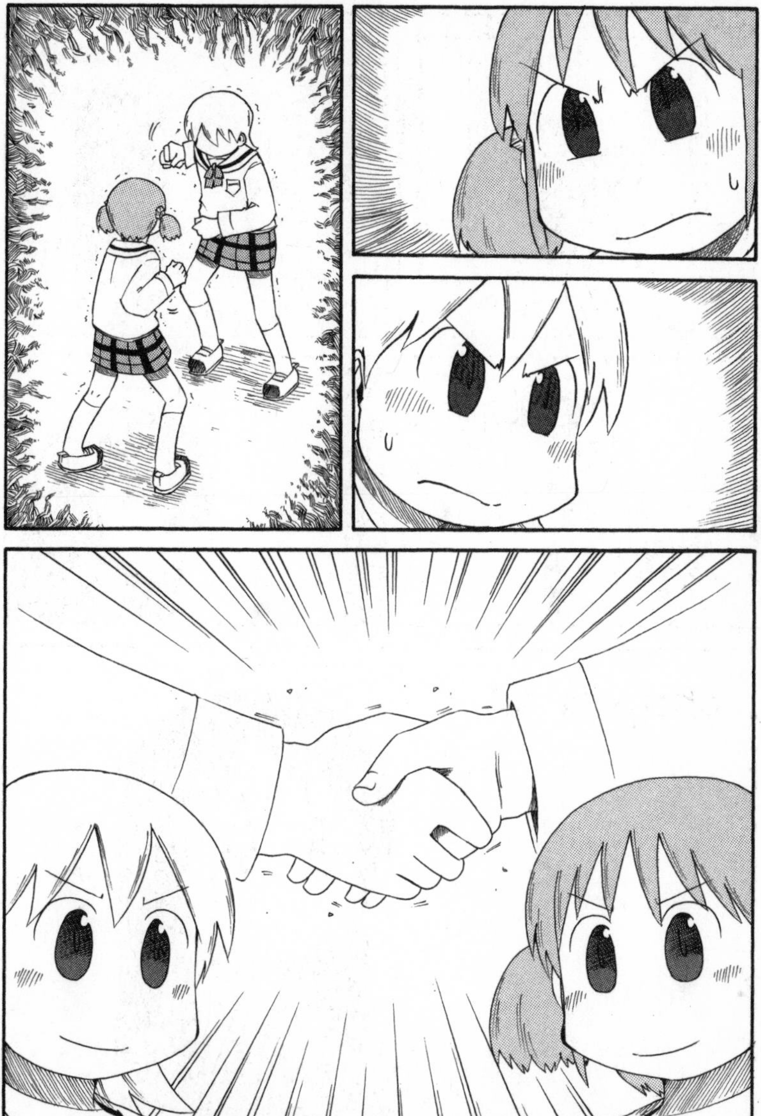

chapter 46: end

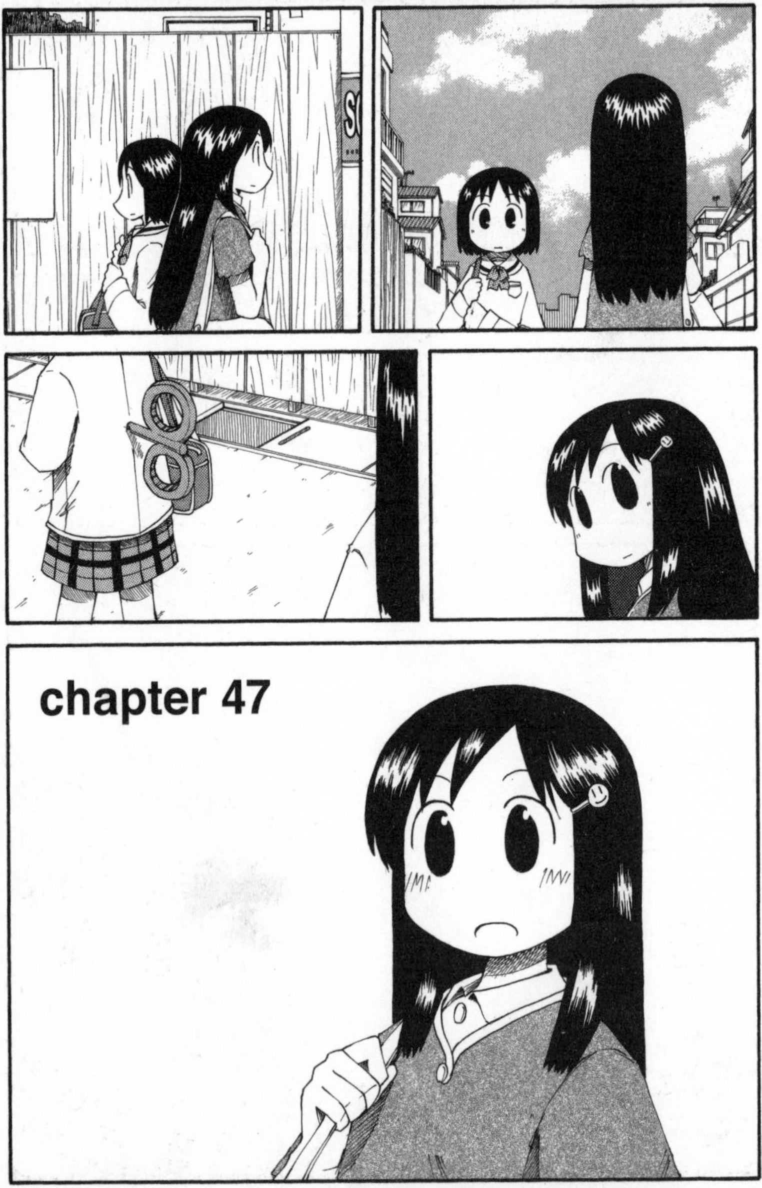
chapter 47

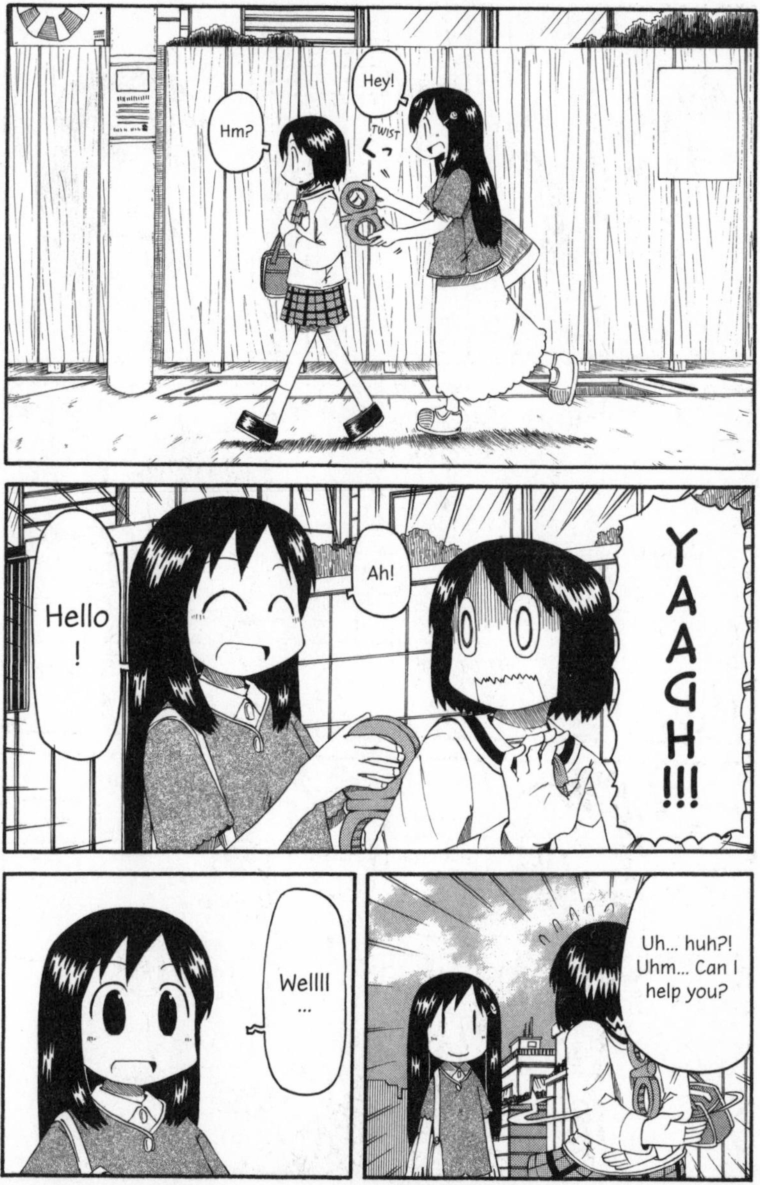

Hey!
TWIST
くっ
Hm?
YAAGH!!!
Ah!
Hello!
Uh... huh?! Uhm... Can I help you?
Wellll...

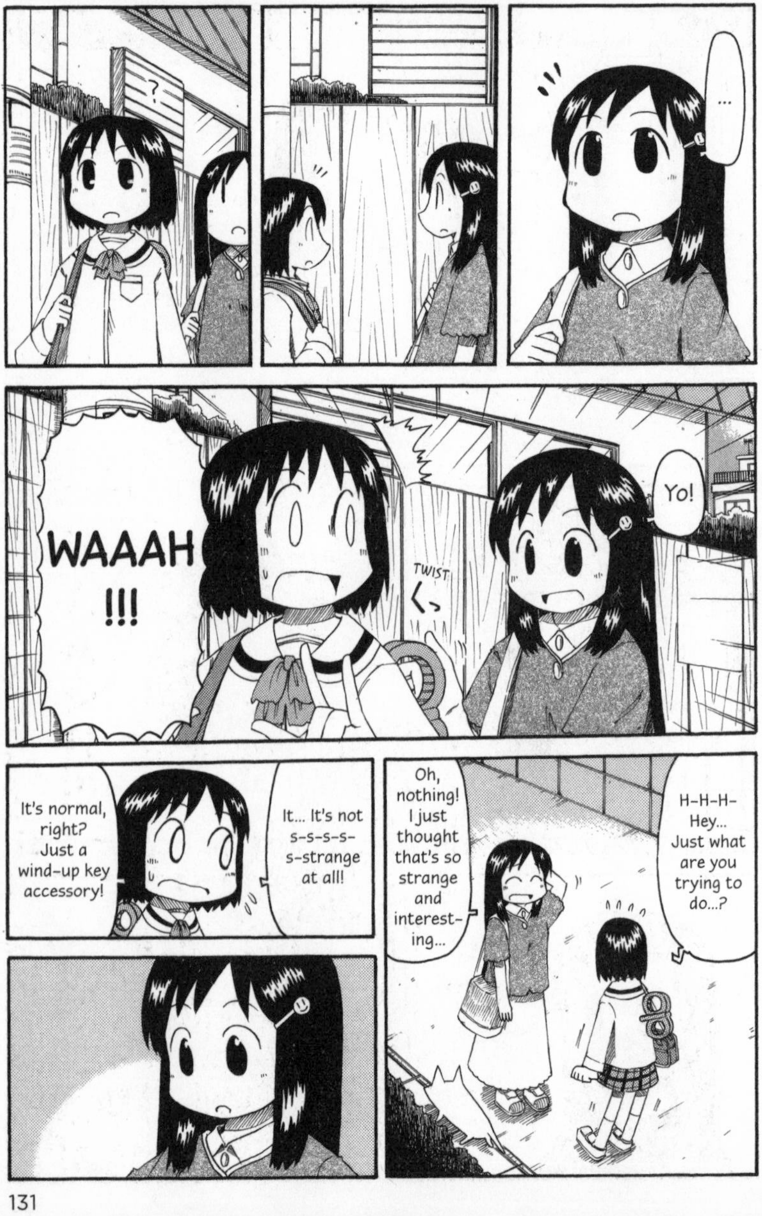

...
?
Yo!
TWIST
WAAAH !!!
H-H-H- Hey... Just what are you trying to do...?
Oh, nothing! I just thought that's so strange and interest- ing...
It... It's not s-s-s-s- s-strange at all!
It's normal, right? Just a wind-up key accessory!

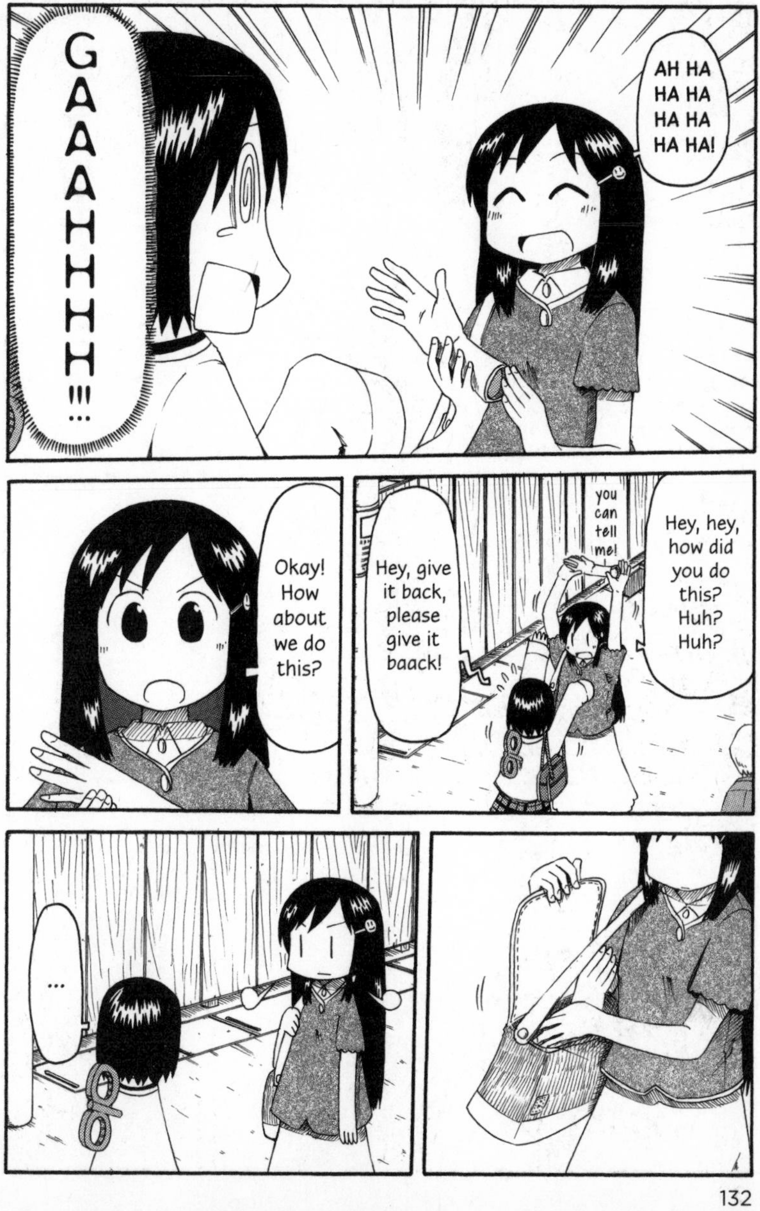
AH HA HA HA HA HA HA HA!
GAAAHHHH!!!
Hey, hey, how did you do this? Huh? Huh?
you can tell me!
Hey, give it back, please give it baack!
Okay! How about we do this?
...

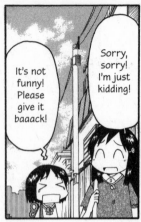

TURN
るっ
WHYYY?!!
Sorry, sorry! I'm just kidding!
It's not funny! Please give it baaack!
すっ
SHFF
Left or right?
IT'S IN YOUR BAG!!
Please don't follow me anymore!!
Okay, okay, sorry.
KACHINK
Ah...

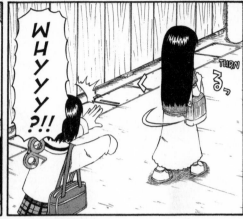

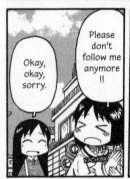

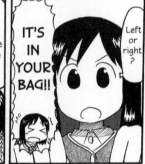

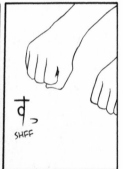

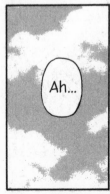

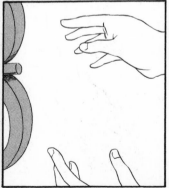

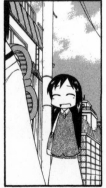

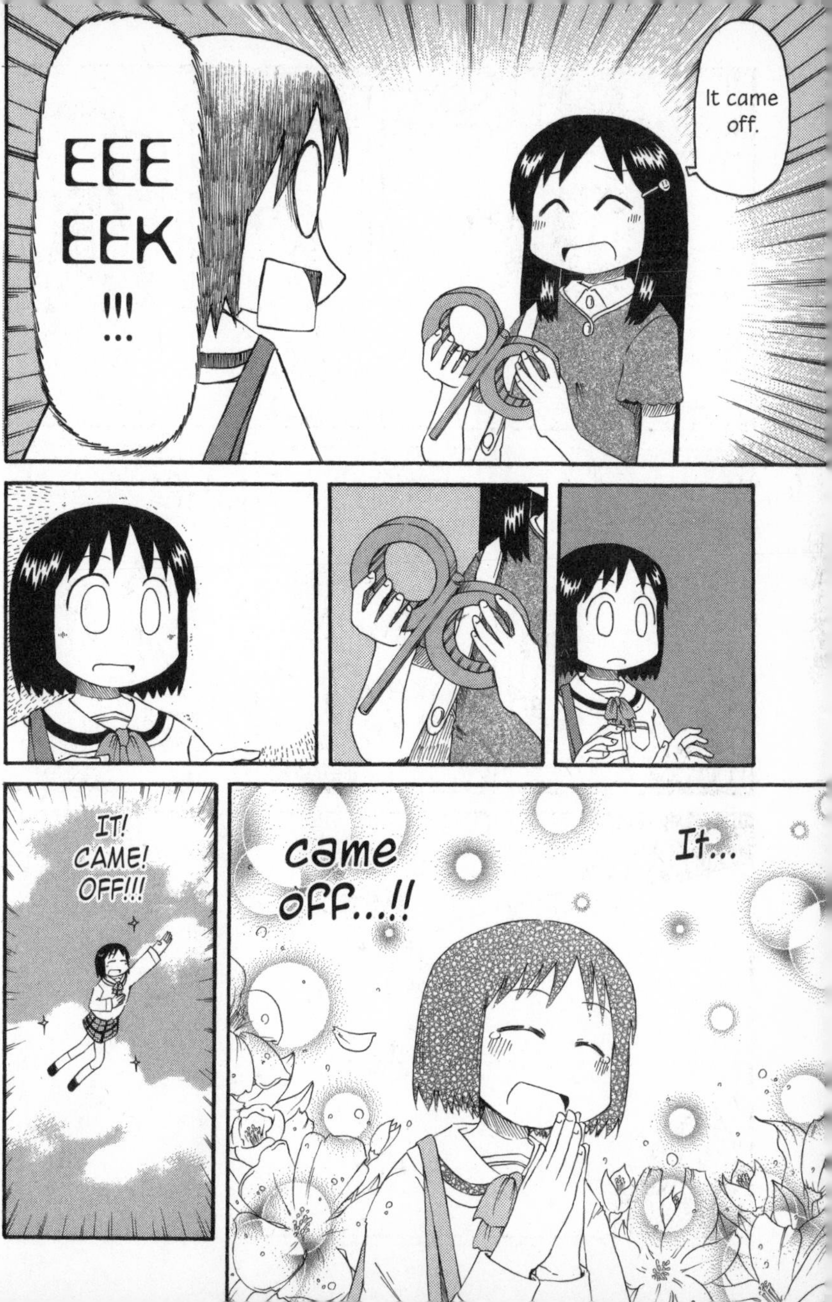

It came off.
EEEEEK!!!...
It...
came off...!!
IT! CAME! OFF!!!

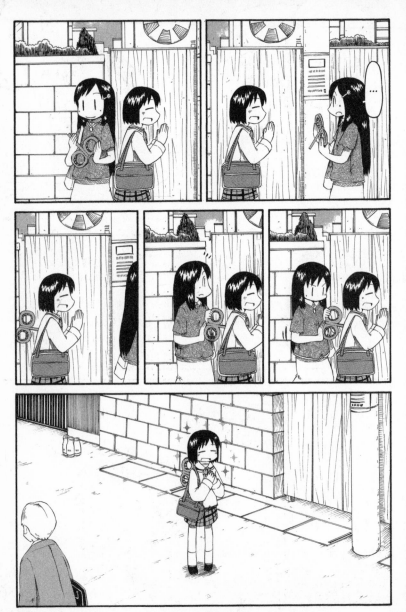

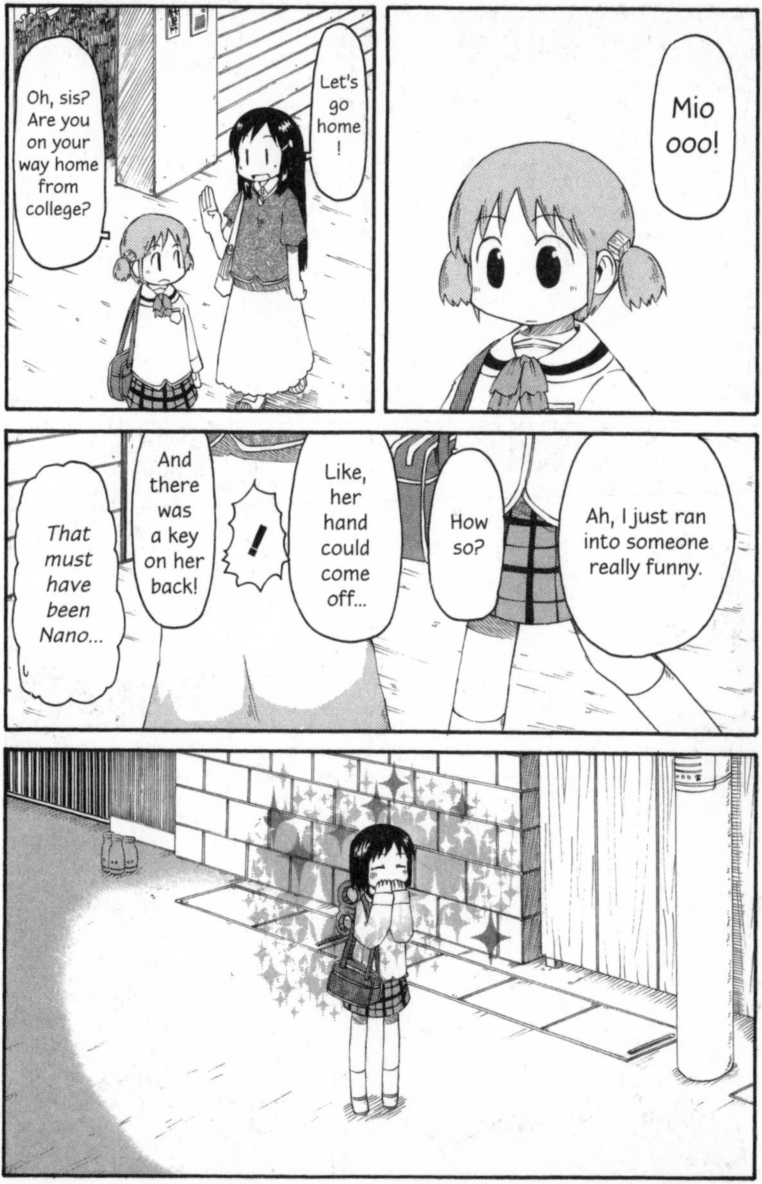
Mio ooo!
Let's go home!
Oh, sis? Are you on your way home from college?
Ah, I just ran into someone really funny.
How so?
Like, her hand could come off...
!
And there was a key on her back!
That must have been Nano...

chapter 47: end

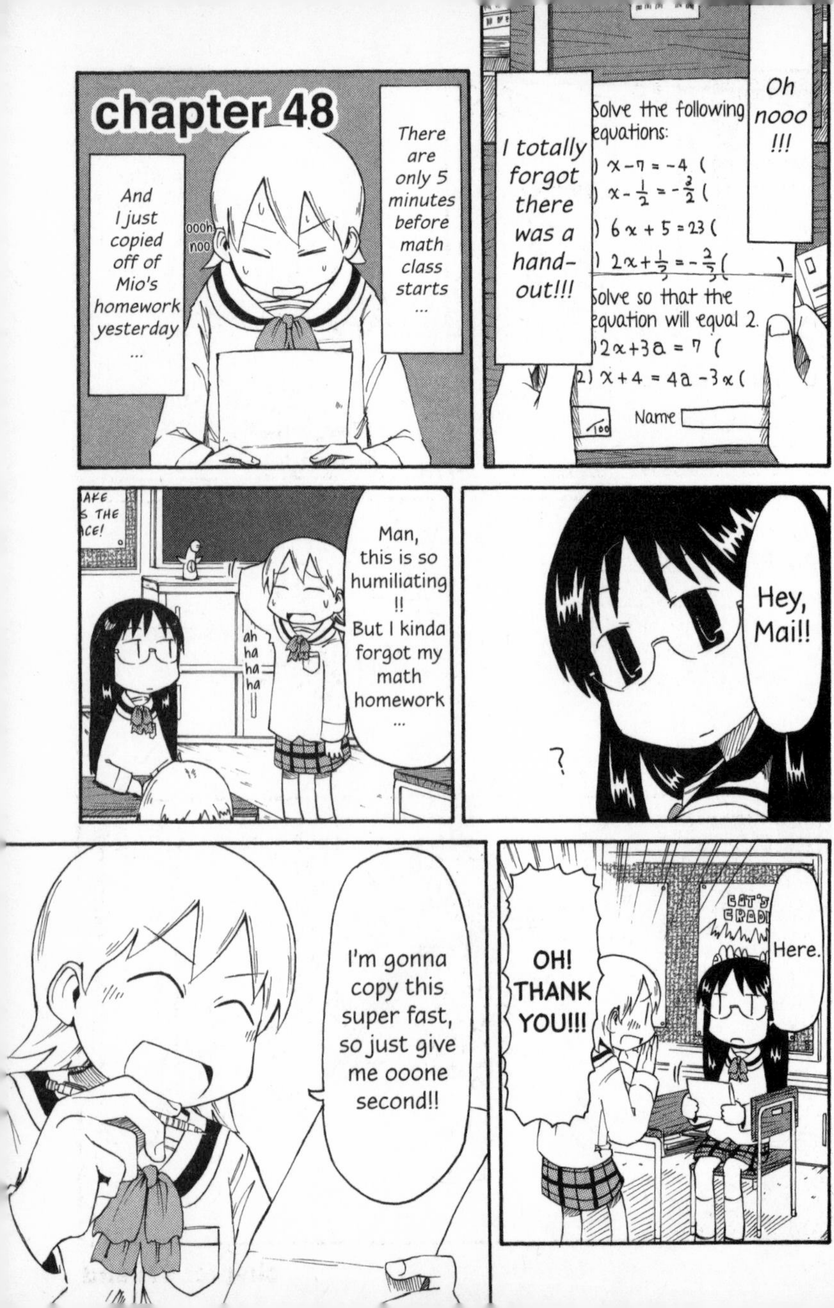
Oh nooo !!!
I totally forgot there was a handout!!!
Solve the following equations:
Solve so that the equation will equal 2.
Name
chapter 48
There are only 5 minutes before math class starts ...
oooh noo
And I just copied off of Mio's homework yesterday ...
Hey, Mai!!
?
Man, this is so humiliating !! But I kinda forgot my math homework ...
ah ha ha ha
Here.
OH! THANK YOU!!!
I'm gonna copy this super fast, so just give me ooone second!!

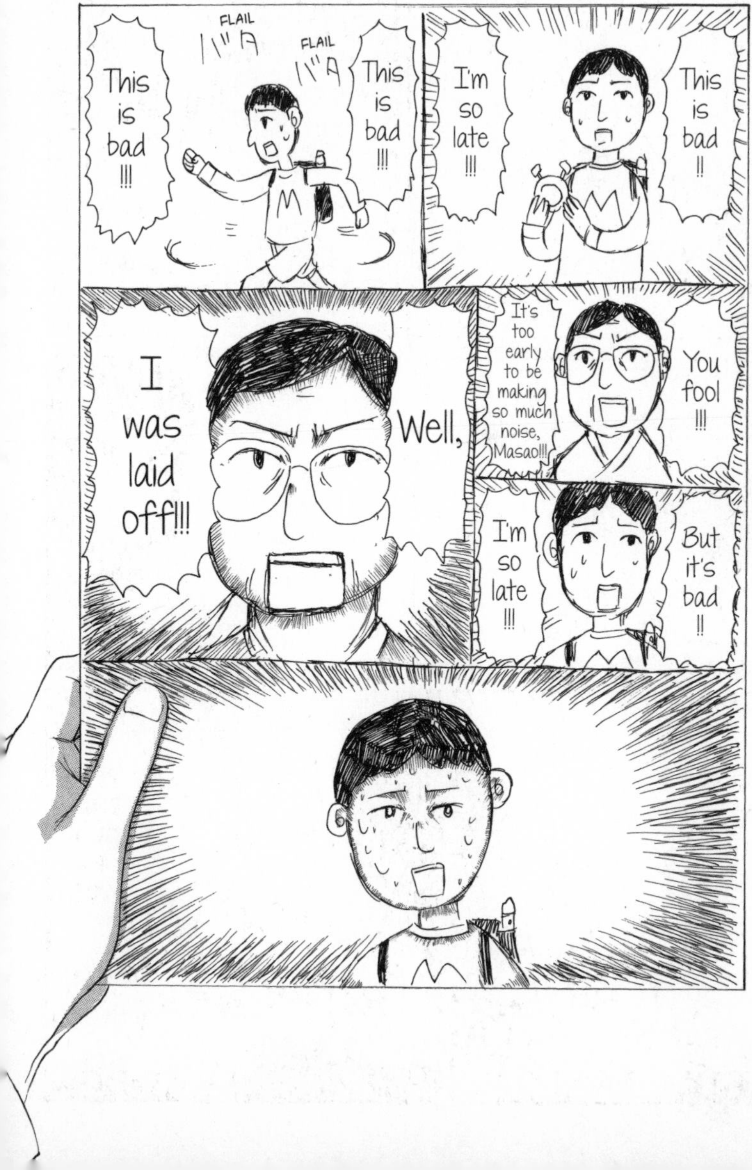
This is bad !!
I'm so late !!!
This is bad !!!
FLAIL
バタ
FLAIL
バタ
This is bad !!!
You fool !!!
It's too early to be making so much noise, Masao!!!
But it's bad !!
I'm so late !!!
Well,
I was laid off!!!

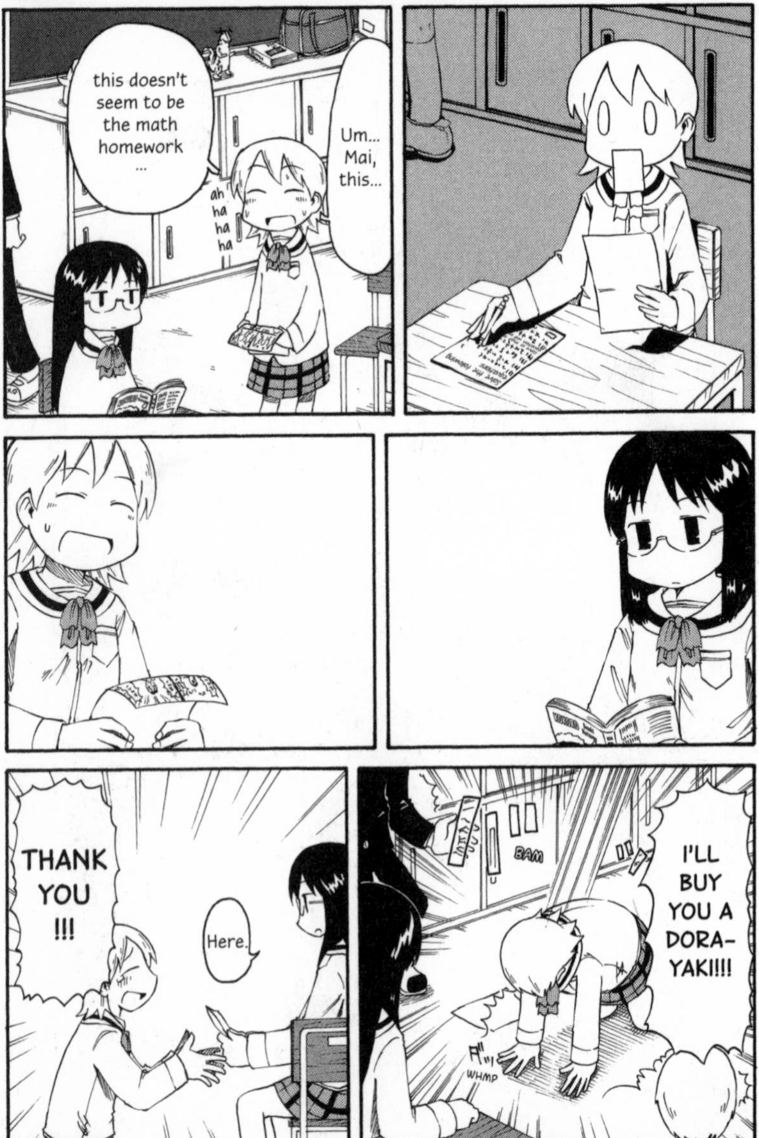
Um... Mai, this...
this doesn't seem to be the math homework ...
ah ha ha ha !!
I'LL BUY YOU A DORA-YAKI!!!
BAM
WHMP
Here.
THANK YOU !!!

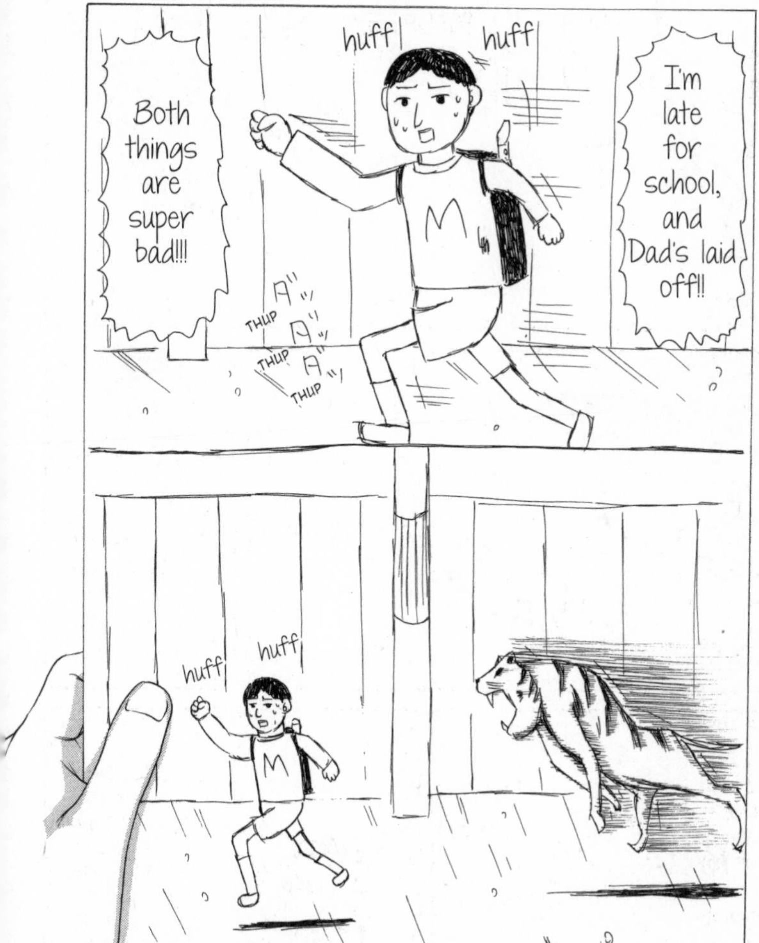
huff huff
I'm late for school, and Dad's laid off!!
Both things are super bad!!!
THUP
THUP
THUP
huff huff

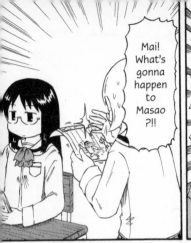

Mai! What's gonna happen to Masao?!!

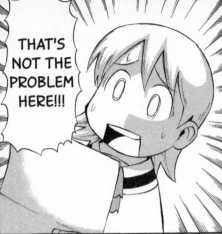

THAT'S NOT THE PROBLEM HERE!!!

MAI, PLEASE GIVE ME THE HANDOUT!!!

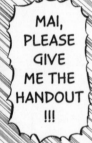

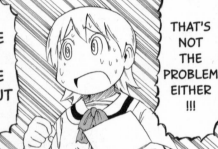

THAT'S NOT THE PROBLEM EITHER!!!

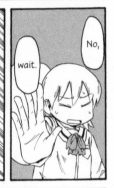

No, wait.

THIS IS IT!!! GEEZ, WHY DIDN'T YOU START WITH THIS?!!

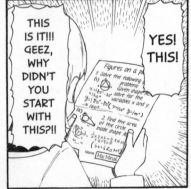

YES! THIS!

Figures on a pl...
1. Solve the following problems.
(1) Given shape...
solve for the variables x and y.

2. Find the area of the circle inside shape A.

Name [Mai Minak...]

Here.

WHP

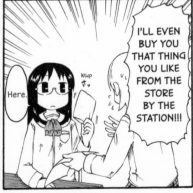

I'LL EVEN BUY YOU THAT THING YOU LIKE FROM THE STORE BY THE STATION!!!

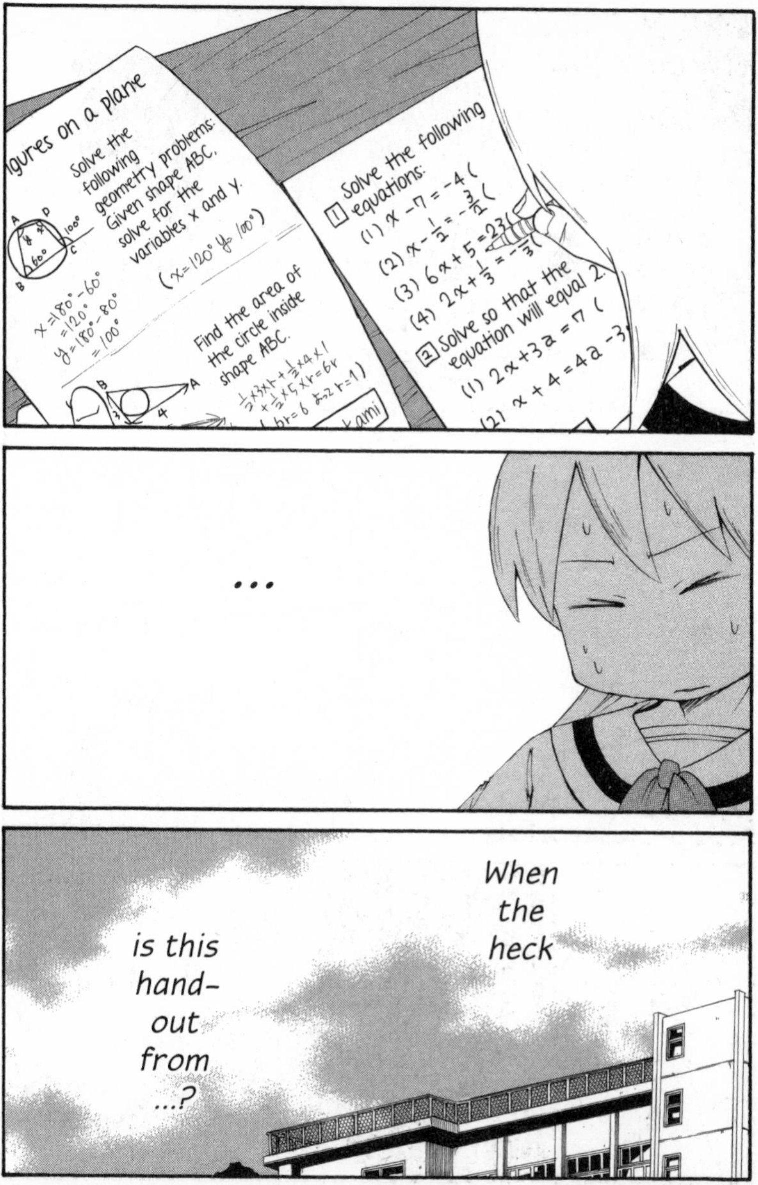
Solve the following equations:
(1) x − 7 = −4
(2) x − 1/2 = −3/2
(3) 6x + 5 = 23
(4) 2x + 1/3 = −1/3
Solve so that the equation will equal 2.
(1) 2x + 3a = 7
(2) x + 4 = 4a − 3
...gures on a plane
Solve the following geometry problems:
Given shape ABC, solve for the variables x and y.
(x=120° y=100°)
x=180°−60°
=120°
y=180°−80°
=100°
Find the area of the circle inside shape ABC.
...
When the heck
is this hand-out from ...?

chapter 48: end

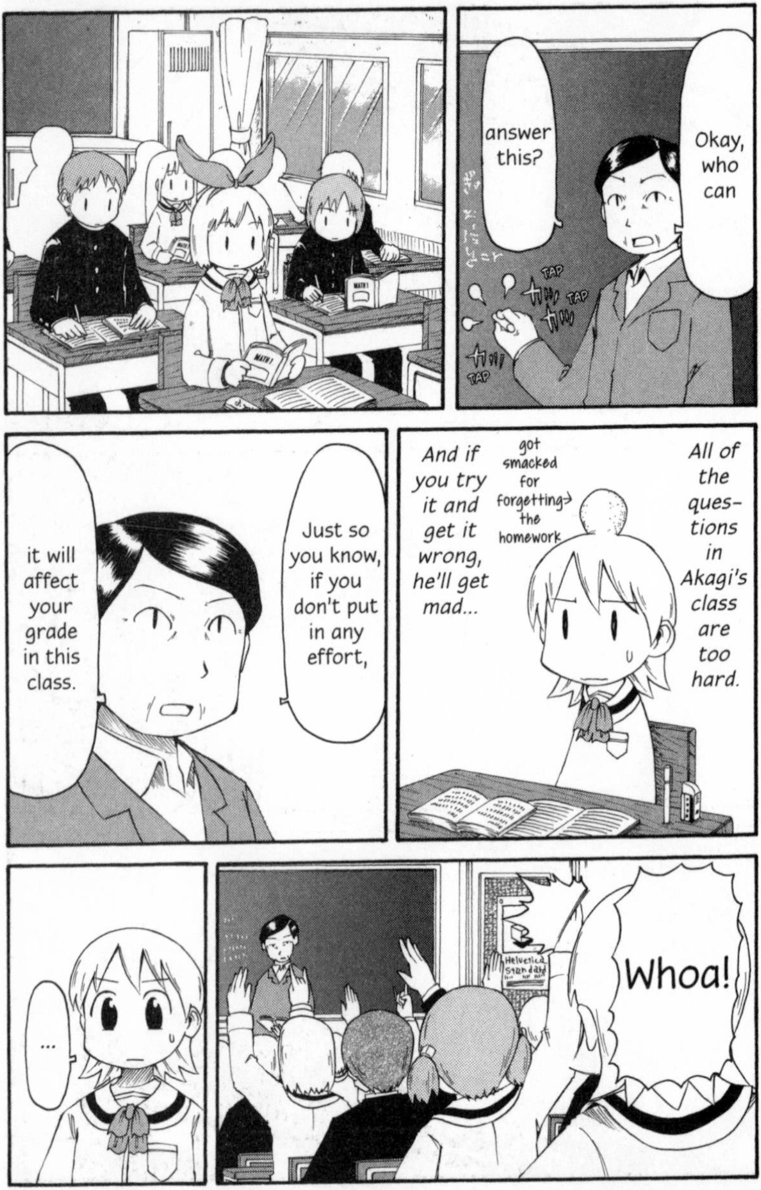
Okay, who can
answer this?
TAP
TAP
TAP
All of the questions in Akagi's class are too hard.
And if you try it and get it wrong, he'll get mad...
got smacked for forgetting the homework
Just so you know, if you don't put in any effort,
it will affect your grade in this class.
Whoa!
Helvetica standard
...

chapter 49

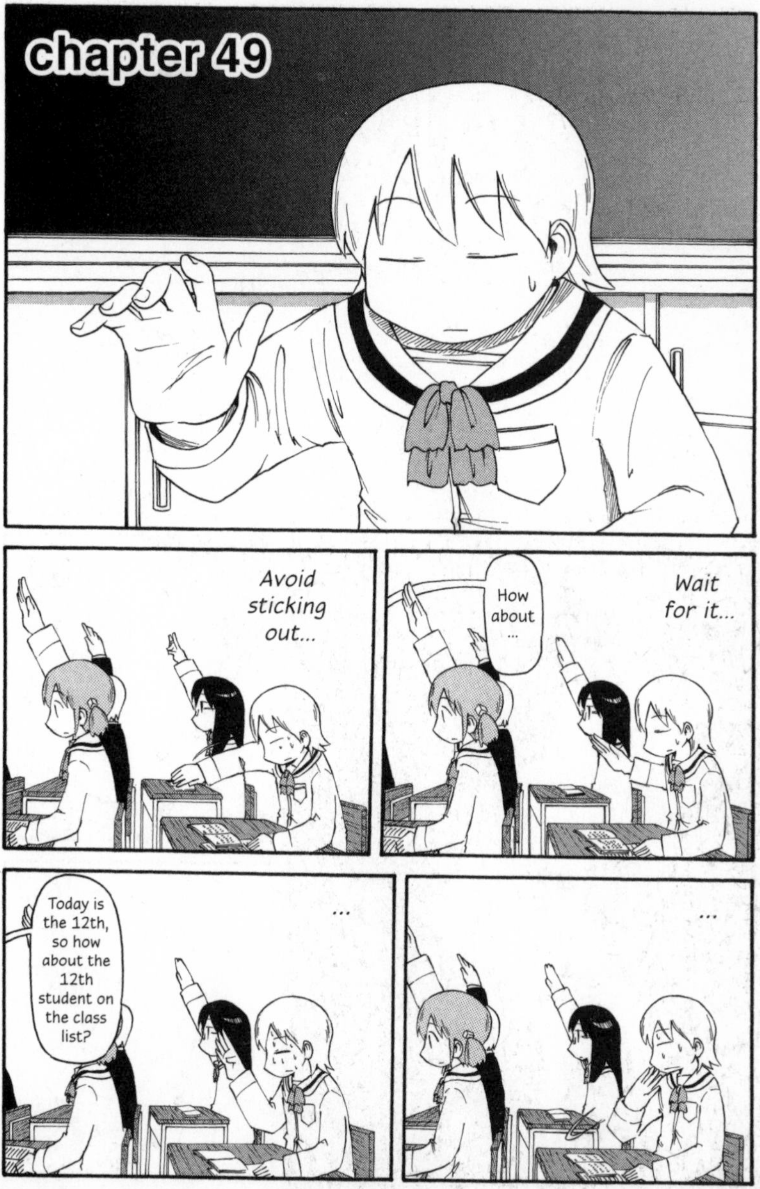

Wait for it...
How about ...
Avoid sticking out...
...
...
Today is the 12th, so how about the 12th student on the class list?

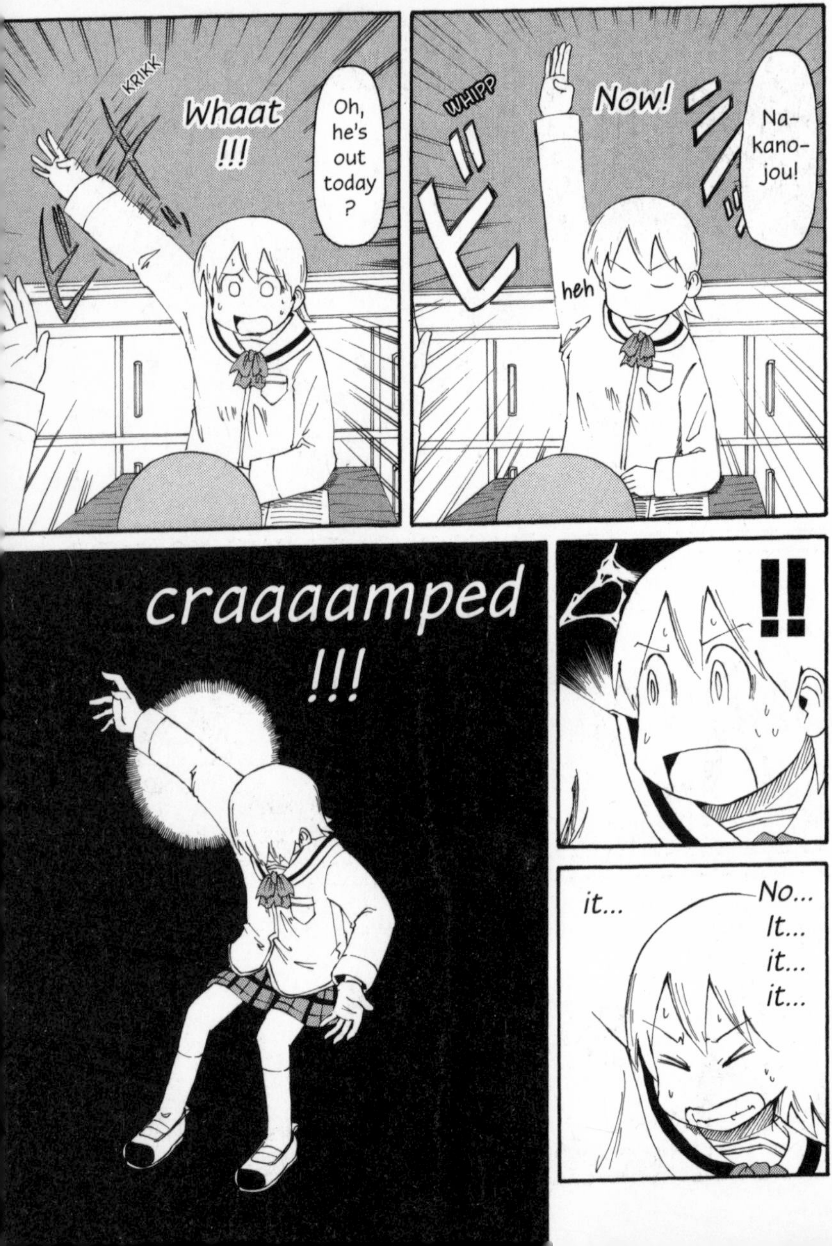
Na-
kano-
jou!
Now!
WHIPP
heh
Oh, he's out today?
Whaat !!!
KRIKK
!!
No... It... it... it...
it...
craaaamped !!!

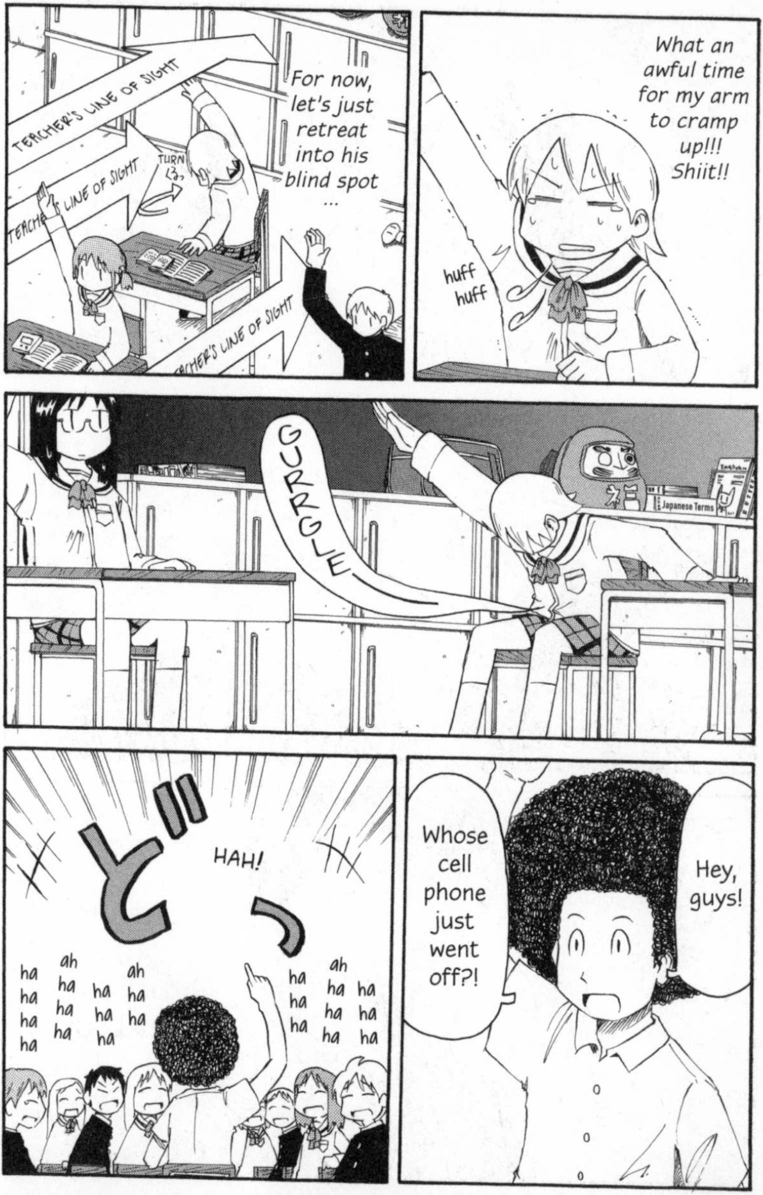
What an awful time for my arm to cramp up!!! Shiit!!
huff huff
For now, let's just retreat into his blind spot ...
TEACHER'S LINE OF SIGHT
TURN くるっ
LINE OF SIGHT
TEACHER'S LINE OF SIGHT
GURRGLE
Japanese Terms
Hey, guys!
Whose cell phone just went off?!
HAH!
どっ
ha ah ha ha ha ha ha ha
ah ha ha ha ha ha ha
ha ha ha ha
ah ha ha ha
ha ha ha
ah ha ha ha
ha ha ha ha

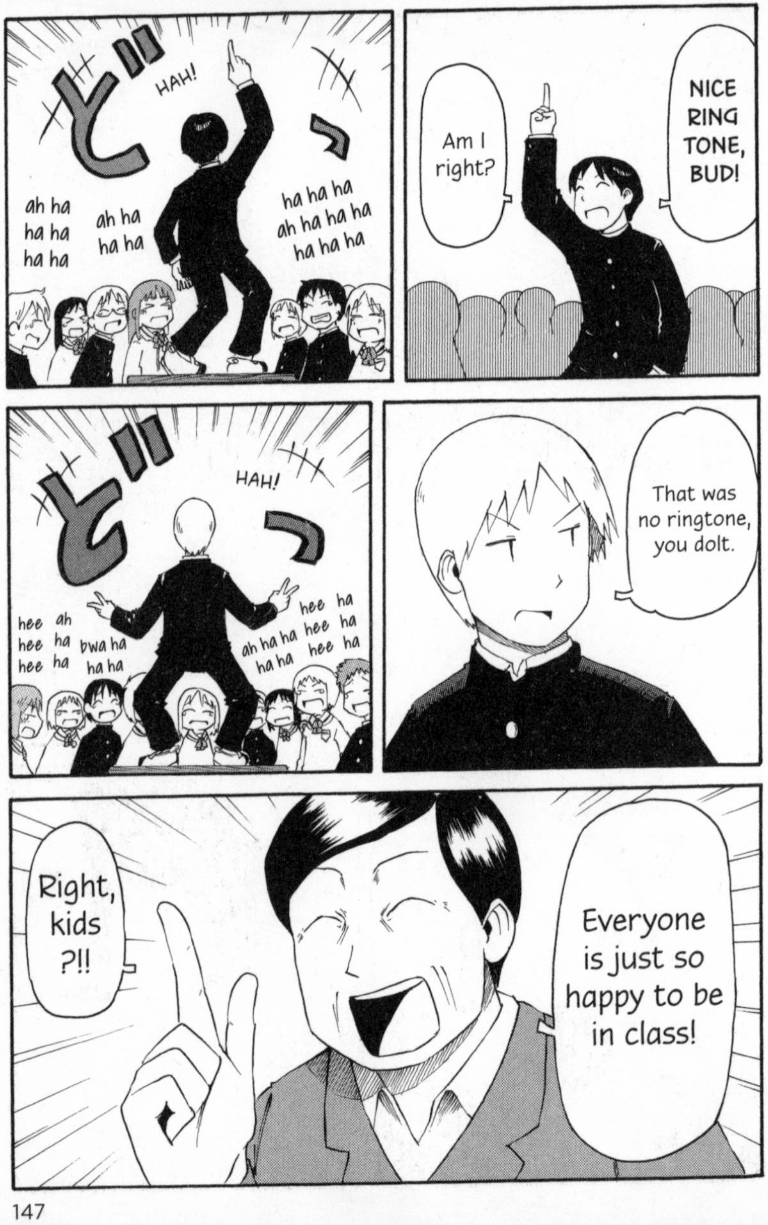
NICE RING TONE, BUD!
Am I right?
HAH!
どっ
ha ha ha ah ha ha ha ha ha ha
ah ha ha ha
ah ha ha ha ha ha
That was no ringtone, you dolt.
HAH!
どっ
hee ha hee ha hee ha
ah ha ha ha ha
bwa ha ha ha
ah ha ha
hee hee hee
Everyone is just so happy to be in class!
Right, kids ?!!

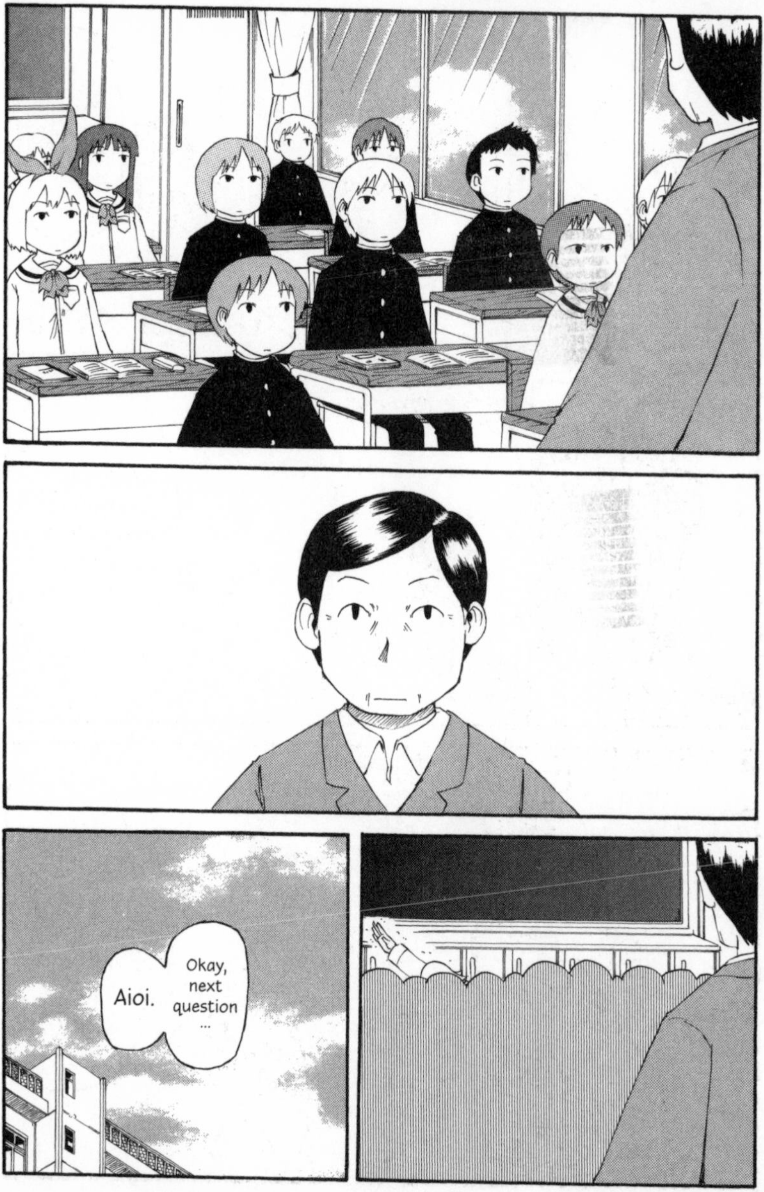
Okay, next question ...
Aioi.

chapter 49: end

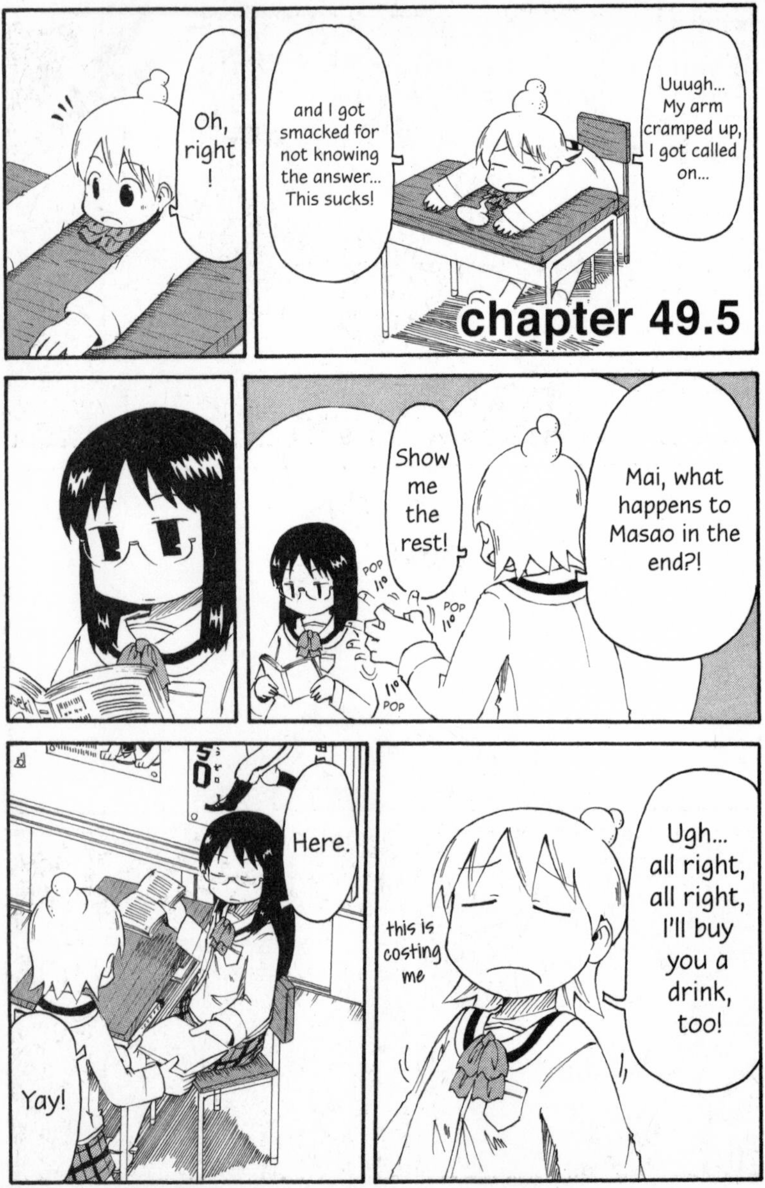
Uuugh... My arm cramped up, I got called on...
and I got smacked for not knowing the answer... This sucks!
chapter 49.5
Oh, right!
Mai, what happens to Masao in the end?!
Show me the rest!
POP
POP
POP
Ugh... all right, all right, I'll buy you a drink, too!
this is costing me
Here.
Yay!

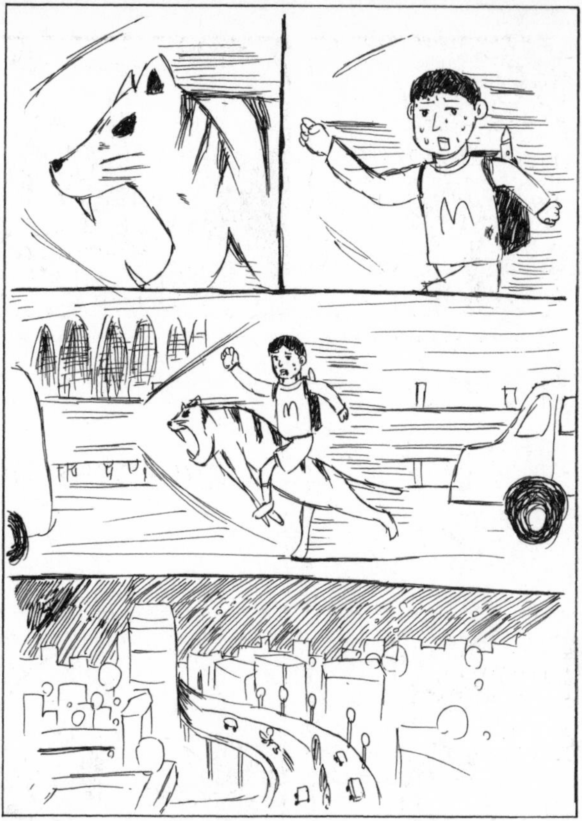

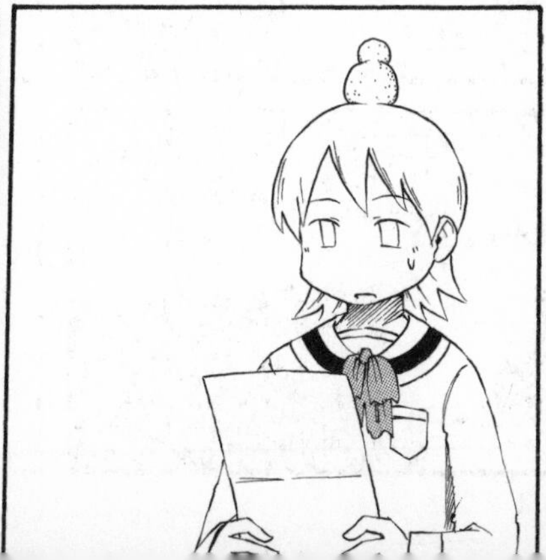

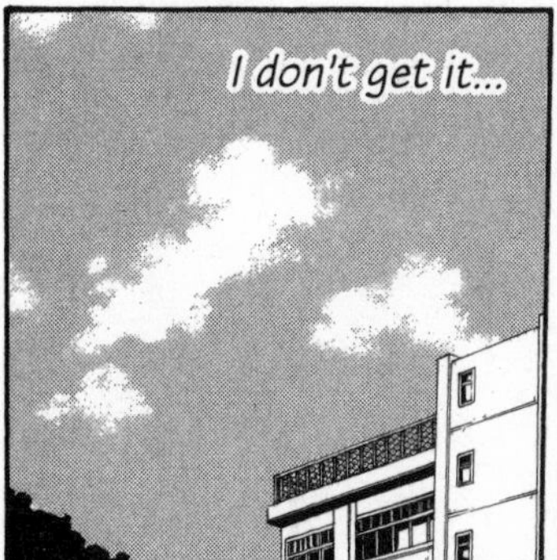
I don't get it...

chapter 49.5: end

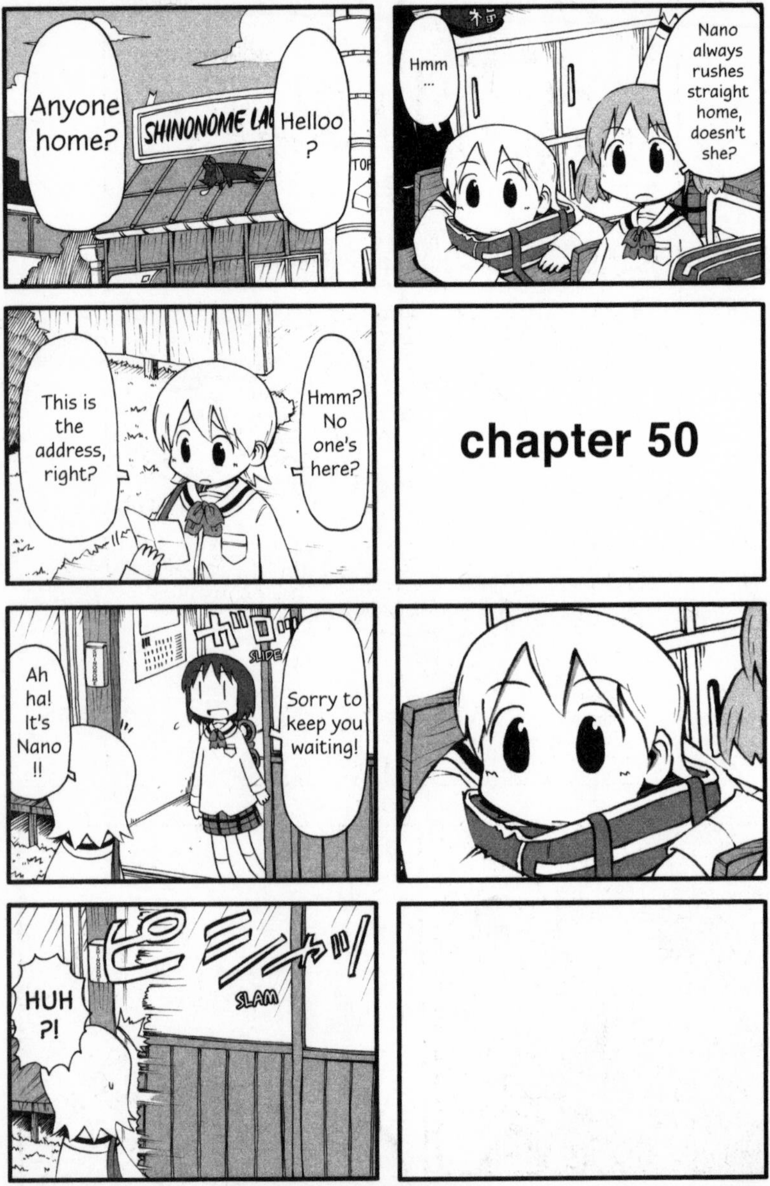
Nano always rushes straight home, doesn't she?
Hmm ...
chapter 50
Helloo ?
Anyone home?
SHINONOME LAB
Hmm? No one's here?
This is the address, right?
SLIDE
Sorry to keep you waiting!
Ah ha! It's Nano !!
SLAM
HUH ?!

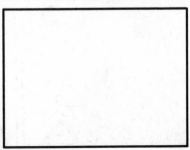

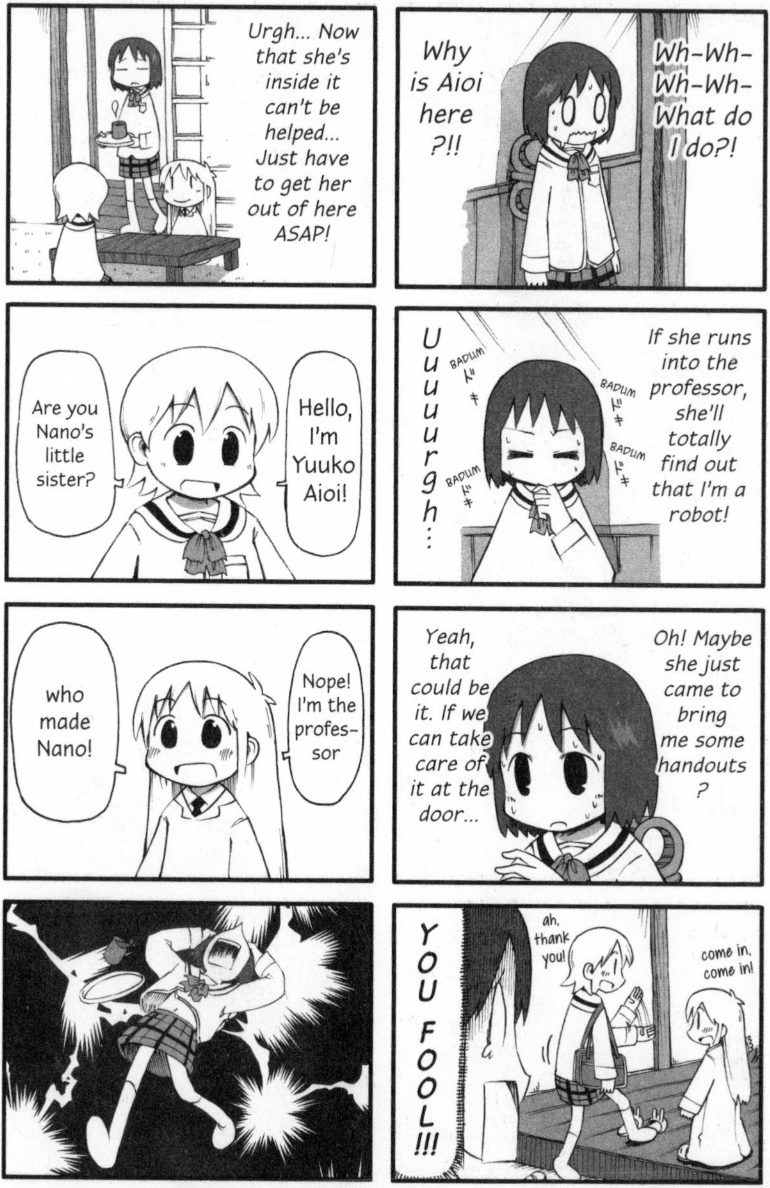
Wh-Wh-Wh-Wh-What do I do?!
Why is Aioi here?!!
Urgh... Now that she's inside it can't be helped... Just have to get her out of here ASAP!
If she runs into the professor, she'll totally find out that I'm a robot!
BADUM ドキ
BADUM ドキ
BADUM ドキ
BADUM ドキ
Uuuuurgh...
Hello, I'm Yuuko Aioi!
Are you Nano's little sister?
Oh! Maybe she just came to bring me some handouts?
Yeah, that could be it. If we can take care of it at the door...
Nope! I'm the profes-sor
who made Nano!
come in, come in!
ah, thank you!
YOU FOOL!!!

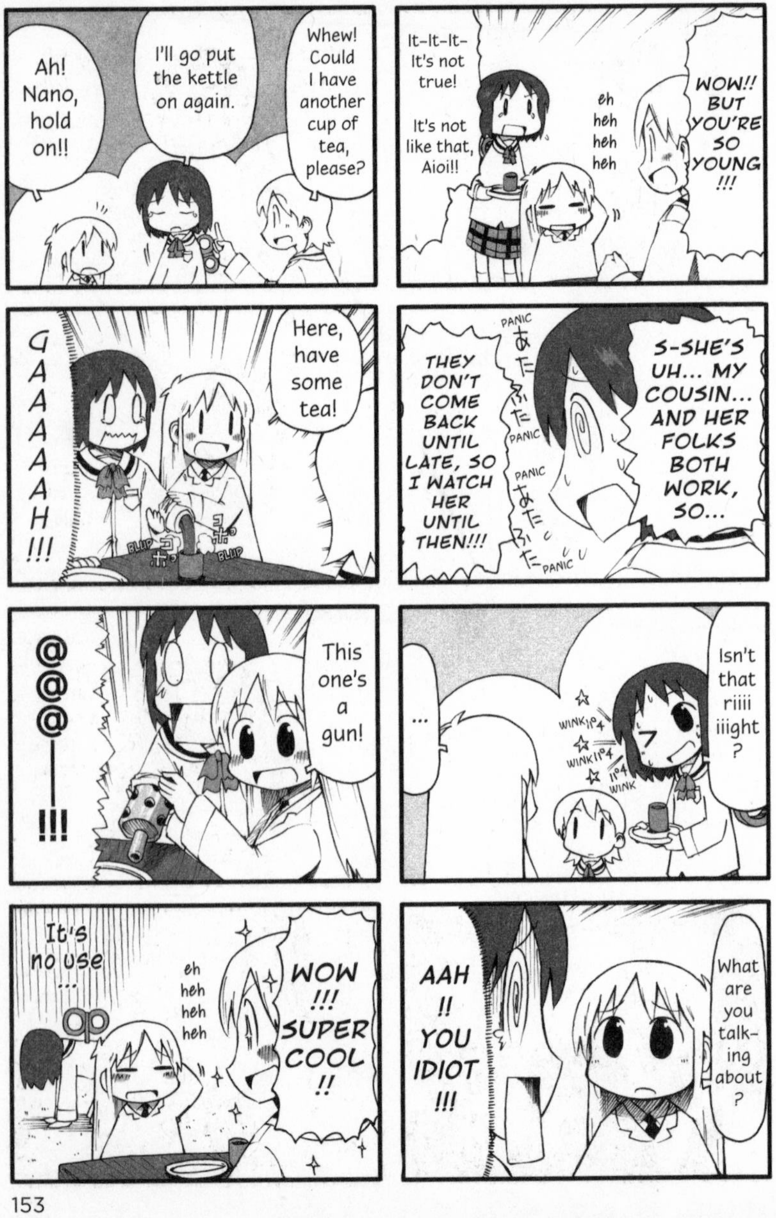
WOW!! BUT YOU'RE SO YOUNG!!!
eh heh heh heh
It-It-It-It's not true!
It's not like that, Aioi!!
Whew! Could I have another cup of tea, please?
I'll go put the kettle on again.
Ah! Nano, hold on!!
S-SHE'S UH... MY COUSIN... AND HER FOLKS BOTH WORK, SO...
PANIC あたふた PANIC
PANIC あたふた PANIC
THEY DON'T COME BACK UNTIL LATE, SO I WATCH HER UNTIL THEN!!!
Here, have some tea!
BLUP BLUP
GAAAAAAAH!!!
Isn't that riiiiiiight?
WINK WINK WINK
...
This one's a gun!
@@@—!!!
What are you talking about?
AAH!! YOU IDIOT!!!
WOW!!! SUPER COOL!!
eh heh heh heh
It's no use...

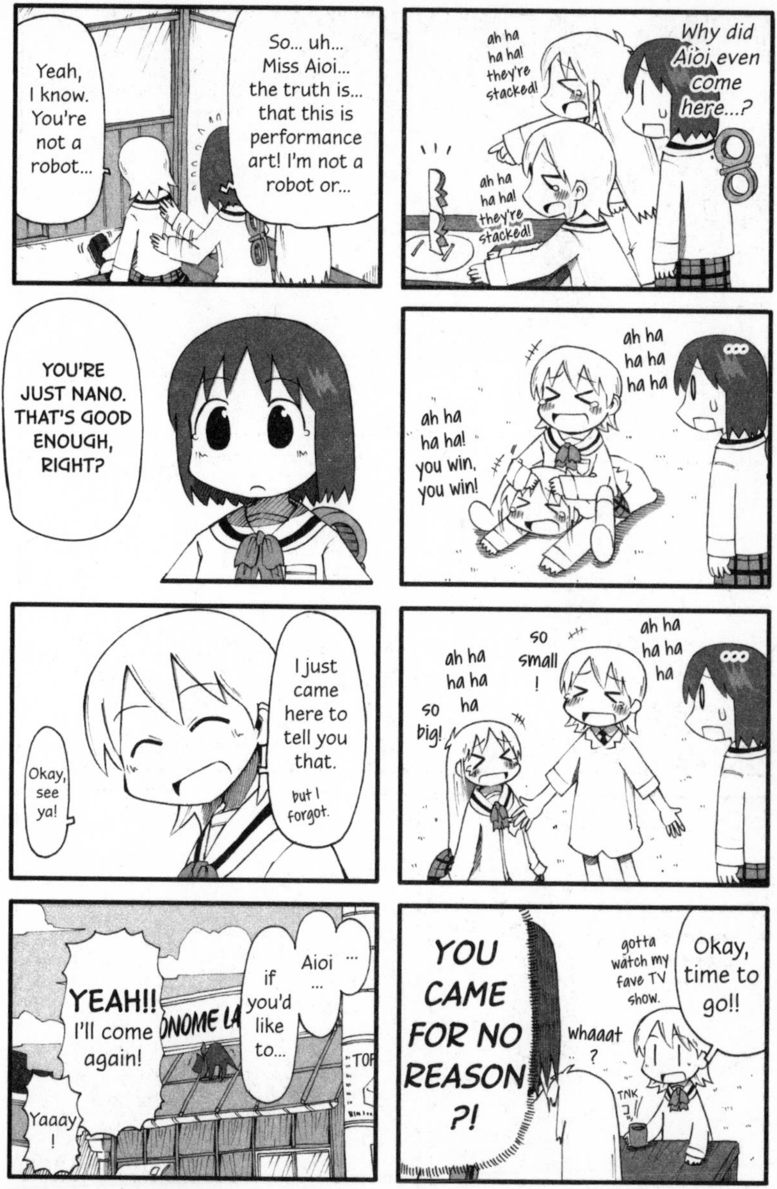

ah ha ha ha! they're stacked!
Why did Aioi even come here...?
ah ha ha ha! they're stacked!
ah ha ha ha ha ha
ah ha ha ha! you win, you win!
ah ha ha ha ha
so small !
ah ha ha ha ha
so big!
Okay, time to go!!
gotta watch my fave TV show.
TNK
Whaaat ?
YOU CAME FOR NO REASON ?!
So... uh... Miss Aioi... the truth is... that this is performance art! I'm not a robot or...
Yeah, I know. You're not a robot...
YOU'RE JUST NANO. THAT'S GOOD ENOUGH, RIGHT?
I just came here to tell you that.
but I forgot.
Okay, see ya!
Aioi ...
if you'd like to...
YEAH!! I'll come again!
Yaaay !

chapter 50: end

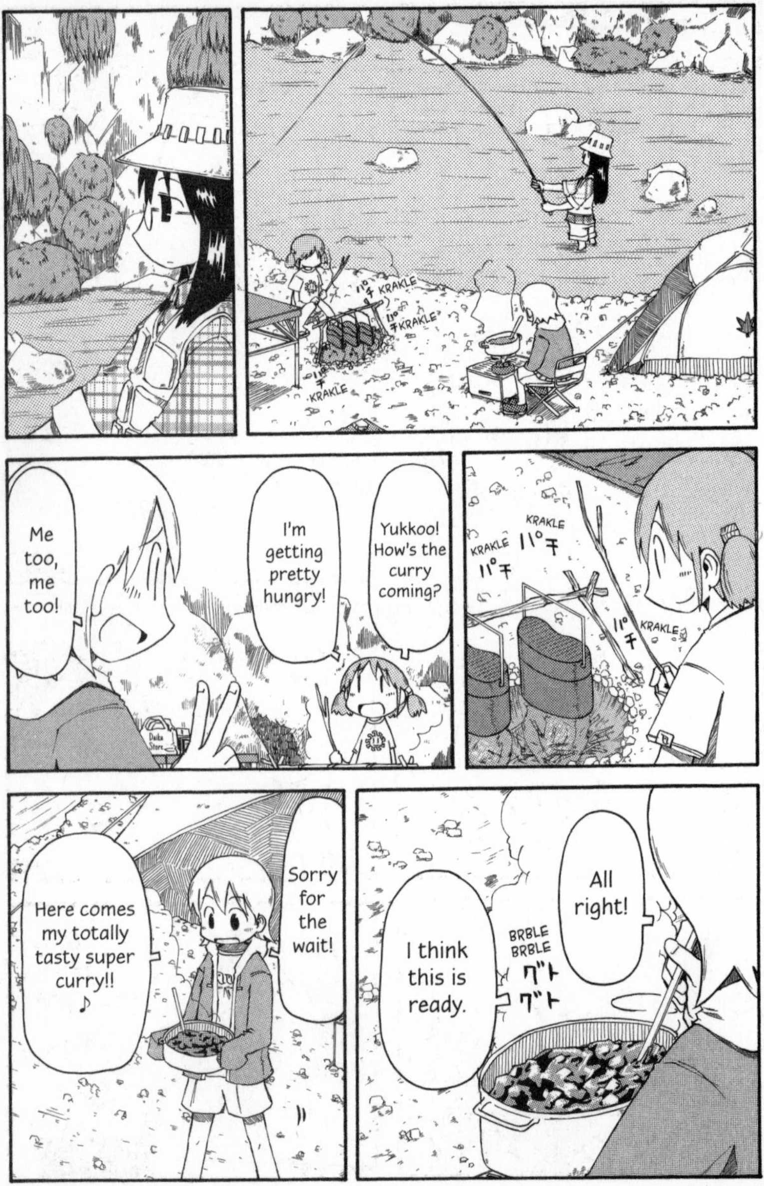
パチ KRAKLE
パチ KRAKLE
パチ KRAKLE
KRAKLE パチ
KRAKLE パチ
パチ KRAKLE
Yukkoo! How's the curry coming?
I'm getting pretty hungry!
Me too, me too!
All right!
BRBLE BRBLE グトグト
I think this is ready.
Sorry for the wait!
Here comes my totally tasty super curry!! ♪

chapter 51

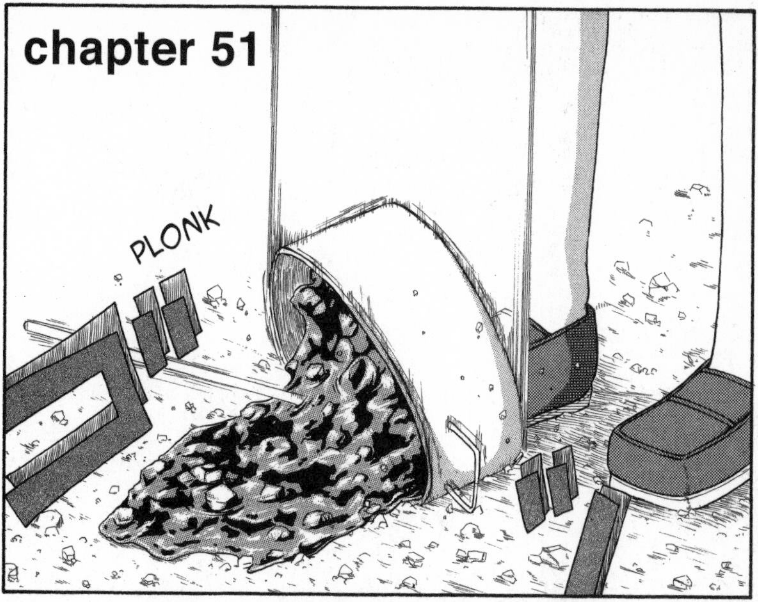
PLONK

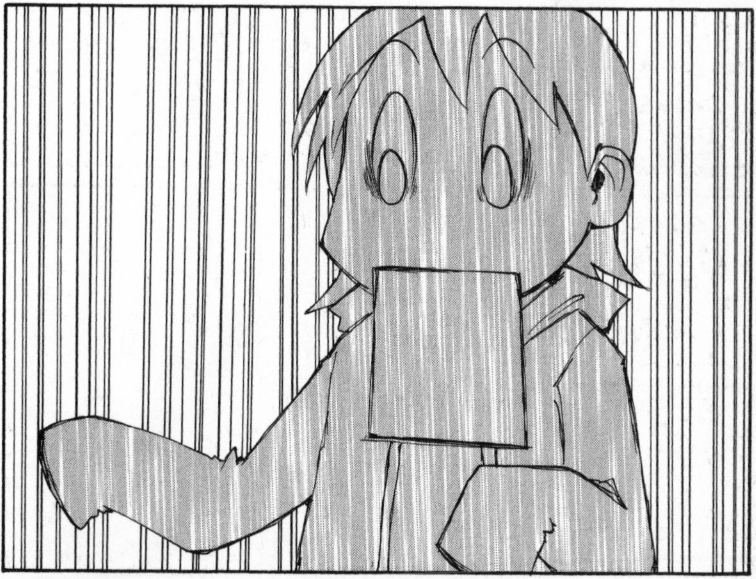

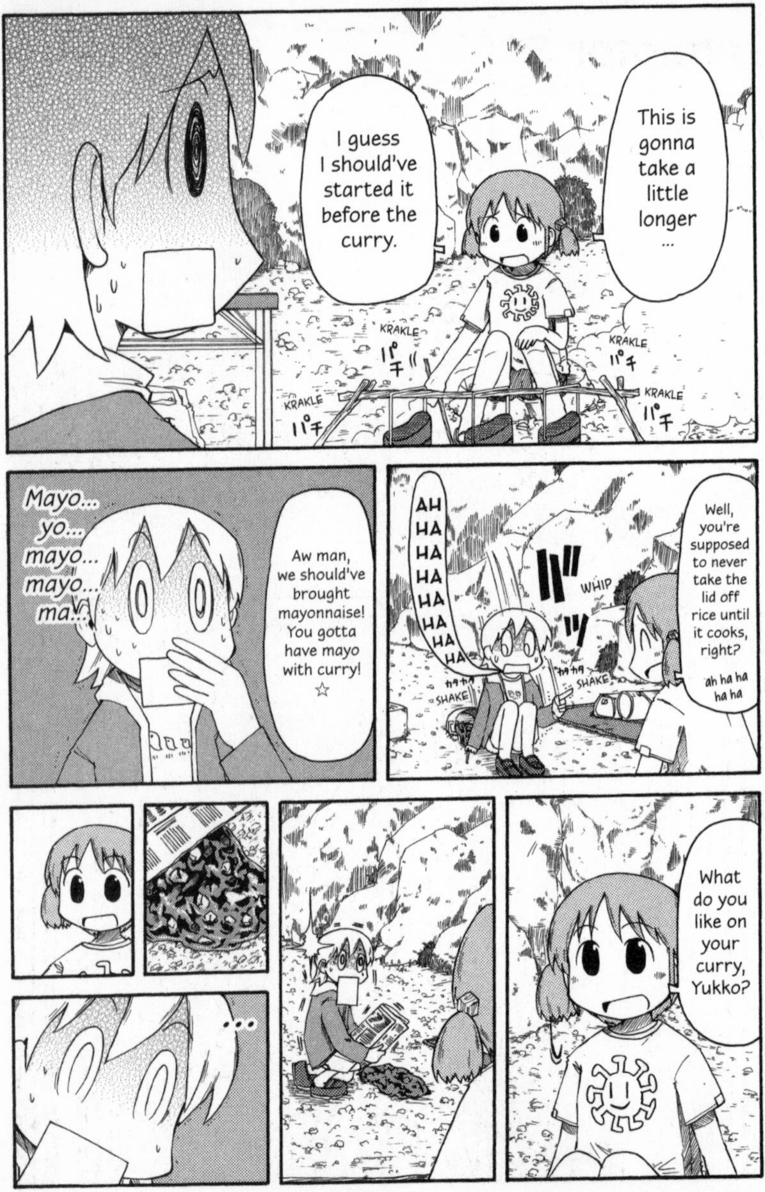
This is gonna take a little longer ...
I guess I should've started it before the curry.
KRAKLE
パチ
KRAKLE
パチ
KRAKLE
パチ
KRAKLE
パチ
Well, you're supposed to never take the lid off rice until it cooks, right?
ah ha ha ha ha
WHIP
SHAKE
SHAKE
AH HA HA HA HA HA HA HA
Aw man, we should've brought mayonnaise! You gotta have mayo with curry! ☆
Mayo... yo... mayo... mayo... ma...
What do you like on your curry, Yukko?
...

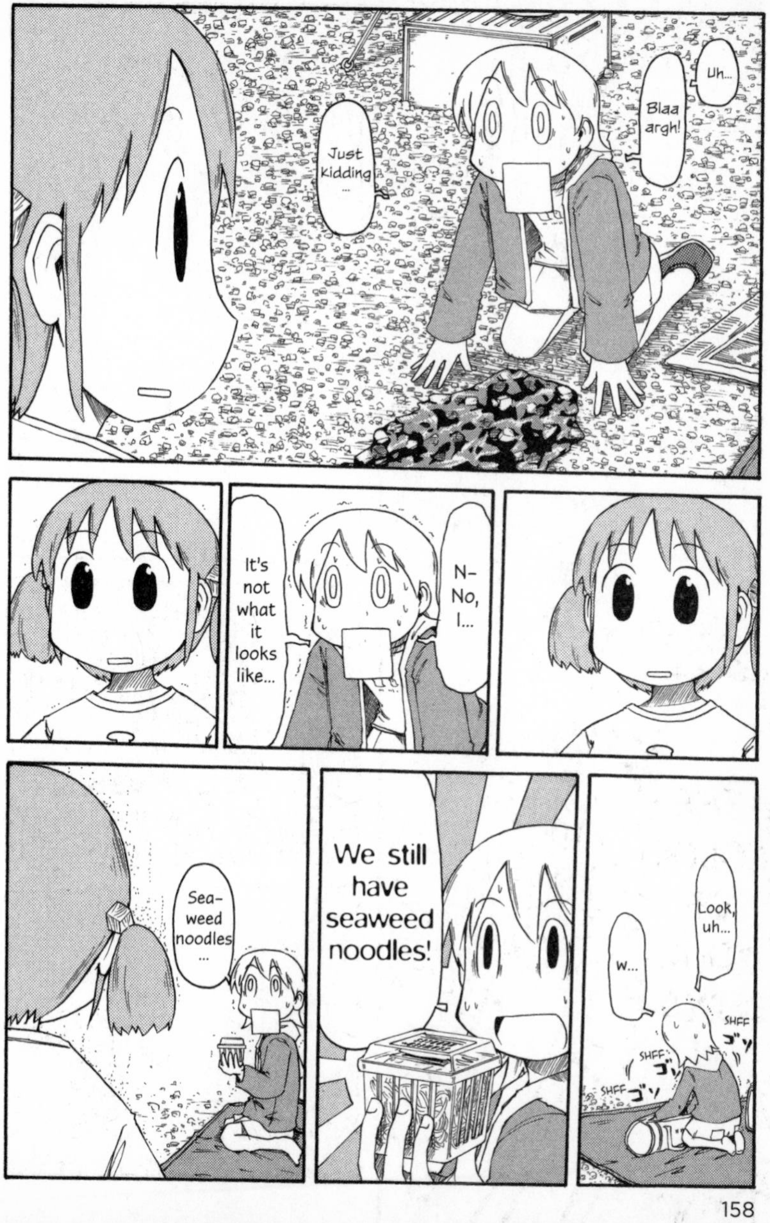
Uh...
Blaa argh!
Just kidding...
N-No, I...
It's not what it looks like...
Look, uh...
W...
SHFF ゴッ
SHFF ゴッ
SHFF ゴッ
We still have seaweed noodles!
Sea-weed noodles...

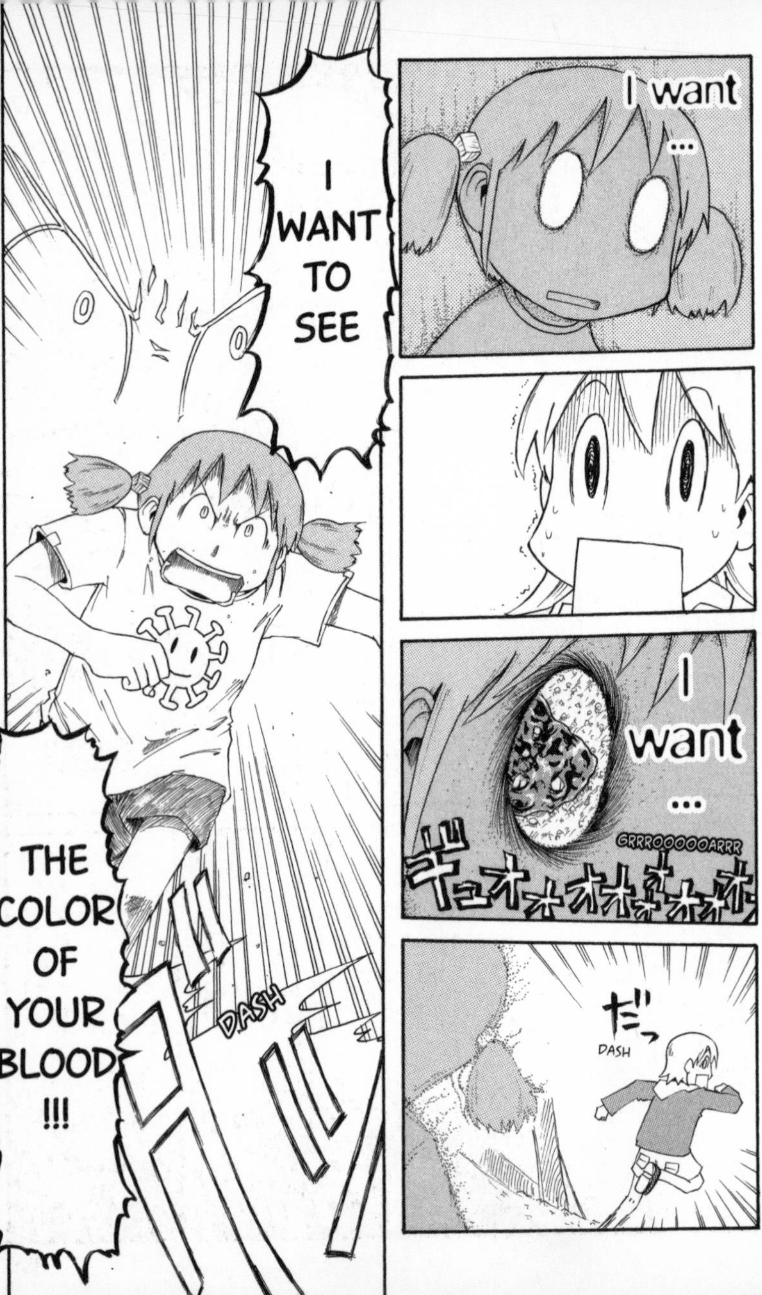
I want ...
I want ...
GRRROOOOOARRR
だっ
DASH
I WANT TO SEE
THE COLOR OF YOUR BLOOD !!!
DASH

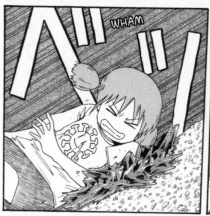

WHAM

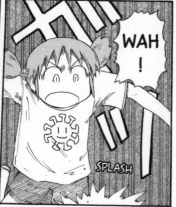

WAH!

SPLASH

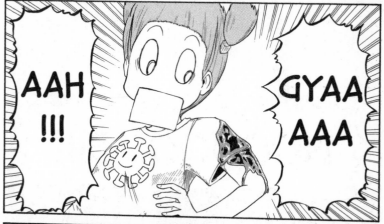

AAH!!!

GYAAAAA

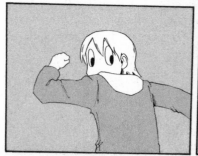

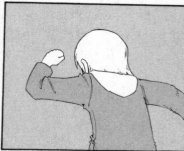

160

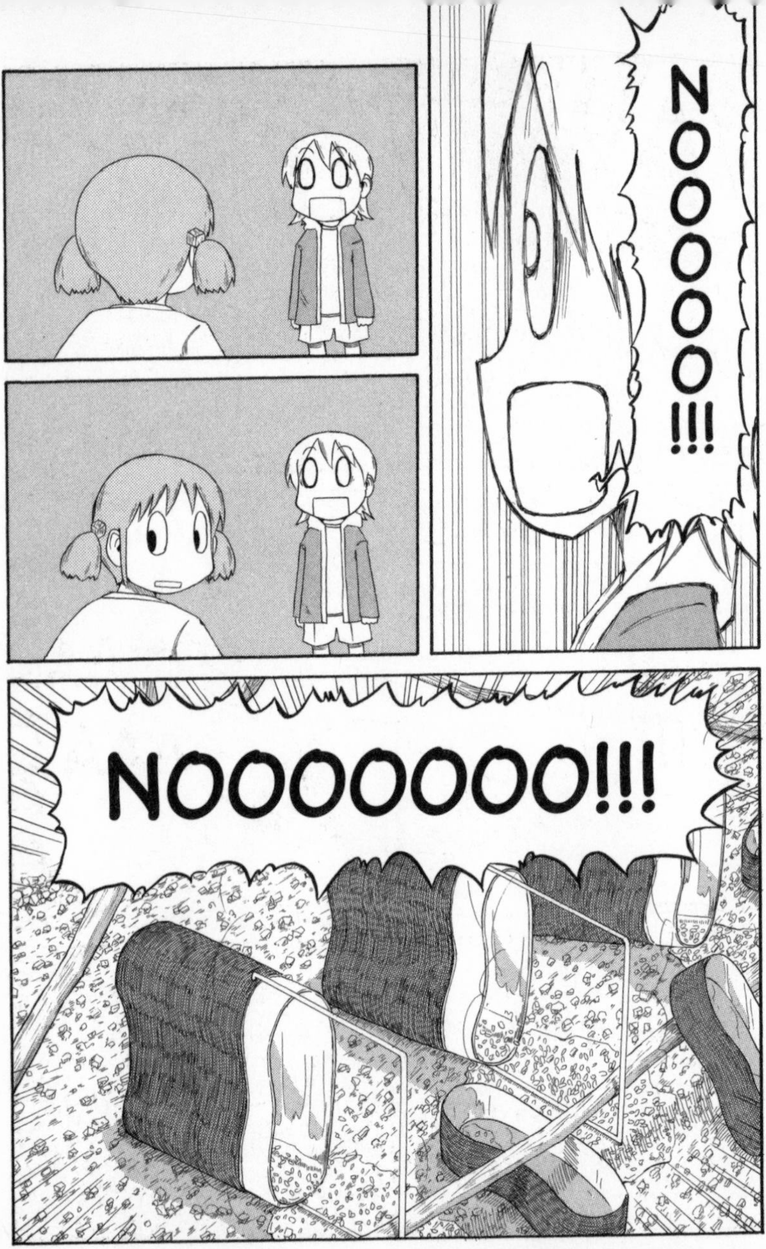
NOOOOO!!!
NOOOOOOO!!!

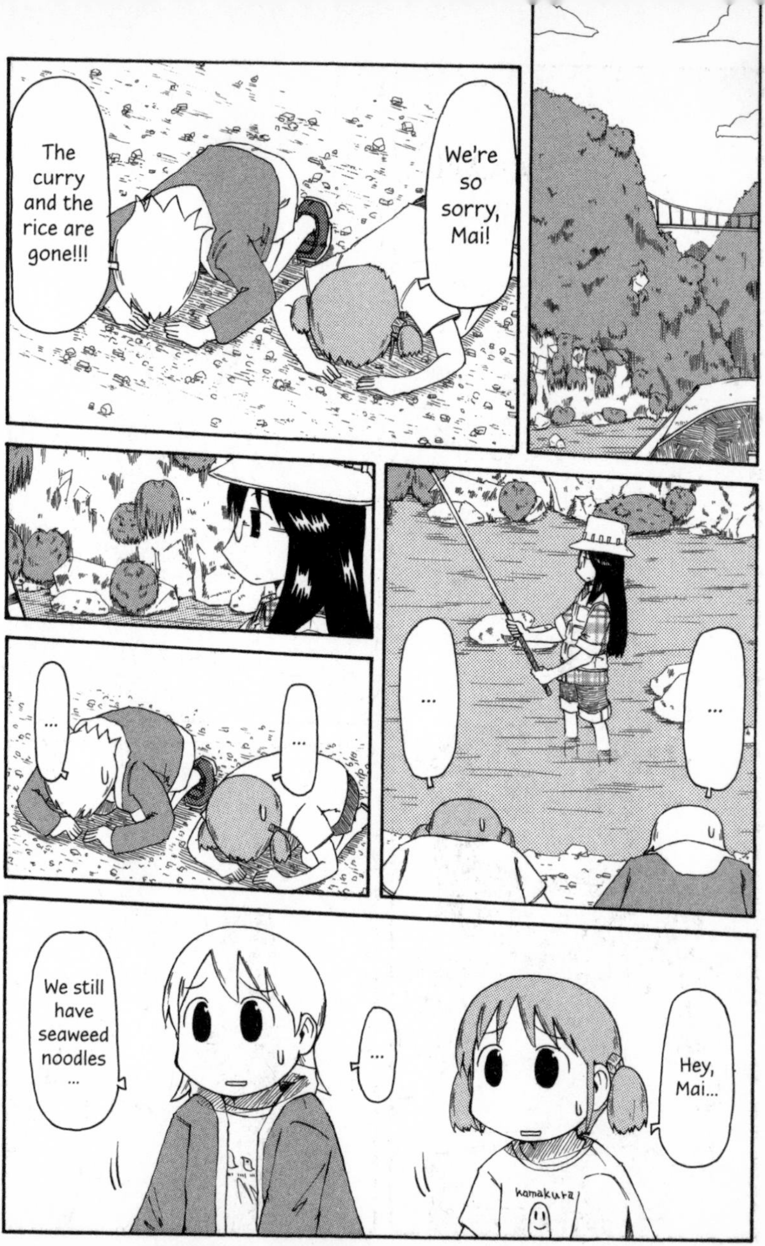
We're so sorry, Mai!
The curry and the rice are gone!!!
...
...
...
...
Hey, Mai...
kamakura
...
We still have seaweed noodles ...

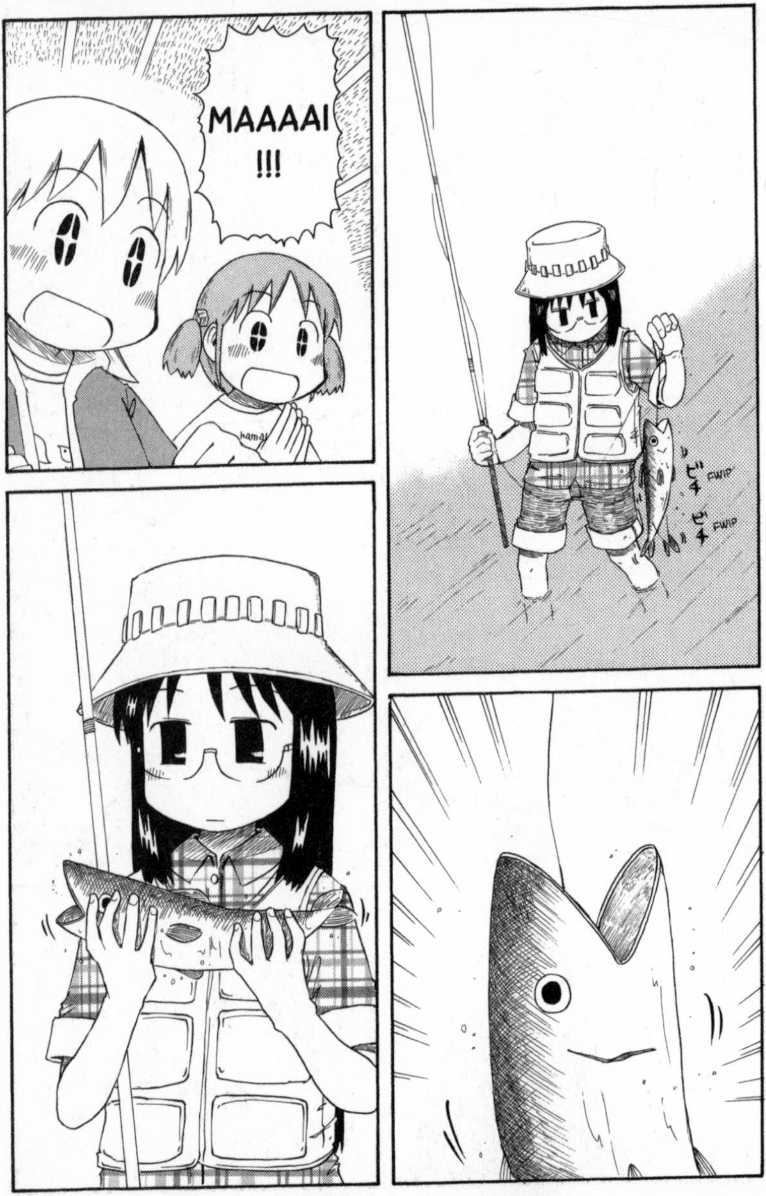
ビチ FWIP
ビチ FWIP
MAAAAI !!!

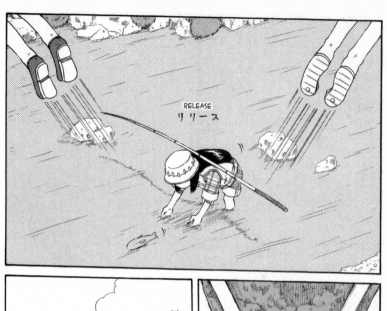

RELEASE
リリース

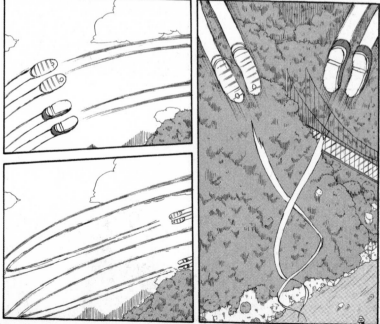

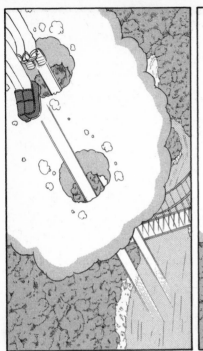
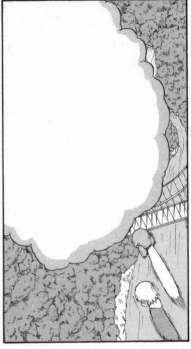
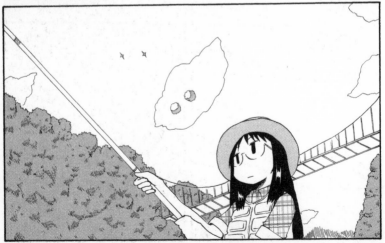

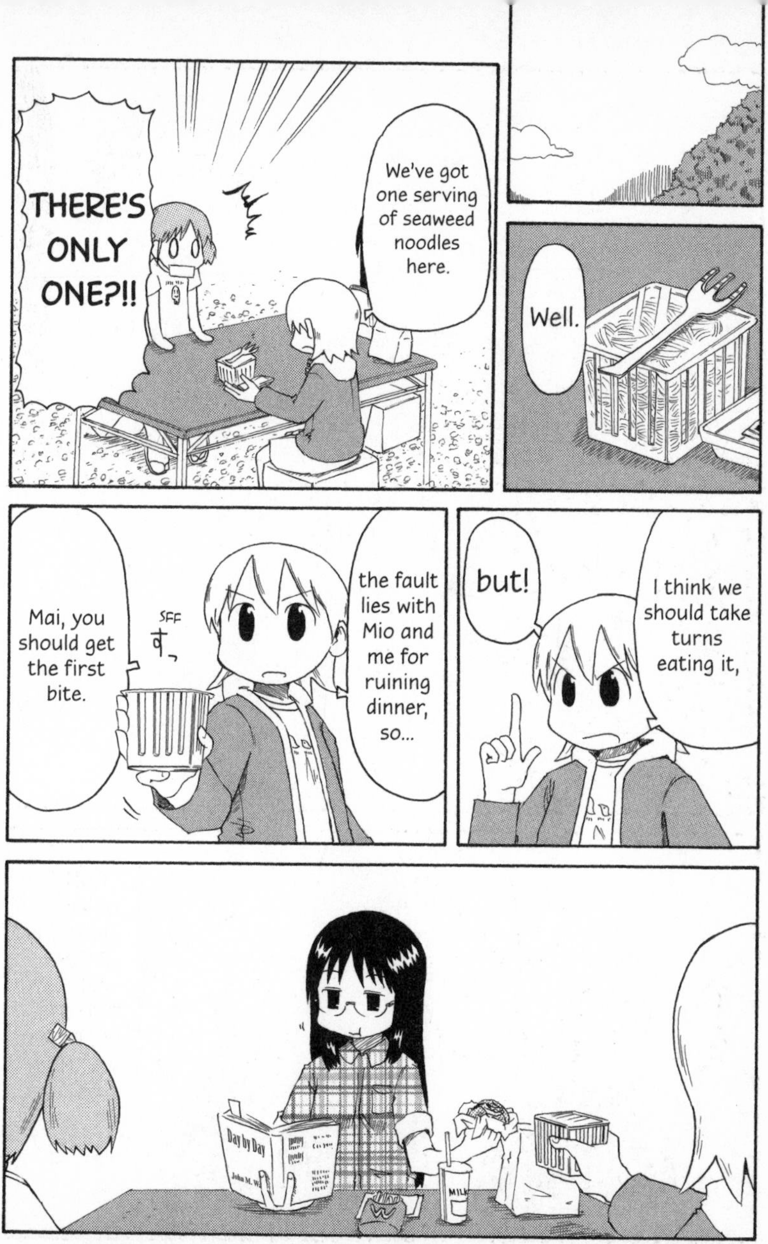
Well.
We've got one serving of seaweed noodles here.
THERE'S ONLY ONE?!!
I think we should take turns eating it,
but!
the fault lies with Mio and me for ruining dinner, so...
SFF
Mai, you should get the first bite.
Day by Day
MILK

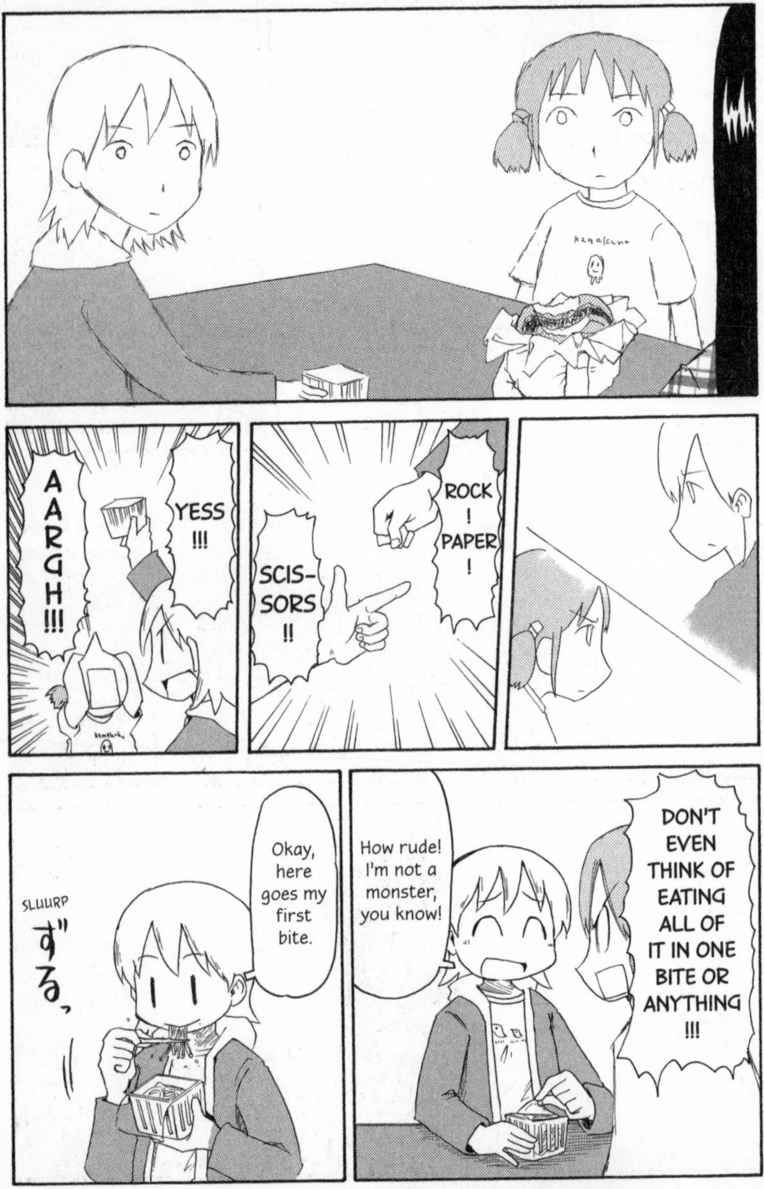
ROCK! PAPER!
SCISSORS!!
YESS!!!
AARGH!!!
DON'T EVEN THINK OF EATING ALL OF IT IN ONE BITE OR ANYTHING!!!
How rude! I'm not a monster, you know!
Okay, here goes my first bite.
SLUURP
ずるっ

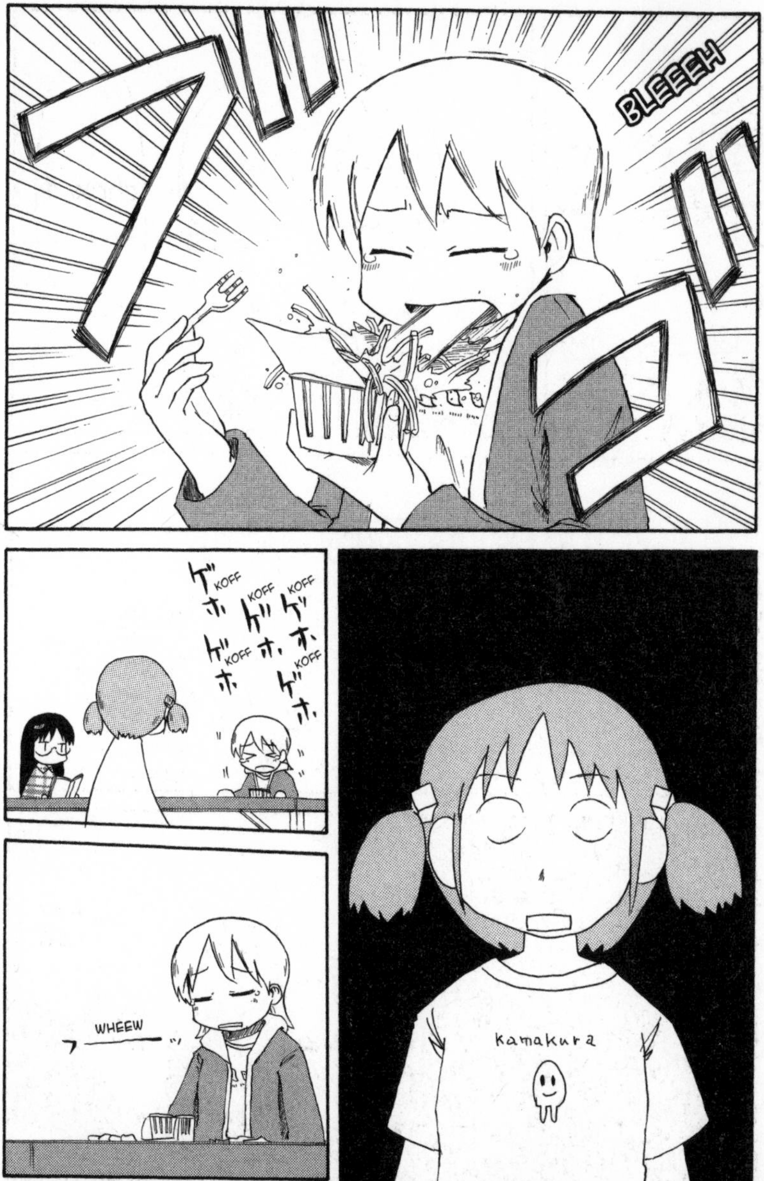
BLEEEH
ゲホ、ゲホ
KOFF
ゲホ、
KOFF
ゲホゲホ
KOFF
KOFF
KOFF
kamakura
フ———ッ
WHEEW

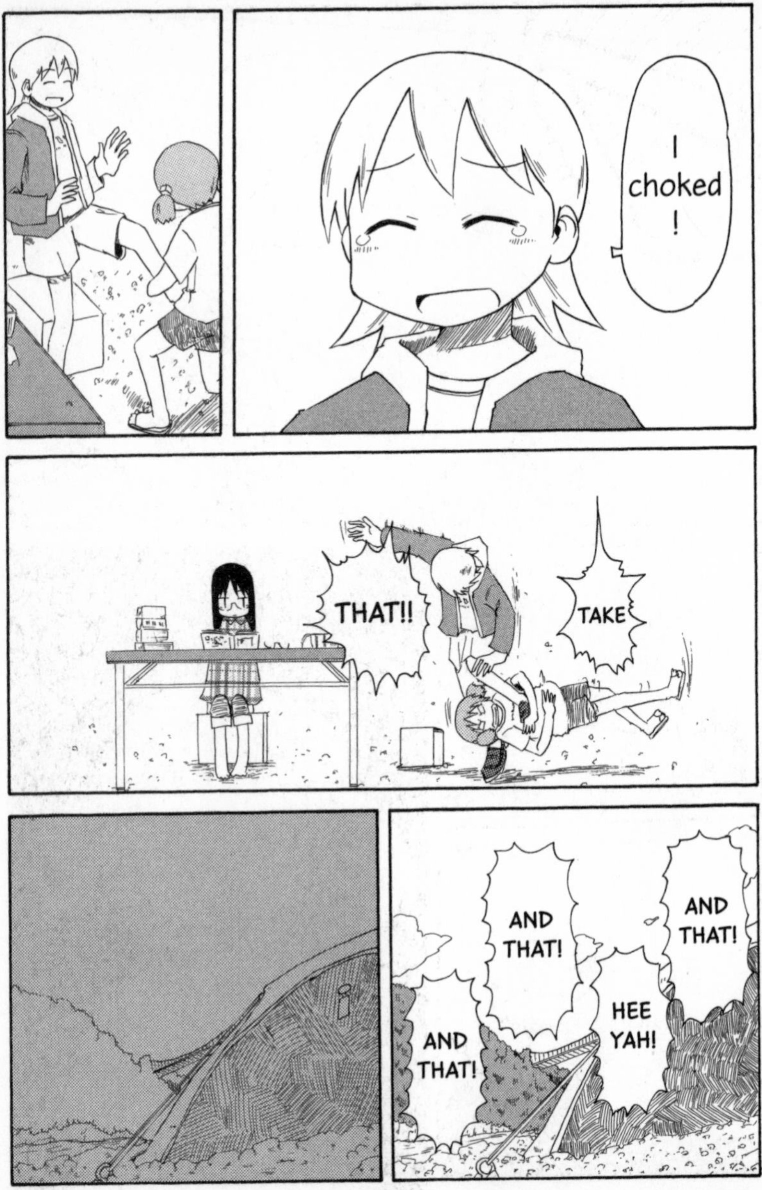
I choked!
TAKE
THAT!!
AND THAT!
AND THAT!
HEE YAH!
AND THAT!

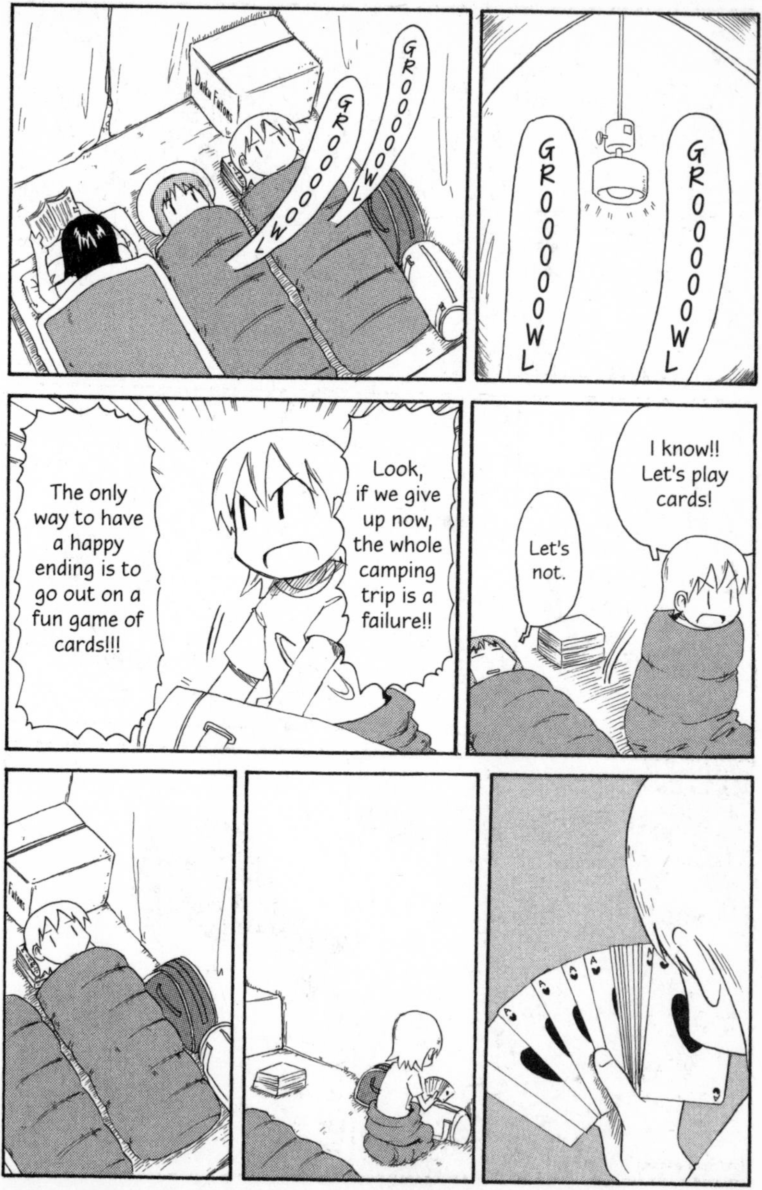
GROOOOOOWL
GROOOOOOWL
GROOOOOOWL
GROOOOOOWL
Daiku Futons
I know!! Let's play cards!
Let's not.
Look, if we give up now, the whole camping trip is a failure!!
The only way to have a happy ending is to go out on a fun game of cards!!!
Futons

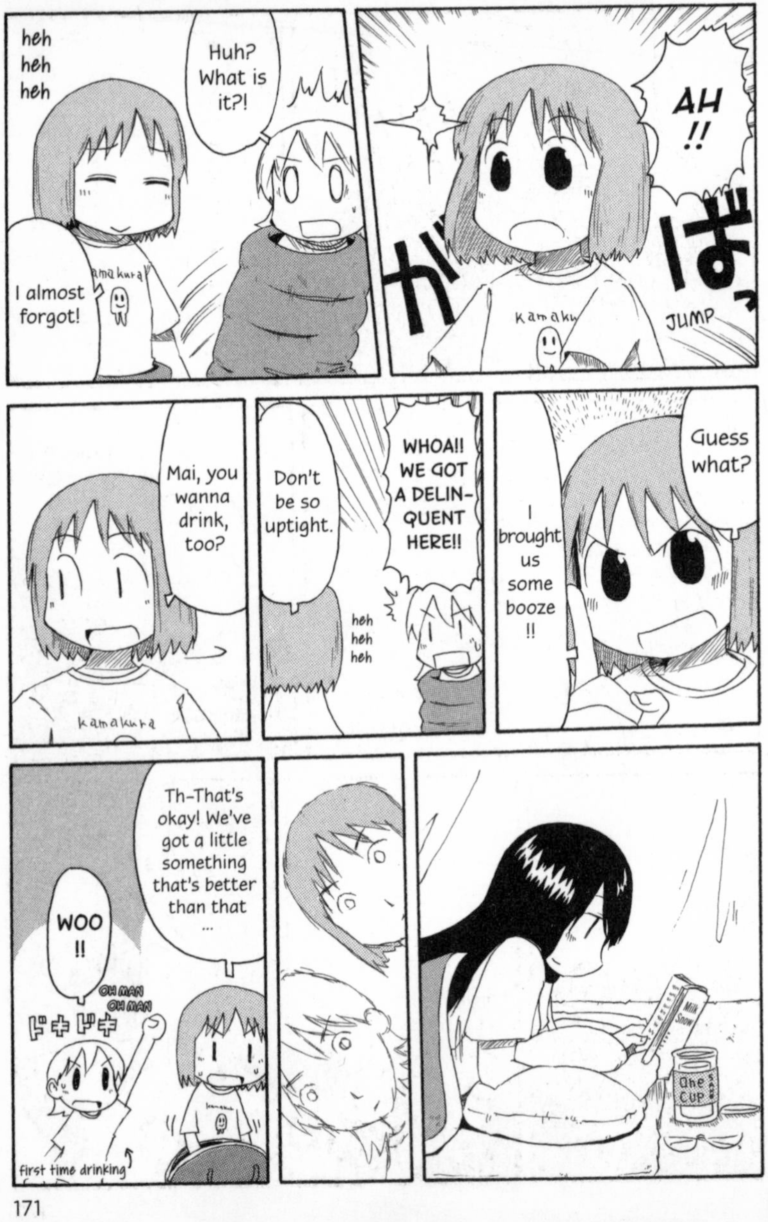
AH !!
がばっ
JUMP
Huh? What is it?!
heh heh heh
I almost forgot!
Guess what?
I brought us some booze !!
WHOA!! WE GOT A DELINQUENT HERE!!
Don't be so uptight.
heh heh heh
Mai, you wanna drink, too?
Milk Snow
One Cup
Th-That's okay! We've got a little something that's better than that ...
WOO !!
OH MAN OH MAN
ドキドキ
first time drinking

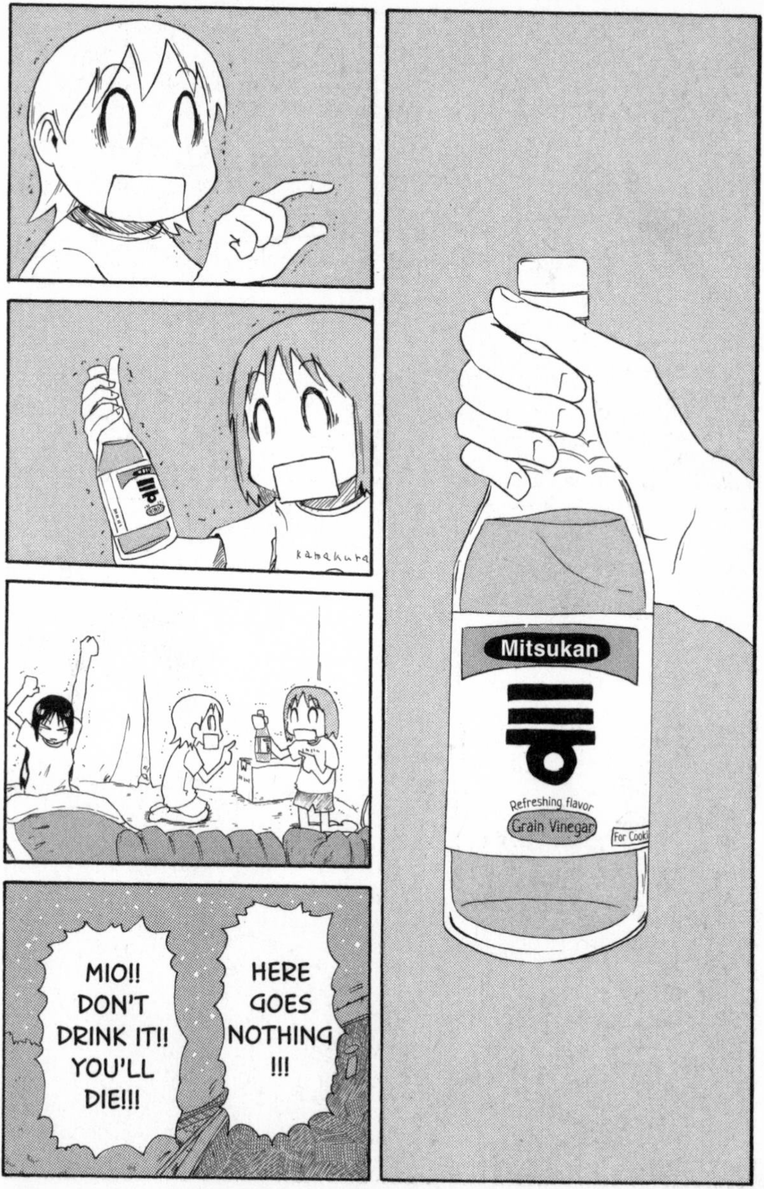
Mitsukan
Refreshing flavor
Grain Vinegar
HERE GOES NOTHING!!!
MIO!! DON'T DRINK IT!! YOU'LL DIE!!!

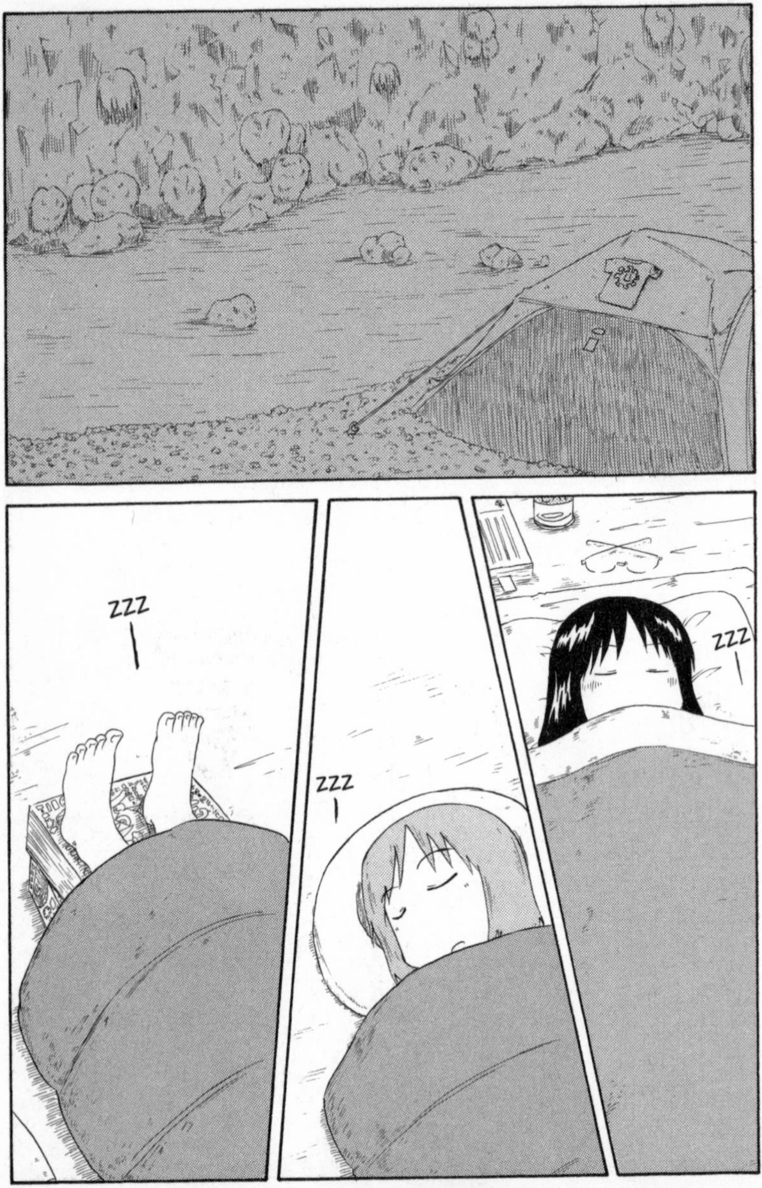
ZZZ
ZZZ
ZZZ

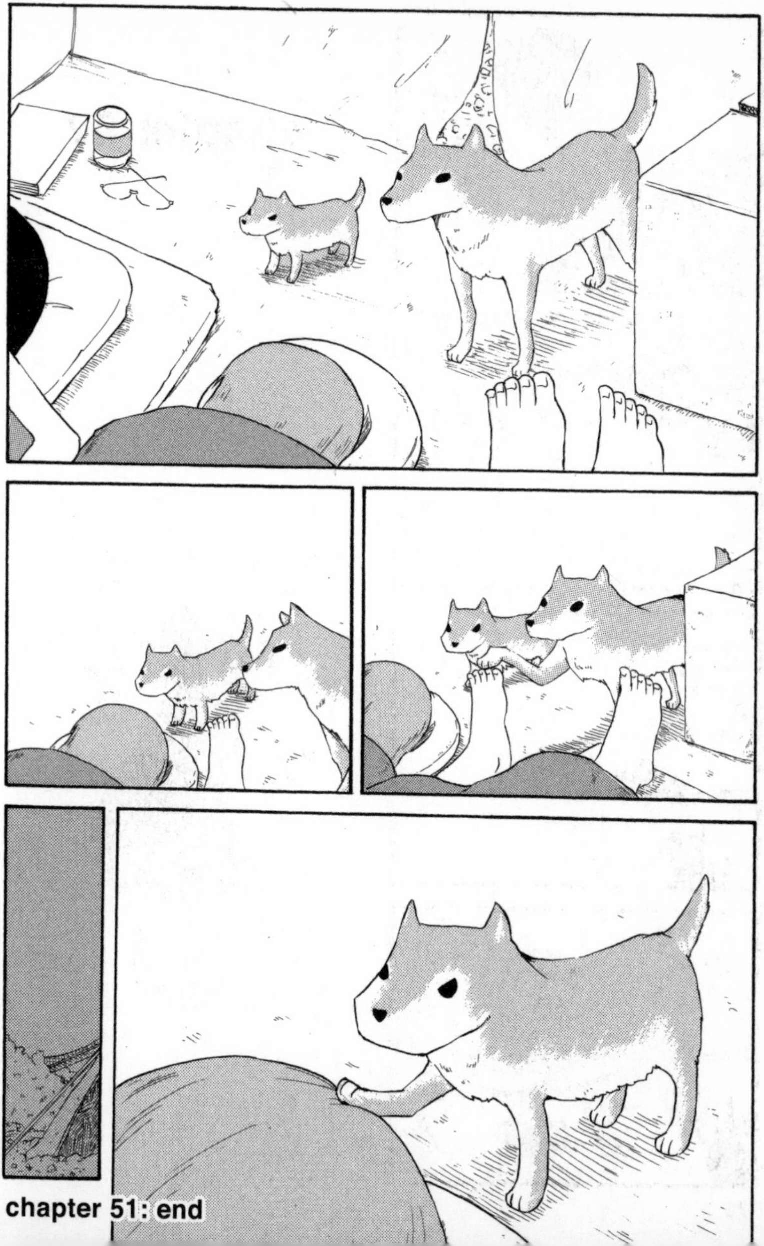
chapter 51: end

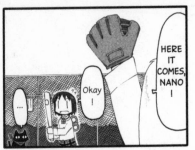

... / Okay! / HERE IT COMES, NANO!

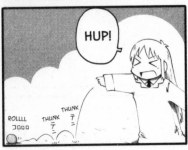

HUP!

ROLLL コロロ / THUNK テン / THUNK テン

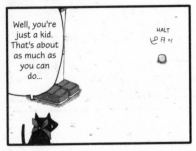

Well, you're just a kid. That's about as much as you can do... / HALT ピタッ

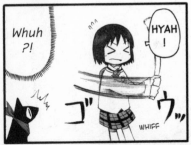

Whuh?! / HYAH! / ゴ / ウッ / WHIFF

chapter 52

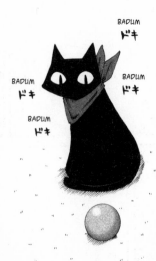

BADUM ドキ / BADUM ドキ / BADUM ドキ / BADUM ドキ

175

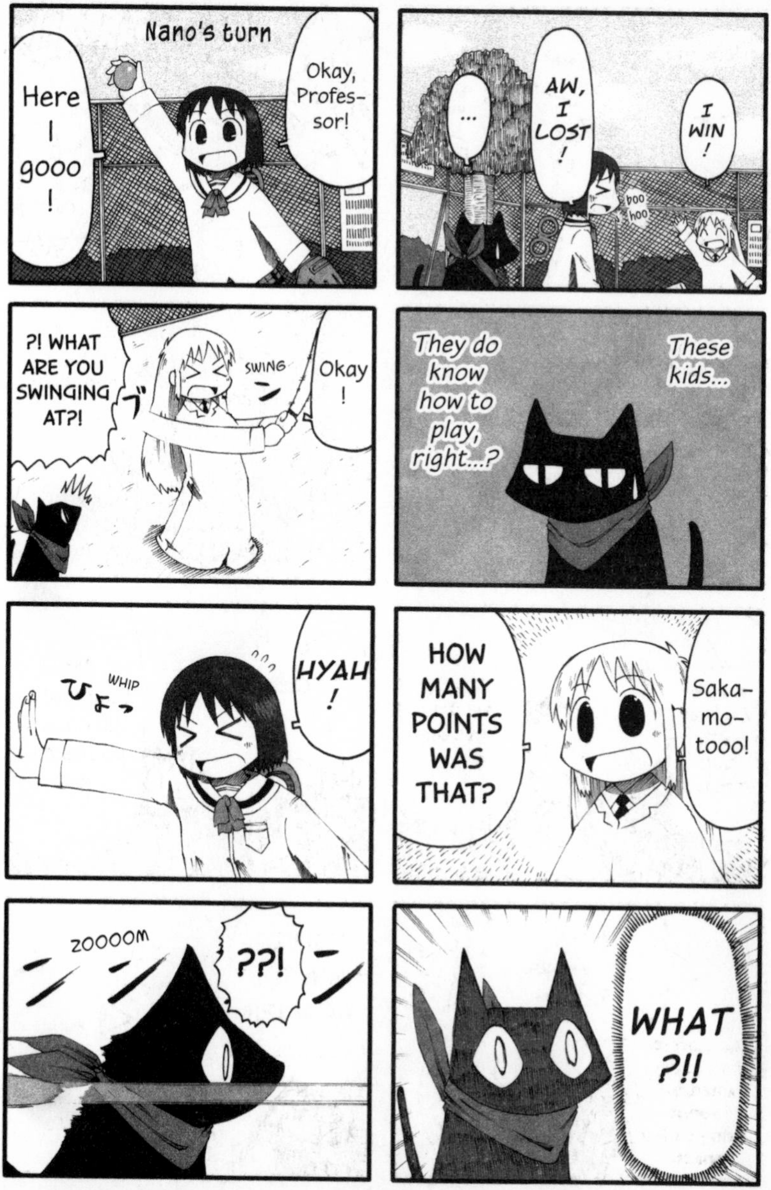

I WIN!
boo hoo
AW, I LOST!
...
These kids...
They do know how to play, right...?
Sakamotooo!
HOW MANY POINTS WAS THAT?
WHAT?!!
Nano's turn
Okay, Professor!
Here I gooo!
Okay!
SWING
?! WHAT ARE YOU SWINGING AT?!
HYAH!
WHIP
??!
ZOOOOM

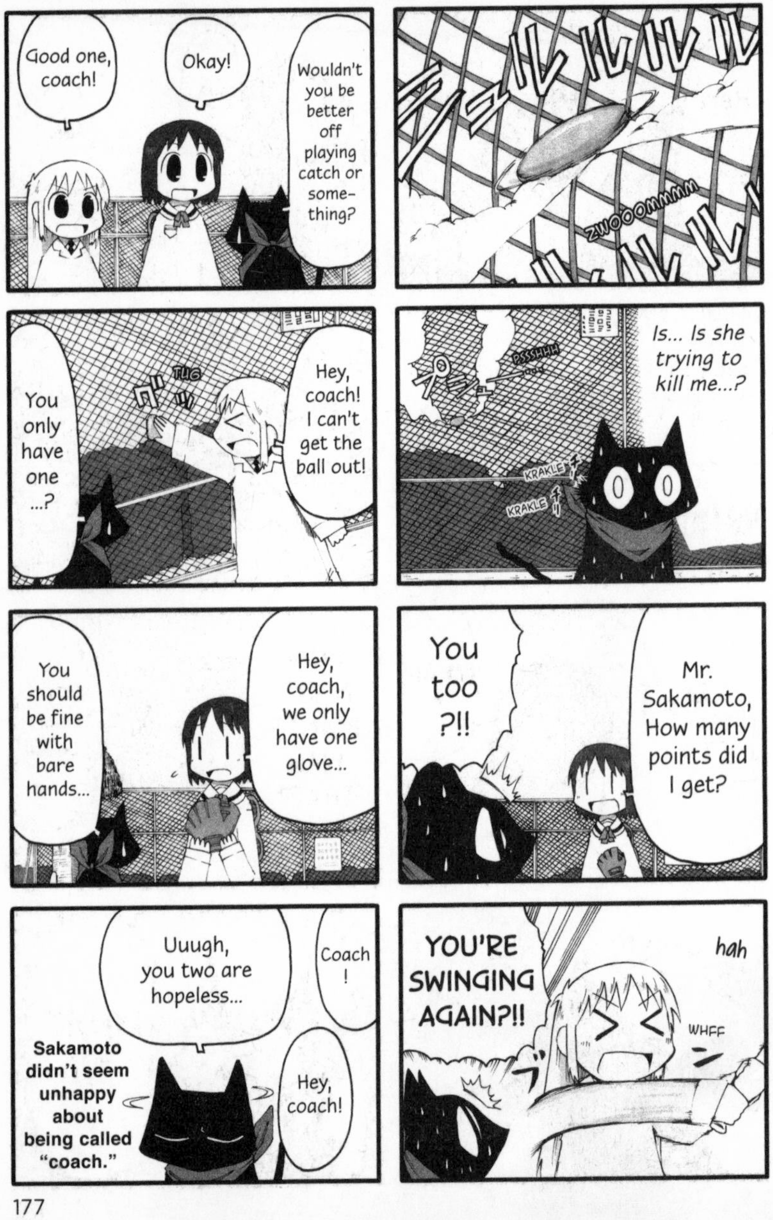
ZWOOOMMMM
Is... Is she trying to kill me...?
PSSSHHH
KRAKLE
KRAKLE
Mr. Sakamoto, How many points did I get?
You too ?!!
hah
WHFF
YOU'RE SWINGING AGAIN?!!
Wouldn't you be better off playing catch or something?
Okay!
Good one, coach!
Hey, coach! I can't get the ball out!
TUG
You only have one ...?
Hey, coach, we only have one glove...
You should be fine with bare hands...
Coach !
Uuugh, you two are hopeless...
Hey, coach!
Sakamoto didn't seem unhappy about being called “coach.”

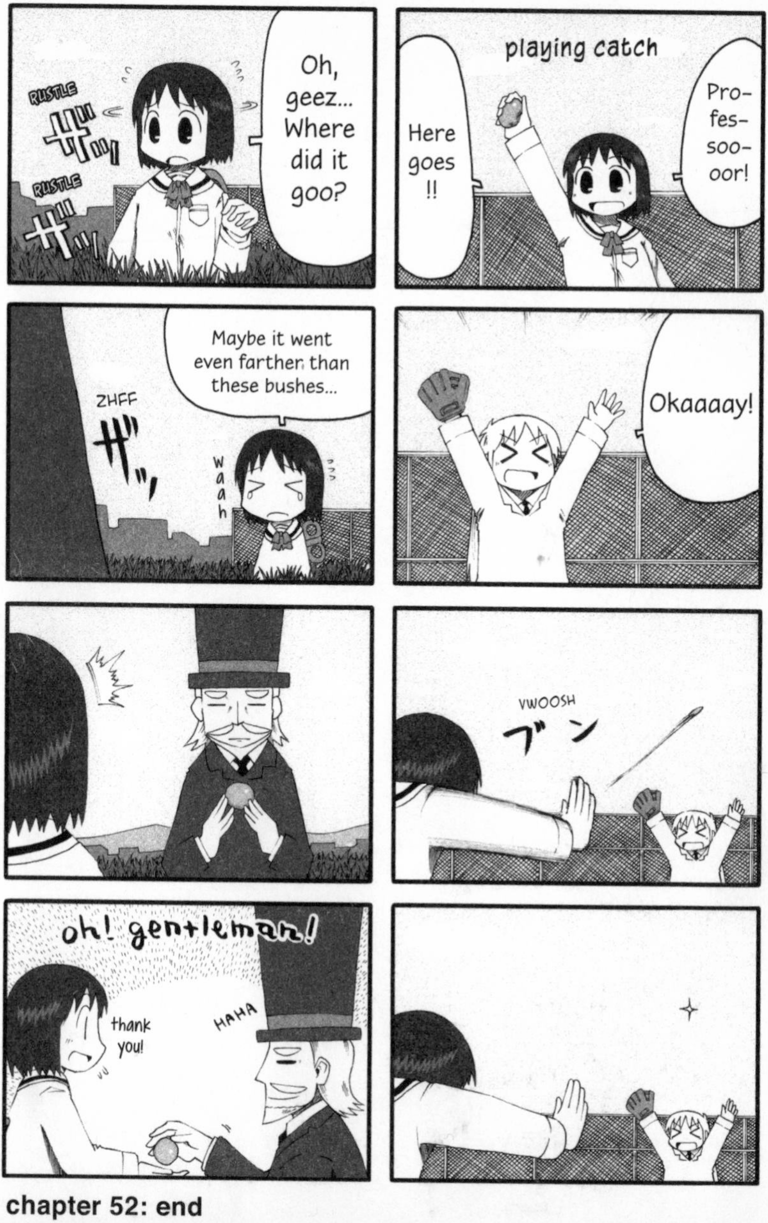
playing catch
Pro-fes-soo-oor!
Here goes !!
RUSTLE
RUSTLE
Oh, geez... Where did it goo?
Okaaaay!
Maybe it went even farther than these bushes...
ZHFF
waah
VWOOSH
ブン
oh! gentleman!
HAHA
thank you!

chapter 52: end

to be continued in volume 4!

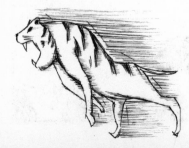

nichijou 3

my ordinary life

A Vertical Comics Edition

Translation: Jenny McKeon
Production: Grace Lu
　　　　　 Hiroko Mizuno

© Keiichi ARAWI 2008
First published in Japan in 2007 by KADOKAWA CORPORATION, Tokyo.
English translation rights arranged with KADOKAWA CORPORATION, Tokyo
through TUTTLE-MORI AGENCY, INC., Tokyo.

Published by Vertical Comics, an imprint of Vertical, Inc., New York

Originally published in Japanese as *nichijou 3* by Kadokawa Corporation, 2007
nichijou first serialized in *Monthly Shonen Ace,* Kadokawa Corporation, 2006-2015

This is a work of fiction.

ISBN: 978-1-942993-32-2

Manufactured in Canada

First Edition

Second Printing

Vertical, Inc.
451 Park Avenue South
7th Floor
New York, NY 10016
www.vertical-comics.com

Vertical books are distributed through Penguin-Random House Publisher Services.

nichijou

my ordinary life

(3)

keiichi arawi

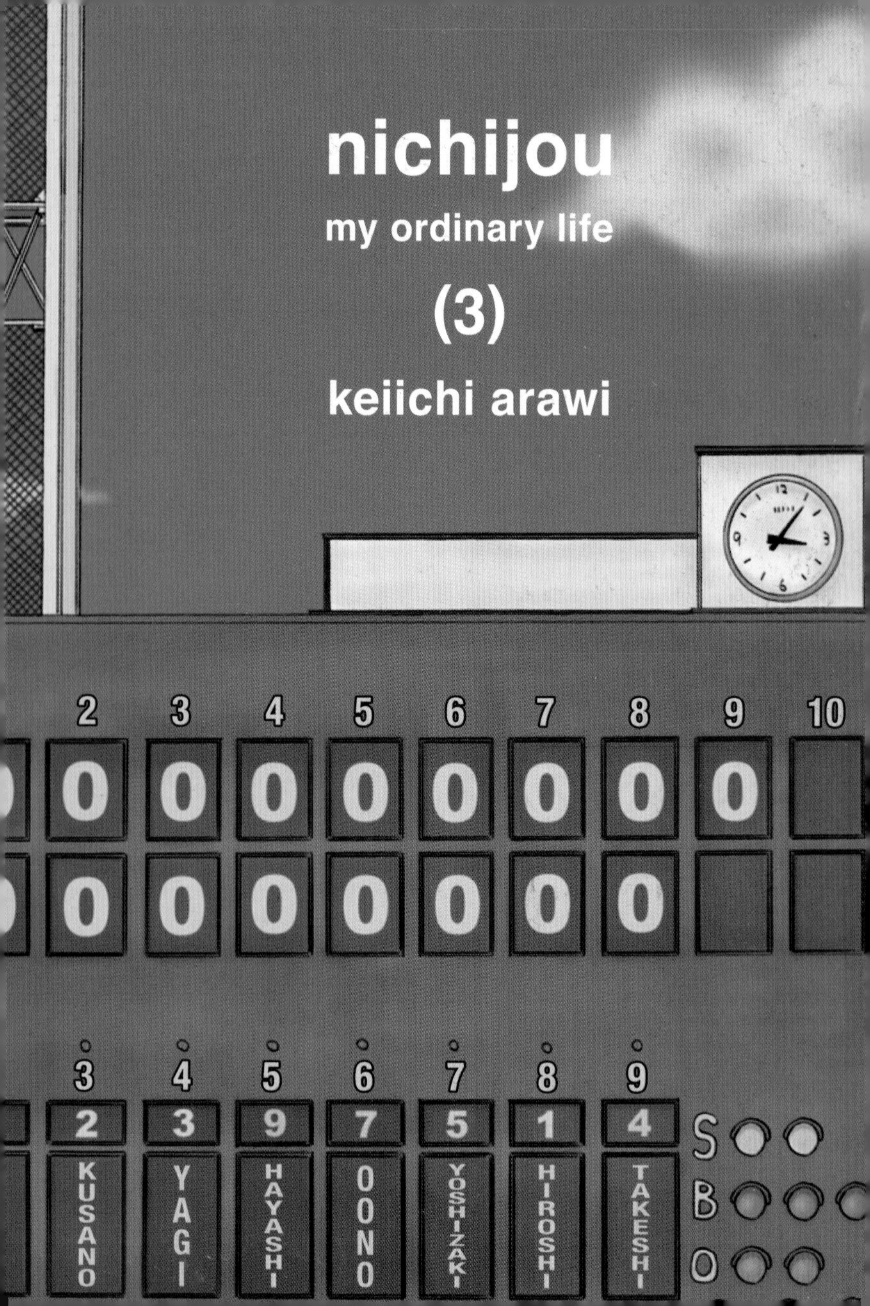

2 3 4 5 6 7 8 9 10
0 0 0 0 0 0 0 0
0 0 0 0 0 0 0
3 4 5 6 7 8 9
2 3 9 7 5 1 4
KUSANO
YAGI
HAYASHI
OONO
YOSHIZAKI
HIROSHI
TAKESHI
S
B
O

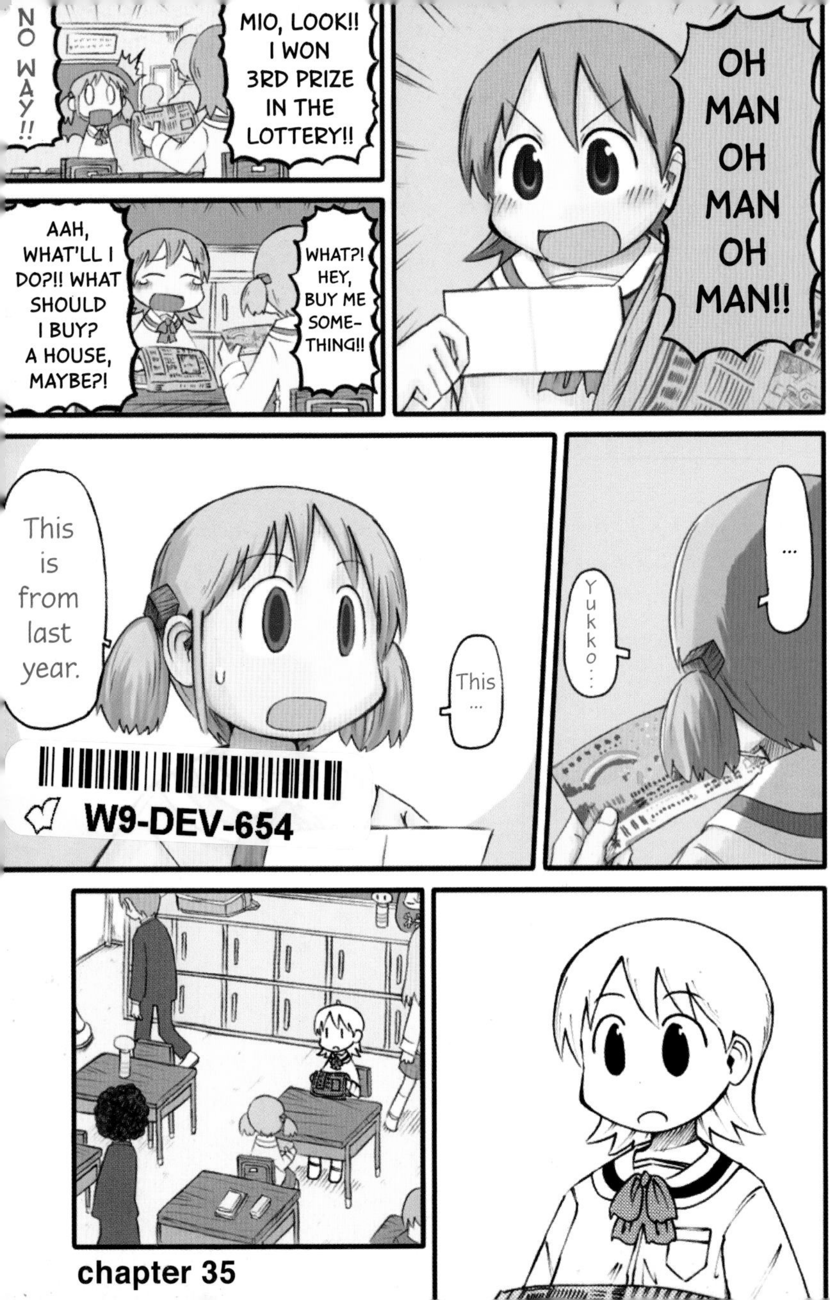
OH MAN OH MAN OH MAN!!
MIO, LOOK!! I WON 3RD PRIZE IN THE LOTTERY!!
NO WAY!!
WHAT?! HEY, BUY ME SOME-THING!!
AAH, WHAT'LL I DO?!! WHAT SHOULD I BUY? A HOUSE, MAYBE?!
...
Yukko...
This...
This is from last year.

chapter 35